D0066392

Cultural Foundations of Education

Cultural Foundations of Education

■ ■ ■ ■

FOURTH EDITION

Young Pai

University of Missouri–Kansas City

Susan A. Adler

University of Missouri–Kansas City

Linda K. Shadiow

Northern Arizona University

PEARSON

Merrill
Prentice Hall

Upper Saddle River, New Jersey
Columbus, Ohio

Library of Congress Cataloging in Publication Data

Pai, Young
   Cultural foundations of education / Young Pai, Susan A. Adler, Linda Shadiow.-- 4th ed.
    p. cm.
   Includes bibliographical references and index.
   ISBN 0-13-170281-5
   1. Educational anthropology--United States--Case studies. 2. Multicultural education--
United States--Case studies. 3. Pluralism (Social sciences)--United States--Case studies.
4. Educational psychology--Case studies. 5. Learning--Case studies. I. Adler, Susan A.
II. Shadiow, Linda. III. Title.

LB45.P35 2006
306.43--dc22

2005006704

Vice President and Executive Publisher: Jeffery W. Johnston
Executive Editor: Debra A. Stollenwerk
Associate Editor: Ben M. Stephen
Editorial Assistant: Mary Morrill
Production Editor: Kris Roach/Alexandrina Wolf
Production Coordination: PublishWare
Design Coordinator: Diane C. Lorenzo
Cover Designer: Terry Rohrbach
Cover image: Corbis
Production Manager: Susan Hannahs
Director of Marketing: Ann Castel Davis
Marketing Manager: Darcy Betts Prybella
Marketing Coordinator: Tyra Poole

This book was set in ITC New Baskerville by PublishWare and was printed and bound by
R. R. Donnelley & Sons Company. The cover was printed by Phoenix Color Corp.

Copyright © 2006, 2001, 1997, 1990 by Pearson Education, Inc., Upper Saddle River, New Jersey 07458.
Pearson Prentice Hall. All rights reserved. Printed in the United States of America. This publication is
protected by Copyright and permission should be obtained from the publisher prior to any prohibited
reproduction, storage in a retrieval system, or transmission in any form or by any means, electronic,
mechanical, photocopying, recording, or likewise. For information regarding permission(s), write to:
Rights and Permissions Department.

Pearson Prentice Hall™ is a trademark of Pearson Education, Inc.
Pearson® is a registered trademark of Pearson plc
Prentice Hall® is a registered trademark of Pearson Education, Inc.
Merrill® is a registered trademark of Pearson Education, Inc.

Pearson Education Ltd.   Pearson Education Australia Pty. Limited
Pearson Education Singapore Pte. Ltd.   Pearson Education North Asia Ltd.
Pearson Education Canada, Ltd.   Pearson Educación de Mexico, S.A. de C.V.
Pearson Education—Japan   Pearson Education Malaysia Pte. Ltd.

10 9 8 7 6 5 4 3 2 1
0-13-170281-5

To
Sunok, a wellspring of my growth,
in whom the East and the West meet
ever so gracefully,
and our grandchildren,
Vanessa, Nathan, and Chelsea,
whose lives shall be enriched
by the confluences of the two cultures

To
Natalya, Karolyn, Ethan, and Alex—
for education is about the future

To
Kaye, Bob, Petra, and Regan—
for the joy of lessons learned

Preface

Educators generally agree that education takes place in a specific sociocultural context. But we are not always clear and precise about the myriad ways that cultural factors influence the process of schooling, teaching, and learning. More often than not, our insensitivity to and lack of knowledge regarding the role of culture in education lead to unsound educational policies, ineffective school practices, and unfair assessment of learners. Accordingly, the primary purpose of this book is to examine education as a cultural phenomenon and the implications of this perspective for schooling, multicultural education, educational development, and the process of teaching and learning.

Cultural Foundations of Education is designed to provide educators and prospective educators with knowledge essential to making decisions about teaching and learning. It is not a methods textbook; rather, as the title implies, it is intended as a foundation for thinking about curricula and pedagogy. This is a time of sociocultural as well as educational change, and educators must be equipped with the knowledge and understanding necessary for effective analysis of educational issues. Teachers cannot close their classroom doors on cultural influences on education. It is our intention that this book contribute to more thoughtful dialogue about education in its cultural context.

Uses of This Text

Most of the concepts, theories, and issues presented in this text, along with their educational ramifications, will require further probing and elaboration; therefore, instructors are encouraged to introduce their own materials, experiences, and insights to these topics as well as to the influence of political, economic, and religious variables on education and schooling.

"Cases For Reflection" involving African American, Asian American, Hispanic American, Native American, and white American groups are presented at the end of each chapter. The contents of individual chapters will help readers analyze the cases; also, additional sources in anthropology and education, opinions of other students, and the instructor's guidance will be useful in gaining varied and alternative insights.

New to This Edition

A number of significant changes have been incorporated into this fourth edition:

- Chapter 1 opens with a vignette depicting ethnic and cultural diversity found in our schools today to illustrate how diversity influences teaching and learning.
- The concepts of "private" and "operating" cultures and syncretism have been brought back into chapter 2 from the first edition to explore how a new cultural identity may be developed by combining different cultural elements. The section on core values has been updated to reflect current times.
- Chapter 3 contains a discussion of the role of history in understanding cultural foundations of education and an updated examination of both the Head Start and achievement gaps.
- Significant sections on No Child Left Behind legislation and the place of religious diversity in cultural pluralism have been added to chapter 4.
- An examination of the holistic perspective's implications for the role of schools is a new feature of chapter 5.
- The ethic of care and culturally responsive teaching are discussed in chapters 6 and 7, respectively.

This edition pays special attention to how generalizations about groups can be made useful while avoiding the pitfalls of stereotyping.

Other modifications and updates, while changing the text in only minor ways, keep the text connected with current trends and theories, as well as with the experience of readers.

Acknowledgments

Our thanks to Beth Hall for her research support and to the NAU graduate students in the cultural foundations classes over the years for their insights and questions. We also want to thank our reviewers for their insightful comments: Malcolm B. Campbell, Bowling Green State University; William S. Forney, University of North Texas; Frances O'Neill, Northern Michigan University; and Roberta Kyle, Marist College.

Educator Learning Center: An Invaluable Online Resource

Merrill Education and the Association for Supervision and Curriculum Development (ASCD) invite you to take advantage of a new online resource, one that provides access to the top research and proven strategies associated with ASCD and Merrill—the Educator Learning Center. At **www.educatorlearning center.com**, you will find resources that will enhance your students' understanding of course topics and of current educational issues, in addition to being invaluable for further research.

How the Educator Learning Center Will Help Your Students Become Better Teachers

With the combined resources of Merrill Education and ASCD, you and your students will find a wealth of tools and materials to better prepare them for the classroom.

Research
- More than 600 articles from the ASCD journal *Educational Leadership* discuss everyday issues faced by practicing teachers.
- A direct link on the site to Research Navigator™ gives students access to many of the leading education journals, as well as extensive content detailing the research process.
- Excerpts from Merrill Education texts give your students insights on important topics of instructional methods, diverse populations, assessment, classroom management, technology, and refining classroom practice.

Classroom Practice
- Hundreds of lesson plans and teaching strategies are categorized by content area and age range.
- Case studies and classroom video footage provide virtual field experience for student reflection.
- Computer simulations and other electronic tools keep your students abreast of today's classrooms and current technologies.

Look into the Value of Educator Learning Center Yourself

A 4-month subscription to Educator Learning Center is $25 but is free when packaged with any Merrill Education text. In order for your students to have access to this site, you must use this special value-pack ISBN number when placing your textbook order with the bookstore: 0-13-168653-4. Your students will then receive a copy of the text packaged with a free ASCD pincode. To preview the value of this Web site to you and your students, please go to **www.educatorlearningcenter.com** and click on "Demo."

Brief Contents

Contents

Prologue: "The Teachers' Office"

Mr. Kim, a junior high school teacher in Korea, asked Namsik, one of forty students in his social studies class, to see him about a paper Namsik had turned in. Namsik dreaded the thought of having to meet with Mr. Kim because he must go to "The Teachers' Office," a large room in which all of the teachers in the school have their assigned desks. To children, it is not an open, friendly, or easily accessible place. For Namsik, going to see Mr. Kim is an intimidating, if not traumatic, experience. He must walk past other teachers' desks because Mr. Kim is at the far end of the large office.

As Namsik enters the room, a teacher asks, "Hey, Namsik, are you behaving yourself?" Another teacher wonders, "Why are you here, Namsik?" Still another teacher tries to put Namsik at ease, "Leave him alone, he is a good kid." Namsik is nervous, a bit scared, and even feels somewhat demeaned because it is never easy to deal with older people, particularly his teachers, to whom he must be deferential and obedient. Namsik thinks, "Boy! This is no democracy. I hope I don't ever have to come back to this office again!"

As Namsik observes, this arrangement seems inconsistent with the ideals of democratic and open education. "The Teachers' Office," in all Korean schools during the period of Japanese colonial rule (1910–1945), still exists today. Despite numerous educational reform efforts made to democratize Korean education for more than half a century, why is Namsik's experience still commonly shared by schoolchildren today? How effective have the reform efforts been?

According to the Ministry of Education in the Republic of Korea[1], the objective of educational reform, or the ideal of New Education for the twenty-first century, lies in the establishment of an Open Education Society in which anyone can receive the kind of varied and high-quality education he or she desires (p. 144). Education in such a society is to be learner-centered so that self-realization, originality, personality (character) development, and autonomy rather than school grades and rote memorization of facts are central (pp. 145–146). Teachers, students, and parents are to participate actively in school administration as well as

---

[1]Ministry of Education, Republic of Korea, 1997, *Education in Korea:* 1997–1998, Seoul, Korea: Author, 1997).

curriculum development and evaluation. Implicit in these ideals is the notion that the teaching–learning process should not be seen as mere transmission of factual knowledge from those who have it (teachers) to those who do not have it (students). Accordingly, teachers and students should not be seen as masters and disciples but as helpers/collaborators and learners, respectively.

While the reform efforts from the 1950s to the 1980s had different organizational and programmatic measures, making Korean education open and democratic remained the fundamental goal for educational reforms throughout the past five decades (pp. 29–36). As a result of these efforts suggested by many education experts in the United States, many institutional and curricular changes have been made. Yet it appears that teaching continues to be a primarily teacher-dominated activity and learning is seen as the process of receiving knowledge from its provider, the teacher. Similarly, Namsik's experience of visiting Mr. Kim in "The Teachers' Office" suggests that the reform measures have done little to change how educators view teaching, learning, and the respective roles of teachers and students.

Though there is no simple answer to why schools in Korea still have "The Teachers' Office," historical, economic, and even political factors probably contribute to this phenomenon. But it is important to remember that education always occurs in a particular sociocultural context. This means that institutional, programmatic, and policy changes are not likely to be effective unless their underlying premises about teaching and learning are consistent with the society's cultural beliefs regarding how self-identity and its relationships with other persons are defined. It would appear that while Korean culture reflects a hierarchical view of individuals, the democratic education reform measures are founded on an egalitarian perspective. Indeed, "The Teachers' Office" as an educational practice is more consistent with the former than the latter.

We have used "The Teachers' Office" story to point out that an understanding of the nature of educational as well as teaching–learning processes requires looking beyond institutions and programs. We must examine how cultural contexts assign meanings and values to what we do in education and schooling, for they are the criteria by which we decide what is important and worthwhile. This book examines the specific ways cultural factors influence various dimensions of education so that our understanding may help us become more effective in teaching and learning.

PART ONE

Culture and the Educative Process

1

Introduction

KEY *Concepts:*
- Anthropology
- Culture
- Cultural anthropology
- Ethnography

Azzie, a high school junior, always dressed modestly. She was the daughter of Syrian immigrants who taught their children to respect and cherish their Muslim beliefs and heritage. Although Azzie did not wear a head scarf, she always wore long-sleeved tops and long skirts or loose-fitting slacks. Her parents felt she was too young to date, and they closely monitored her social activities. Azzie had no problem with her parents' demands, except that her non-Muslim friends didn't seem to understand. They teased her about her conservative dress and didn't understand why she stayed aloof from the boys. Azzie thought that her girlfriends were foolish to dress the way they did. She believed that cropped shirts and low-cut, skin-tight pants showed a lack of respect for one's self. She didn't say this, but increasingly she felt herself drifting away from old friends.

It was Ms. McGee's first year of teaching. She loved her second graders. Her predominantly African American class was full of enthusiasm and enjoyed learning. One would think this would be an ideal classroom, but Ms. McGee wondered how to get the children to quiet down without dimming their enthusiasm for learning. The children seemed to be constantly calling out, interrupting her and one another. She struggled to get them to raise their hands, to keep quiet until called upon, and to wait patiently for their turn. She worried that the principal would give her a poor rating if the chaos in her classroom continued.

Ms. Romano spotted the fight before it began. Johnny, one of the two boys arguing loudly in the cafeteria, was in her fifth-period class. Ms. Romano and Mr. Buchanan approached the two boys, hoping to stop the fight before it began. "Johnny," she said. "We've talked about this before; coming to blows is no way to settle disagreements with dignity." Meanwhile, Mr. Buchanan gently took the other boy's arm. "You can settle this like gentlemen," he explained. The boys backed down, and the four of them sat down to discuss the problem.

Inside and outside the classroom, Ms. Romano, like many of the teachers in her school, treated students with respect, caring, and high expectations. Most teachers were supportive, yet demanding. They held high expectations, academically and socially. The school climate was described by many as emotionally warm, with clear and consistent rules and expectations. Students often said they felt cared for and supported. They also said that they felt that school was a place where they could learn.

"I'm never going near the teacher's lounge again," said Katie after her first week of student teaching at a middle school. "Everyone complains about how bad the students are. It's one big gripe session. Not only that, but the teachers sit in cliques and it's impossible for a new person like myself to feel accepted. No one seems to really care!"

Each of these teachers and students has encountered the effects of culture in schools, classrooms, and education generally. Learners bring to school beliefs, values, and behaviors they have already learned. In other words, they bring with them their home cultures, and these in turn influence their behavior in school. Furthermore, schools themselves have their own cultures. A school's climate, whether supportive of learners and learning, or angry and isolating, is an example of the culture of a school.

WHAT CHARACTERIZES CULTURE?

Scholars debate the exact meaning of the term *culture;* nonetheless, there are certain key elements that many agree characterize the concept of culture. **Culture** may be seen as the knowledge, beliefs, values, skills, and behaviors of a social group. Culture is learned and transmitted from one generation to the next. Culture also changes as situations and the needs of a people change. In short, culture is learned, shared, and changed (Banks & Banks, 2004). Culture is constructed; that is, it is not "natural," it is not something that exists apart from human history and experience. Culture may be identified as the ways in which a group of people have come to solve the problems of survival and existence.

Any human social organization, whether large or small, may be said to have a culture. We can make generalizations about the culture of a nation, such as the United States, or of subgroups within a nation, such as Irish Americans or adolescents. We can also make generalizations about institutions within a society. Servers in diners or cocktail lounges can be said to share a common culture of "waitressing" (Spradley, 1975), just as firefighters share elements of a common culture. Schools have cultures as well. (See, for example, McLaren, 1994, *Life in Schools* and Lesko, 1988, *Symbolizing Society.*) As a teacher, understanding the culture of your school and the culture that you and your students bring with you to school can greatly enhance your abilities as an effective teacher.

WHY STUDY THE CULTURAL FOUNDATIONS OF EDUCATION?

Effective teachers know their students as individuals, and they also recognize that each individual is a member of multiple sociocultural groups. The children in your classroom are also family members, community members, members of ethnic and perhaps religious groups, and so on. You may share some common cultural experiences with the students in your class, or you may share few cultural commonalities with your students.

The United States has seen a rise in immigration in recent years. According to the Population Reference Bureau (2001), in 2000 there were 19.5 million people in the United States age five or older who did not speak English well. Children ages 5–17 accounted for about 15 percent of the population who had difficulty speaking English. Children with this difficulty have difficulty succeeding in school and, later, encounter obstacles in the labor market. The Population Reference Bureau also predicts that by 2025 the percentage of Hispanics in the United States will rise to 18 percent, while the population of whites will decline to about 62 percent. Only about 13 percent of the population is projected to be African American. If current trends continue, by 2050 nearly half the U.S. population will be composed of today's "minority groups."

Many children in school are from poor and working-class homes in which having the money to make ends meet each week is a challenge. According to the Population Reference Bureau (Mather & Rivers, 2003), the 2000 census showed nearly 38% of school-aged children living in low-income families (below 200 percent poverty level), while 16.6 percent of these children lived below poverty level. More than 20 percent of children lived in poverty neighborhoods. Remember, culture is the way in which social groups cope with their environments. Families and communities in poverty develop ways to cope with this experience. A child working a job that brings income to the family may be more important than that child's regular school attendance. Girls may be expected to care for younger siblings while mom works two jobs. Such common expectations in the home and neighborhood may be at odds with expectations in school.

Not only will you be teaching learners who come to school from varied cultural backgrounds and experience, but you will also be teaching about cultures. The events of September 11, 2001, made clear to all of us how small the world had become. The world has indeed become a "global village," interconnected and interdependent. Communication, transportation, and commerce have brought the diverse cultures of the world closer together. Music, art, foods, and traditions travel to new places in ways unheard of a generation ago. You can buy ice cream at Baskin-Robbins in Cairo, listen to Latin music in New Jersey, and eat pizza in Tokyo. Many see the penetration of Western business, clothes, music, and customs as a threat to local cultures and traditions. Resentment can, and has, boiled over into hatred and violence. Schools can function to help young people find ways to bridge the gulf of misunderstanding, to listen to the grievances and viewpoints of diverse others, or to accept multiple perspectives (Young & Sharifzadeh, 2003). An understanding of diverse cultures doesn't mean that we accept terrorism, but it can provide ways to resolve the grievances and fears of others.

Finally, as a teacher, you will be functioning within a school culture. Individuals occupy certain social positions: student, teacher, administrator, and so forth, each with its own set of behaviors and expectations. Taken together, schools are places in which particular sets of behaviors, values, and beliefs are manifest. Thus schools in general, and each school in particular, have a culture that, as a teacher, you will be part of. As a new teacher, you will be socialized into the appropriate behaviors of teachers generally and of teachers in your building in particular. That is, you will be taught, sometimes in very subtle ways, the acceptable beliefs, behaviors, and values of your school.

There is no escaping the fact that education is a sociocultural process. Hence, a critical examination of the role of culture in human life is indispensable to the understanding and control of educative processes. From a cultural perspective, school can be viewed as the means by which each society attempts to transmit and perpetuate its notion of the good life, which is derived from the society's beliefs about the nature of the world, knowledge, and values. These beliefs vary from society to society and culture to culture. To put it differently, if we view culture as a system of knowledge, beliefs, values, attitudes, artifacts, and institutions, then we may regard education as the intentional attempt to pass on such a complex whole from one generation to another. Because education is used to relay cultural content to the next generation, the structure of the educational system, the role of the school, and the teacher–learner relationship reflect the social organization and the cultural norms of the society. For example, in a society where individuals treat each other as equals, the teacher–learner relationship, like the parent–child relationship, tends to be informal, and communication styles tend to be open, with frequent reciprocal exchanges. On the other hand, in a culture where individuals see others as either above or below their own status (a hierarchical perspective), we are likely to find a formal teacher–pupil relationship with a communication style characterized by commands and demands issued from teachers to learners, who are seen as occupying a lower status.

In another sense, the aims and ways of educating the young are not only influenced by the conditions of society and its culture, but they may also be viewed as responses to societal and cultural needs. This means that in a culturally diverse society such as ours, the various educational agents, especially the schools, must deal with the issues, problems, and needs arising out of the relationship between the dominant and minority cultures. Thus, no part of the educative process, neither its contents nor its products, is free from cultural influence. Educators need to realize that the processes of teaching and learning are influenced by the core values, beliefs, and attitudes, as well as the predominant cognitive and communication styles and linguistic patterns, of a culture. Further, the educative process, whether formal or informal, is equally affected by the socioeconomic status of the learner, peer pressures, the nature of the relationships between dominant and minority groups, and the impact of technology on the society.

As inextricable as the connection between culture and education is, education as a field of study has not always been concerned with this important relationship. Traditionally, the study of education and teacher education programs has placed much greater emphasis on the psychological rather than the sociocultural dimensions of teaching–learning processes. As well-known educational anthropologist George D. Spindler (1973) points out:

> Educational psychology has clearly dominated the scene, partly because of a historical accident that institutionally wedded psychology and education rather early in America and partly because the need for tests and measurements and applied principles of learning have been particularly obvious in the educational milieu of American schools and have been appropriate for psychological applications. (p. 101)

Even in other foundational fields, the sociocultural areas that are usually called *educational sociology* are primarily concerned with the relationships among socioeconomic stratification, social change, bureaucracy, sex roles, demographic trends, and so on, in education and schooling. It is true that in the early 1900s Edgar C. Hewet wrote about anthropology and education (1904) and ethnic factors in education (1905), and a significant number of works on education and culture by such well-known scholars as Margaret Mead, Jules Henry, Clyde Kluckhohn, Solon Kimball, Dorothy Lee, and others appeared in the 1940s and 1950s. But serious attempts to utilize the tools and the findings of anthropology in dealing with matters related to general education, schooling, and teacher education did not begin until the early 1960s. Even today, cultural foundations of education are usually subsumed under educational sociology, educational psychology, social foundations of education, or even history and philosophy of education.

Although the study of the cultural foundations of education is not yet a clearly established, distinct discipline, this should not diminish its importance as practitioners attempt to examine how cultural variables affect education, teaching, learning, and the growth and development of all learners. The relevance of such a field in the study of education rests on the fact that worldviews, values, cognitive and communication styles, linguistic patterns, child-rearing practices, tool making, knowledge acquisition, and the different ways people relate to each other are all culturally bound. They also have substantial impact on how people of all ages learn and become educated. Moreover, our knowledge of how these and other related factors influence human behavior may enable us to expose the cultural assumptions underlying the ways we and others think, analyze, and observe. Indeed, studying cultural foundations (bases) of education may give us a critical tool with which we can more accurately assess our work as educators and facilitate the development of more effective and just educational strategies and resource allocations to assure optimal learning for all.

A CAVEAT

There are many ways of using "culture" to help children learn optimally and develop necessary skills for dealing effectively with a wide range of intellectual, social, vocational, and even emotional needs and problems. However, an over-simplified use of culture and overgeneralization of cultural traits often lead to erroneous and even harmful judgments about individuals from other cultures. *Culture* represents complex patterns of behaviors, interpersonal relationships, attitudes, uses of language, and definitions of roles that reflect the fundamental worldviews of a particular society. *Culture* also refers to certain general patterns of behaviors, attitudes, thinking and communication styles, and social relationships that a society expects from its members. Hence, no culture specifically spells out how each individual incorporates and expresses cultural expectations in any given life situation.

The extent to which a society's cultural norms are manifested in the daily lives of its people depends on the nature of their circumstances, personality traits, emotional dispositions, socioeconomic factors, and even familiarity with other cultural patterns. We should not assume that every member of a particular culture will act and think in exactly the same way. Our knowledge of another culture can give us only some general clues or a different perspective with which possible alternative explanations of a person's behavior or attitude can be understood. Teachers and counselors should be sensitive to the points of conflict between the cultures of minority groups and the mainstream society. The behaviors of the culturally different should be understood in this context. That is, if a minority child is found hitting another child, this should not automatically be judged as "picking a fight" or an expression of some strange cultural practice. Children in certain minority cultures play with each other by hitting and kicking, and the child's act of hitting may be a non-English-speaking child's way of saying, "Let's play together." But such a judgment should not be made without knowing the circumstances surrounding the relationship between the mainstream and culturally different children and the points at which their cultural practices may conflict. Depending on the behavioral patterns of the minority child, his or her act of hitting may indeed be a hostile reaction to a frustrating situation, or it may be an invitation to play.

Without detailed clinical observations or experiences and in-depth ethnographic (observer–participant) studies of individuals in their life situations, we cannot gain insightful information about the whys and the wherefores of other people's actions and attitudes. For this reason, the education of teachers and other school personnel should include components in which they are asked to observe, encounter, and evaluate cross-cultural experiences. One author recalls reading a teacher's handbook on Southeast Asian students. The handbook, prepared by a state department of education, explained that people in Southeast Asian countries and Korea always write their last names first. The book then went on to suggest that when a Southeast Asian student initially reports to school, his or her names should be reversed so that the last name follows the first name. But following this suggestion would be "correcting" a nonmistake because many students from these parts of the world come to the United States with their last names already placed after the given names. A more appropriate procedure is for school personnel to simply ask the child, "What is your surname?", "Which is your surname?", or "Is this your surname?"

ANTHROPOLOGY AND EDUCATION

Given the nature and function of the cultural foundations of the education field as just described, anthropology should be considered its parent discipline and knowledge base. Anthropology, a science *(logos)* of man *(anthro),* is concerned with describing, analyzing, and comparing the physical, social, psychological, and linguistic aspects of human behaviors as they manifest themselves in different cultural patterns. These patterns are investigated regardless of whether they existed in remote places in prehistoric times or exist at home today. When we consider the wide range of topics and the immense variations of space and time in which investigations are carried out, anthropology may be considered the discipline with the broadest scope and the most holistic approach to understanding human behavior and institutions.

ANTHROPOLOGY AND TEACHING

The relevance of anthropology to educational inquiry and the practice of teaching has already been intimated in this chapter. Moreover, because the specific implications of anthropological concepts and findings will be discussed in the remaining portions of this book, we will look at only two broad aspects of the relationship between anthropology and teaching. One is the value of anthropology as a part of the general education of teachers; the other is the relevance of anthropological findings and methods in the professional development of teachers and prospective teachers.

A primary role of schools as specialized agents of human society is to transmit the fundamental worldviews, values, beliefs, and behavioral norms of the society to the young. In an ethnocentric society, schools tend to cultivate and reinforce attitudes that encourage learners to regard only their own beliefs, values, and ways of thinking as right and worthy of respect and admiration. Because all societies are more or less ethnocentric, most of us may be seen as products of ethnocentric education. According to Solon Kimball (1974), it is because of this kind of education that "few individuals possess the capacity to view themselves and the world around them either objectively or as parts of an interrelated system," and most individuals have been intellectually "isolated from new insights through adherence to established formulas, dogmas, or other rigid systems of beliefs" (p. 56).

An unfortunate consequence of ethnocentric education is that it robs people of respect for and appreciation of other cultural patterns and therefore robs them of the flexibility to utilize other ways of coping with a wide range of problems. Through comparative and analytic studies of other cultures, teachers can develop a broader perspective and critical understanding of these cultures and their alternative means of dealing with divergent human needs and problems. In the words of Robert Redfield (1973), anthropological studies may

> lead the young person to look back upon his own culture from a vantage point secured in the understanding gained of other cultures and thus achieve that objectivity and capacity to consider thoughtfully his own conduct and the institutions of his own society which are, in part, a result of thinking as if within another culture. Further, the individual will be able to see that there are ways other than his or her own which are compatible with human needs and with the dignity of the individual . . . to develop the power to think well about one's own way of life so that that way may be improved. (p. 205)

The liberalizing influence of anthropology is bound to have a positive impact on teacher education programs. Indeed, effective teaching in a pluralistic society such as the United States needs to be based on an understanding of the various ways that cultural factors and conflict influence the pupils' modes of thinking, learning, communicating, and relating to others. The infusion of anthropological studies in teacher education is relevant and necessary, because applying the insights of anthropology may help teachers to develop sensitivity to the varying patterns of motivation, intergroup and intragroup relationships, and the manners of relating school-taught concepts to out-of-school life. Ideally, the knowledge and skills to deal effectively with learning and behavioral difficulties stemming from cultural differences and conflicts should be integrated into the entire teacher education curriculum as a basis for formulating instructional strategies and resources to facilitate optimal learning for all.

USES OF ANTHROPOLOGICAL METHODS IN EDUCATION

A productive approach to applying anthropology in the study of education is to utilize the investigative methods of anthropology in educational inquiry. As might be inferred from the preceding discussions of the different branches of anthropology, anthropological studies use three major methods: (1) the fieldwork approach, (2) the organismic approach, and (3) the comparative approach.

The Fieldwork Approach

The fieldwork approach, first pioneered by Franz Boas (1858–1942), is based on the assumption that the most reliable data about cultural patterns should be obtained through objective observation of a society by an investigator who is also closely involved in the life of that society. Ethnography and other qualitative field approaches to the study of education, such as observation and in-depth interviewing, have become increasingly popular over the past several years. The methodologies and the assumptions undergirding these approaches differ in several ways from the experimental designs that dominated research in education during much of the twentieth century. Sherman and Webb (1988) identified several characteristics common to qualitative field studies. First, such studies are premised on the assumption that events can be understood only if they are seen in context. The contexts of inquiry are natural, not contrived or designed. Those who are studied are allowed to speak for themselves, to describe their perspectives and behaviors. Researchers attend to the experience as a whole, not to separate variables, and in this way, they seek to understand experience holistically:

> [Q]ualitative research implies a direct concern with experience as it is "lived" or "felt" or "undergone." . . . Qualitative research, then, has the aim of understanding experience as nearly as possible as its participants feel or live it. (Sherman & Webb, 1988, p. 7)

In this approach, the anthropologist becomes a participant as well as an objective observer. Observation in the field rather than the study of other people's reports is central to this method. While the fieldwork approach is the most widely used anthropological method in educational research, the other two approaches have also influenced research in education.

The Organismic Approach

The organismic approach rests on the belief that a culture should be seen as a living organism—an integrated system of institutions, folkways, and mores. Hence, a study of conditions or artifacts in any society must be done in the context of a culture as an integrated system. Because functions of the various sectors of a culture are all interrelated, changes in one area are bound to have ripple effects on the others. Two separate perspectives constitute the organismic approach. The structuralist view holds that societal needs provide the unifying force in people's lives. An early proponent of this view was English anthropologist A. R. Radcliffe-Brown (1881–1955). The second perspective is founded on the belief that the individual's needs give the integrating thrust in human life. The best-known early believer of this view was Polish anthropologist Bronislav Malinowski (1884–1943). When the organismic approach is utilized in education, schools and classrooms may be seen as an independent culture or a social system. In this way we not only look for the characteristics that distinguish schools from other institutions, but we can also examine the influence of the school's unique values, customs, traditions, and behavioral norms on students. The effects of the school's general climate on the institution's instructional effectiveness can also be examined via the organismic approach.

Cultural Materialism

Although cultural materialism is not considered an organismic perspective, some attention should be given to this relatively new but major contemporary mode of anthropological thinking. Not unlike advocates of the organismic view, cultural materialists argue that culture should be seen as a system. As leading cultural anthropologist Marvin Harris points out, seemingly strange and irrational cultural practices in another society have rational bases when viewed as an integral part of a system. Moreover, what determines the nature of human institutions, social interactions, and even philosophies and religions are not ideals and logic but rather the manner in which the society stores and uses energy (Harris, 1968).

The East Indian belief in the sacred cow, which may seem irrational and self-defeating from the Western point of view, illustrates Harris's point. When seen as an integral part of the people's attempt to cope with the harsh ecological conditions for survival, however, the belief has a perfectly rational basis. Consider this: India is an agricultural land lacking many important natural resources, such as oil, coal, wood, and steel. In such an environment, using oxen as traction animals, their milk as a source of nutrition, and even dried cow dung as a source of fuel and floor-covering material has provided an efficient and adaptive means of harnessing and using energy for survival. On the other hand, treating cattle as a main food source would have been an inefficient and maladaptive means of expending energy for livelihood. Eating beef would have deprived the people of many critical measures for living and perpetuating the Indian people. The religious significance of the cows then must have evolved from tales about their pivotal role in life that were passed on from one generation to another through informal education—for example, storytelling (Harris, 1974). Thus, the religious belief about the sacred cow did not originate from some theological or philosophical idea regarding the nature of reality, because "livelihood eventually dominates social organization, which in turn governs ideology and logic" (Burger, 1975, p. 107).

From the cultural materialist point of view, what is taught, how people learn, and how schools function are not determined by the ideals held by educators and philosophers but rather by modes of harnessing and expending energy. Consequently, the ways of storing and using energy determine teacher–pupil, administrator–pupil, and even school–community relationships and define what constitutes usable technology—for example, computers, calculators, word processors, and other electrical or electronic hardware and software. Because cultural materialists are concerned with the efficient use of energy, they do not believe that cultures are relative or that all cultures are equally "good." Quite to the contrary, they insist that cultures can be compared with each other in terms of the efficiency with which energy is stored and used. For example, the efficiency of a culture can be measured by studying the amount of energy used in relation to the amount of food produced according to the long-term consequences. Similarly, cultures can be compared according to their use of human and technological resources in proportion to the effectiveness of their educational institutions.

It is important to note that cultural materialism should be viewed more as a strategy for empirical study of human society than as a philosophical system such as Marxism. Marxism, also known as dialectical materialism, is founded on the assumption that the modes of producing and distributing goods determine the nature of social organization and human ideologies. Further, the dialectical process of the struggle between workers and their "masters" in a capitalistic society is believed to result in the inevitable destruction of the latter followed by the appearance of a classless society. Hence, dialectical materialism entails political activism, which cultural materialists consider inimical to an objective empirical investigation of human culture.

In respect to the place of cultural materialism in education, the specific implications of this point of view for educational plans and strategies and teacher education have yet to be worked out. However, cultural materialism as a fundamental perspective may give us unique insight into the connection between culture and education. In an era in which technological changes are rampant and their influence pervasive, the findings of cultural materialists ought to be taken seriously for an explanation of the present and possible control of the future.

The Comparative Approach

Advocates of the comparative approach, as the term itself suggests, study cultures by comparing a set of data from a particular culture with similar information about other cultures. Studies in international and comparative education are examples of the comparative approach applied to educational inquiry. In recent years, many educators and the public have been interested in learning about the Japanese educational system. This curiosity occurs partly because, compared with our schoolchildren, Japanese pupils are significantly more proficient in mathematics and science. Some argue that Japanese children in general are better educated than children in the United States. In investigating the relative effectiveness of Japanese and U.S. schools, we may compare the impact of respective cultures on children's attitudes toward schooling, teachers, intellectual activities, learning, and other people. In the area of school administration, data regarding the behavioral norms for interpersonal relationships in Japanese and U.S. cultures may tell us about the nature of administrator–teacher and teacher–pupil relationships as they impinge upon teaching–learning effectiveness. Through this kind of study, we may find that transplanting an educational measure from another culture may not be helpful to our society. On the contrary, such an action may lead us to other unsuspected but more serious difficulties. Cross-cultural studies of education can enable us to avoid counterproductive research studies and self-defeating educational practices.

Although each of the three approaches of anthropological studies just discussed has its own distinctive features, more than one approach could be used in educational inquiry. For example, in doing a comparative study of Japanese and U.S. schools, one may use ethnographic as well as ethnological techniques in analyzing the different systems. Empirical studies of, say, effective schools or bilingualism may follow the fieldwork approach and the comparative method.

Though not detailed here, the historical approach (comparing the present with the past) in the study of cultural development is indeed applicable to the study of educational institutions and their functions. All in all, when we consider the complex and intricate relationship between culture and education, cross-cultural approaches in educational inquiry and teacher education play a pivotal role.

Implications for Practitioners

While teachers are generally not prepared to do full-scale anthropological research, some of the skills of anthropological research can serve classroom teachers in their efforts to become more effective. For example, a teacher beginning a new job might approach the new school as a field site. Through systematic observation and listening and the use of field notes to record impressions and information, the new teacher can begin to understand the culture of the school. What expectations and beliefs guide the behaviors of the participants in the school culture? What does the new teacher have to do to fit in or to avoid counterproductive practices? What are the school's routines? How are decisions made and conflicts resolved? Who holds informal power? What routines and practices support or work against effective teaching practices? If one can begin to understand the school as a system with a history, the reasons for particular practices become clear. This understanding can help practitioners view objectively the values and behaviors of the field site that are taken for granted in order to evaluate their impact on teaching and learning.

The school itself is a cultural site; in addition, the students are members of cultures to which the teacher may not belong. Learning about the communities of students who are culturally different from the teacher can help him or her communicate more effectively with them. This can mean reading about different cultures, but it can also mean talking with parents and others in the community, observing the neighborhood, and participating in local events—in short, getting involved with cultural groups in nonjudgmental ways to better understand the learners. Even when students are members of the same race, class, and ethnic group as the teacher, they are still members of their own youth culture. Understanding young people means listening and observing in order to better see the world as they see it. While effective teachers don't act like adolescents or children, at least not on the job, they are able to understand the world from the perspective of their students and to find ways to make learning more meaningful to them. Seeing students as part of cultural systems and being willing to learn about those systems are important characteristics of effective teachers.

In recent years, teachers have been learning to conduct their own field-based research in a process known as *action research*. Action research can be described as systematic inquiry into the factors that affect one's own teaching practice. Action research first gained prominence in the work of Kurt Lewin (1890–1947) in the 1930s and 1940s. For Lewin, action research was a dynamic, cyclical process in which people examined social issues which affected their lives

(Stringer, 2004). Today the term is used to describe a variety of approaches, generally with a focus on enabling practitioners to better understand and improve their teaching practice and those elements of the schooling process which influence that practice (Noffke & Stevenson, 1995). Most advocates of action research focus on a field-based approach to research borrowed from anthropology. Teachers are taught to gather data in the naturalistic context of their school and classroom. They are "participant–researchers," rather than outside, dispassionate observers. Action research is intended to engage teachers in reflective practice in order to better understand their teaching practices in terms of the perspectives and experiences of the other participants in the classroom (Stringer, 2004). This approach to research can help teachers understand various cultural aspects of their practice. A teacher, for example, might examine how children from different cultural backgrounds respond to a particular pedagogical approach. Teachers might learn, as well, about the nature of the culture of the classroom and school that may facilitate, or limit, the learning of all children. Action research can help teachers unravel the taken-for-granted assumptions of daily life in the classroom. By examining factors previously taken-for-granted, teachers can begin to determine what might be possible to change. Finally, teachers can develop a greater understanding of the cultural factors that influence teaching and learning and how those might be worked with or even changed.

 ## *Cases for Reflection*

The "Cases for Reflection" section of each chapter has a twofold purpose. One is to help readers become aware of the variety and complexity of factors that may contribute to the education of an individual or a group. The other is to stimulate readers to reflect critically about the types of questions we need to raise and the kinds of anthropological methods we may use in attempting to account for the educational achievement of a particular group. Suggested discussion questions follow the excerpt in each chapter.

BECOMING AMERICAN

The Asian Pacific American children must go through life trying to appease many social realities at one time. First, there is the assumed pressure many face to do well in the United States. Success of children gives the family "face." Children represent a future of unlimited possibilities that most first-generation Asian Pacific Americans have been denied. Language, financial, and racial barriers have limited first-generation immigrants and prevented them from attaining the American dream. For many Vietnamese, the hope and aspirations of the rest of the family rest on the shoulders of the children. The children may have left their parents in Vietnam in order to make a better life abroad. . . . Thousands of Chinese children from Taiwan are sent by their parents to complete their education in the United States. These children are often sent as adolescents and may live alone or with friends and relatives that the children hardly know. . . . The pressure to succeed and not disappoint the family is tremendous. The sense of guilt and anxiety is high. . . .

Second, many children are expected to succeed in the United States while maintaining their culture. The need to keep the soul or heart of the family culture is important. Many Asians and Pacific Islanders see America as a land of opportunity in the material sense, but lacking spirituality. Children are asked to become Americanized, but on the parents' terms (observing filial piety, yet at the same time speaking fluent English and reading Shakespeare). Unfortunately, many parents, especially those who do not speak English well, become more alienated as their children become more Americanized. . . . The children are expected to become fully bicultural in order to satisfy the demands of assimilation and upholding traditions. The pressure to be bicultural can be immense and frustrating. . . .

Third, children are faced with stereotypes that limit opportunities for Asian and Pacific Islanders. Perhaps the most popular image to influence Asian Pacific Islander children is that of the model minority. Asian Americans have been portrayed by the media as extraordinary achievers. . . . The exaggerated image centers around students overcoming incredible language and cultural barriers to attain and even surpass the educational achievements of their mainstream counterparts.

Like many stereotypes, the model minority resulted from kernels of truth. Many Asian Pacific Islander parents give up everything in their homelands to improve the lives of their children. In some cases, the children do well and go on to establish successful lives in the United States. However, many Asian Pacific American children do not fit into the model minority mold. The image originated from a number of popular magazines and newspapers (such as U.S. News and World Report, Newsweek, *the* New York Times, Time) *portraying Asian Americans as extraordinary achievers. However, this portrayal is misleading. Asian Americans show not only high educational attainments but relatively higher proportions of individuals with no education compared with Whites. . . . A bimodal distribution of achievement is found where some Asian Pacific Islander groups (such as Chinese, Filipinos, Koreans, Japanese, and Indian) do well compared to Whites while others (some southeast Asian groups) do poorly. . . . Economically, the successful image doesn't always hold up because compared to Whites, many Asian Pacific Islanders (1) live in urban areas, (2) have a higher average number of wage earners per household, and (3) face a "glass ceiling" creating a high percentage of overqualified workers. . . .*

The model minority image often does more harm than good. If students do not fit the model minority stereotype, teachers may become frustrated or blame the students for their poor performance. The students can internalize these stereotypes and feel unworthy and sense that they are unintelligent. Many Asian Pacific American children are pressured to seek academic excellence or risk losing face and family integrity. . . . A model minority stereotype may preempt opportunities for Asian and Pacific Islander students to participate in bilingual programs and justify nonaction with youths who genuinely require other types of assistance. . . . The model minority stereotype can have debilitating social effects. First, other minority groups seen as less "successful" are blamed for not being able to do as well as the Asian achievers. Second, Asians become pitted against other ethnic minorities. When the model minority myth is embraced as true, oppression becomes trivialized because it is seen as easily overcome by hard work and cultural values.

Other images of being lazy or too fun-loving can hurt Pacific Island children. Reports of Asian or Pacific Islander gangs have alienated many people from these groups. For example, the Southeast Asian community of San Diego not only has the highest level of academic achievement, but also has the highest rates of juvenile delinquency. . . .

Fourth, there is often a lack of appropriate role models for Asian Pacific American children. Many schools with a significant Asian or Pacific Islander population do not have Asian Pacific Islander school personnel as positive role models. This is compounded by the feeling among many Asian and Pacific Islander parents that the teaching profession lacks prestige and financial rewards and discriminates against them in the job market.

Source: Russell L. Young (1998), Becoming American. Reprinted by permission from *Struggling to Be Heard: The Unmet Needs of Asian Pacific American Children,* edited by Valerie Ooka Pang and Li-Rong Lilly Cheng, the State University of New York Press ©1998, State University of New York. All rights reserved.

DISCUSSION QUESTIONS

How would the answers to the following questions help you explain why Asian Americans are doing so well or not so well in school and at what cost they pay for their educational performance?

1. Asian Americans come from several different nationality groups. What common cultural characteristics could you infer from the information given in "Becoming American," and how are they related to the academic achievements of Asian Pacific Islander Americans? Could such characteristics have anything to do with the Asian Pacific Islander young people's choice of future occupations?
2. For Asian Pacific Islander American youths, what are possible consequences for being bicultural? Do you think that an Asian Pacific Islander American could be truly (50/50) bicultural? Why or why not? When could a person be truly bicultural? Give some examples.
3. What is meant by "the model minority"? What is wrong with this label if it "resulted from kernels of truth"?
4. What impact might ethnic stereotyping have on the education of Asian Pacific Islander American and other minority students? Could such reasons apply to other minority groups?
5. What are some possible reasons why some Asian Pacific Islander groups do poorly in school as compared with white middle-class children?
6. What role could the model minority stereotype play in perpetuating racism?
7. If Asian Pacific Islander American students have done well in school, why have U.S. schools been less successful in helping other minority young people to do better academically?
8. What makes Asian Pacific Islander Americans succeed or fail in school? Which of the anthropological methods discussed in this chapter might you use to answer this question?
9. What other kinds of questions might you need to raise to obtain additional information to answer question 8?

REFERENCES

Banks, J. A., & Banks, C. E. (2004). *Multicultural education: issues and perspectives*. Hoboken, NJ: Wiley.

Bruner, J. (1996). *The culture of education*. Cambridge: Harvard University Press.

Burger, H. (1975). Cultural materialism: Efficiencies not descriptions. *General Systems, 20,* 107–119. This article provides an excellent summary and review of Marvin Harris's book *The Rise of Anthropological Theory.*

Harris, M. (1968). *The rise of anthropological theory*. New York: Thomas Y. Crowell.

Harris, M. (1974). *Cows, pigs, wars, and witches: The riddles of culture*. New York: Random House.

Kimball, S. T. (1974). *Culture and the educative process*. New York: Teachers College Press.

Lesko, N. (1998). *Symbolizing society*. New York: Falmer Press.

McLaren, P. (1994). *Life in schools* (2nd ed.). New York: Longman.

Mather, M., & Rivers, K. (2003, March). *State results of child well-being: The results from the 2000 Census* [On-line]. Available: http://www.prb.org/AmeristatTemplate.cfm?Section=Education1&template=/ContentManagement/ContentDisplay.cfm&ContentID=8459

Noffke, S. E., & Stevenson, R. B. (Eds.). (1995). *Educational action research: Becoming practically critical*. New York: Teachers College Press.

Population Reference Bureau. (2001, August). Ameristat, Social Science Data Analysis Network [On-line]. Available: http://www.ameristat.org/

Redfield, R. (1973). The contribution of anthropology to the education of teachers. In F. A. J. Ianni & E. Storey (Eds.), *Cultural relevance and educational issues* (pp. 153–159). Boston: Little, Brown.

Sherman, R., & Webb, R. (1988). *Qualitative research in education: Focus and methods*. London: Falmer Press.

Shweder, R. A. (1991). *Thinking through cultures*. Cambridge: Harvard University Press.

Spindler, G. D. (1973). Anthropology and education: An overview. In F. A. J. Ianni & E. Storey (Eds.), *Cultural relevance and educational issues* (pp. 94–115). Boston: Little, Brown. For a historical overview of anthropology in education, see "Theory, research and application in educational anthropology" by Elizabeth M. Eddy (1997), in George D. Spindler (Ed.), *Education and cultural process* (3rd ed.), Prospect Heights, IL: Waveland Press.

Spindler, G. D. (Ed.). (1982). *Doing the ethnography of schooling: Educational anthropology in action*. Prospect Heights, IL: Waveland Press.

Spradley, J. P. (1975). *Cocktail waitress*. NY: Wiley.

Stringer, E. (2004). *Action research in education*. Upper Saddle River, NJ: Pearson.

Young, R. L., & Sharifzadeh, V. (2003). Aftereffect of 9–11: A call to balance patriotism and multiculturalism in the classroom. *Multicultural Perspectives, 5*(2), 34–38.

2

Culture, Education, and Schooling

KEY *Concepts:*

- Acculturation
- Core values
- Culture
- Deficit view
- Education
- Enculturation
- Generalization

- Operating culture
- Private culture
- Schooling
- Stereotyping
- Symboling
- Syncretism

A s has already been suggested, education as a process does not stand for any specific set of activities, such as reading, writing, and figuring; rather, it signifies a deliberate attempt on the part of a group or society to transmit something worthwhile to its members. This transmission may be carried on informally by parents, relatives, and peers or formally through institutions specifically designed for instructional purposes, such as schools and churches. Education is the means by which the members of a society ensure that the behaviors and values necessary to maintain their culture are learned. If education is indeed a cultural process, we must first clarify the meaning of the word *culture*.

WHAT IS CULTURE?

Culture as a System of Norms and Control

In general terms, culture is most commonly viewed as that pattern of knowledge, skills, behaviors, attitudes, and beliefs, as well as material artifacts, produced by a human society and transmitted from one generation to another. Culture is the whole of humanity's intellectual, social, technological, political, economic, moral, religious, and aesthetic accomplishments. Although it is absurd to speak of a culturally deprived child as if there could be a child without any culture, this notion was used in the 1960s and 1970s to describe many minority children for whom compensatory education was designed (Bruner, 1996, p. 73). This view will be discussed in chapter 4.

Central to the concept of culture is the fact that any culture is goal oriented. These goals are reflected in people's behaviors, beliefs, life patterns, and hopes. Hence, culture is more than a collection of disconnected acts and beliefs; rather, it should be seen as an integrated set of norms or standards by which human behaviors, beliefs, and thinking are organized. According to Clifford Geertz (1973):

> Culture is best seen not as complexes of concrete behavior patterns—customs, usages, traditions, habit clusters—as has been the case up to now, but as a set of control mechanisms—plans, recipes, rules, instructions (what computer engineers call "programs")—for governing of behavior. (p. 44)

Culture should, then, be viewed as consisting of the standards and control mechanisms with which members of a society assign meanings, values, and significance to things, events, and behaviors. These norms and control mechanisms are the products of human beings' unique ability to symbol, or to "originate, determine, and bestow meaning upon things and events in the external world and the ability to comprehend such meanings" (White & Dillingham, 1973, p. 1). An ordinary cow becomes a sacred cow and plain water becomes holy water because human beings give them special meanings and significance. This means that the meaning and significance of objects, events, and behavioral patterns should be understood and appreciated within a specific cultural context rather than in terms of their supposed intrinsic properties. As we shall see later, **symboling,** or the process by which people bestow meanings on objects and actions within a specific culture, has many important implications in education.

The process of symboling occurs through thinking, feeling, and acting. The corresponding products—ideas, attitudes, acts, and objects—are indigenous to a culture (White & Dillingham, 1973, p. 27). The patterns of behaviors found in various societies have no inherent meaning apart from their cultural settings, for such patterns are reflections of unique worldviews and value orientations belonging to individual societies. For example, Navajo Indians are said to have a passive view of human beings; they say that "death is taking place within John," implying that human beings belong to a world in which forces of nature make "things" happen to people. On the other hand, white Western people are said to have an active (or aggressive) conception of people; they regard the individual as an agent who causes events to occur in the world, who does "things" to his or her world. Thus, a person in Western society would speak of John dying as if dying were something that a person performs. Similarly, the lack of an appropriate expression for complimenting one's grandmother in certain Far Eastern languages reflects the hierarchical nature of social organizations that do not permit the young to commend their elders directly. In dealing with different cultural beliefs and the behavioral patterns arising from them, we must always take into account the basis of their symboling process.

There is probably no definitive answer explaining why a particular culture assigns certain meanings and worth to a given set of events, objects, or acts. But we can reasonably assume that the dominant worldview of a society is a major source of meanings and values. In turn, a prevailing worldview of a culture results from certain experiences that have enabled a group of people to success-fully solve the problems of daily living. In a very important sense, a culture is a conception of what reality is like and how it works.

Virtually no aspect of human life and its processes is unaffected by culture because it is "in us and all around us, just as the air we breathe" (Erickson, 1997, p. 33). So pervasive is the influence of culture that even our perception of colors and shapes cannot escape its effects. As Russian psychologist A. R. Luria (1976) points out, although there are only twenty or twenty-five names for colors and shapes, the human eye can distinguish up to two or three million different hues and shapes. This means a person perceiving a particular color or shape must identify its primary property and place it in a color or shape category. Thus, perception is not merely a physiological or neurological process. "Seeing" a color or a shape requires making decisions about the category into which a given hue or shape is to be placed. Of course, the number and categories avail-able to a person depend on the language system being used. As Luria puts it:

> Once we recognize that perception is a complex cognitive activity employing auxiliary devices and involving the intimate participation of language, we must radically alter the classical notion of perception as an unmediated process depending only on the relatively simple laws of natural science.
>
> We can thus conclude that, structurally, perception depends on historically established human practices that can alter the system of codes used to process incoming information and can influence the decision assigning the perceived objects to appropriate categories. (p. 21)

Similarly, perception of pain is reported to depend on the linguistic categories available to the person as well as the extent to which a particular culture encour-ages or discourages the expression of thoughts and feelings. What all this sug-gests is that people who live in a culture different from ours may "see" the world differently, for the nature of language and its uses are central to any culture.

The symboling process just discussed occurs not only in the large society but also takes place within its many subunits. These subunits may be social, political, intellectual, economic, educational, religious, racial, ethnic, or generational (chronological). Consequently, a society can be said to have many subcultures or minority cultures, such as Mexican American culture, African American culture, the youth culture, the school culture, and the culture of the poor, each with its own value orientations. Standards and controls of each society or group are established because they enable individuals to deal with the needs and problems arising out of their environment and their associations with others. Cultures then can be seen as different ways of coping with essentially similar problems and needs. They represent various societies' successful experiments in living, which have been developed over time. Human beings become individuals "under the guidance of cultural patterns, historically created systems of meaning in terms of which we give form, order, point and direction to our lives" (Benedict, 1934, p. 278). The culture to which one belongs, then, becomes the root of the individual's identity, because culture gives us a sense of power and confidence by giving us the basis of achieving our goals, determining what is desirable and undesirable, and developing the purpose of our life. Accordingly, to reject or demean a person's cultural heritage is to do psychological and moral violence to the dignity and worth of that individual. Assuming that cultures are various societies' successful experiments in living, it would be unreasonable to argue that any one set of cultural norms is universally good for all societies or is inherently superior to all other cultures, nor should we think that any ideas, attitudes, acts, events, or objects have fixed and absolute meaning and worth.

Culture as a Map

As fundamental as culture is to human life and society, understanding a culture, even if it is our own, does not enable us to know every detail of how a particular group of people acts, thinks, and lives. Nor can we have information about how every segment of a society functions because, as Clyde Kluckhohn (1968) points out, "Culture is like a map. A map just isn't the territory but an abstract description of trends toward uniformity in the words, deeds, and artifacts of a human group. If a map is accurate and you can read it, you won't get lost: if you know a culture, you will know your way around in the life of a society" (p. 35). Though we cannot know all the details of either our own or another people's cultural map, an understanding of the general terrains of the society's culture would help us to be more effective in relating to others and achieving our own purposes. For example, by knowing the cultural maps of our students, we can better facilitate the conditions for effective learning for them, because we can more accurately predict and guide the students' behaviors in teaching–learning situations.

Although culture as a map contains explicit information about the norms and controls of a society, many dos and don'ts are not expressed in a clearly observable way. These cultural standards are implicit and must be inferred through observation of certain consistent and persistent patterns of thinking and acting. For example, in American culture the belief that hard work will lead to success is explicitly manifested in the ways we teach our children about the importance of the work–success ethic. But the fairly widely held view that those who do not succeed are either lazy or stupid has to be inferred from the ways people generally treat those who do not succeed socioeconomically. In a society in which the hierarchical relationships between individuals are believed to be of central importance, many language forms and rules of conduct clearly indicate what is or is not socially and even morally acceptable. In such a culture, children's unwillingness or inability to express their feelings and thoughts in front of their parents or their refusal to maintain direct eye contact with an adult during conversation implicitly reflects the fundamental importance of the hierarchical relationships. This implies that we learn the norms of our culture through direct instructions about explicit cultural standards, but we also acquire our society's culturally sanctioned ways through learning certain specific behaviors. We also learn our cultural norms through the ways people relate to each other and the ways teaching is carried on.

Cultural norms can be learned latently. For example, children learn the values of their society by attending schools because school practices reflect the norms of the culture in which they function. As Hollins (1996) points out,

> It is rather easy to see that [the] hierarchical structure in the governance of schools reflects the bureaucratic governmental structure of the nation and that the interconnected beliefs and values associated with Protestantism, capitalism, and republicanism are present in the focus on individualism, competition, and equality. Those cultural discontinuities that exist in the larger society are also present in the schools in the form of differences in the treatment of students, and at time differences in the quality of education provided, based on classism, racism, and sexism. (p. 31)

For educators, an analysis of the manner in which education is carried on is at least as important as the explicitly stated goals and content of education, because the means or the methods of teaching and educating also inculcate beliefs and attitudes.

More specifically, the modes of social and personal interaction in the school are affected by the cultural conditions of the larger society. The ways that adult members of the society deal with children are likely to be reflected in the teacher's approach to evaluating students' achievements and failures. Similarly, if a culture contains contradictory beliefs and practices, these may be transmitted to students unless the school consciously and deliberately points out and reduces, or eliminates, such contradictions. For example, Americans generally believe that one should always be truthful. But many people also believe that it is all right to "cheat" a little on their income tax returns or to make campaign promises even though they may not be able to fulfill them. At an elementary school, a candidate for the presidency of the student council promised to put Coca-Cola machines in every classroom and provide longer and more frequent recess periods if he were elected to the office. The boy was elected, but the school officials regarded the boy's tactic as merely humorous and imaginative. Although the purpose of forming a student council may have been to teach children the meaning of fair play and the democratic process in operation, the school actually may have helped teach them that whatever means one uses to attain one's goal are justifiable.

CORE VALUES

There are people who believe that the primary function of our schools is to transmit societal values; others insist that the schools ought to be the agent of social reform (transformation). Still others argue that the schools should be agents of both cultural transmission and transformation. Regardless of how we view the proper role of our schools, we cannot deny that, intentionally or unintentionally, the prevailing values, attitudes, and behavioral norms of our society are transmitted to the young through what schools do. It is for this reason that we need to examine the concept of core values in relation to education and schooling.

In attempting to deal with its daily problems, each society develops certain patterns of behavior and attitudes that are useful in meeting human needs and resolving conflicts between individuals and groups. When these patterns become well defined (and even institutionalized) and accepted by the dominant group within a society, they constitute what anthropologist George Spindler calls the **core values** of a culture. These core values become the basis for the standard with which the major institutions of the dominant society evaluate their members. These standards in turn become the criteria for giving people opportunities for advancement and other rewards. The academic as well as the social expectations our schools have of the young are rooted in the core values of our society. However, the core values of the mainstream society are surrounded by other alternative (minority) patterns that often challenge or at least radically differ from the norms of the dominant group. Consequently, the possibility of maintaining social cohesion and cultural diversity depends on the dominant group's ability to deal with value conflicts arising from divergent alternative cultural patterns.

The Core Values of American Culture

Before looking at forces challenging the core values constituting the American conception of the good life—traditionally referred to as the WASP (white Anglo-Saxon Protestant) or the Anglo-American perspective—it may be helpful to examine some of these core values. According to Spindler (1963), the traditional values that make up the core of the Anglo-American pattern fall into the following five general categories: (1) Puritan morality, (2) work–success ethic, (3) individualism, (4) achievement orientation, and (5) future-time orientation (pp. 134–136).

Puritan morality stresses respectability, thrift, self-denial, duty, delayed gratification, and sexual restraint. The second traditional value, the so-called *work–success ethic*, is the belief not only that people should work hard to succeed but also that those who have not become successful are either lazy or stupid, or both. Hence, people must constantly work diligently to convince themselves of their worth. *Individualism*, the third value, emphasizes the sacredness of the individual, which ideally should lead to self-reliance and originality. However, it often manifests itself in a form of egocentrism and disregard for other people's rights and desires. It is this individualism coupled with the work–success ethic that leads many to view welfare programs as giveaways to people who are lazy and unworthy of help. The fourth value, *achievement orientation*, relates to the work–success ethic in that everyone should constantly try to achieve a higher goal through hard work. An individual should not be satisfied with a given position but should always seek something higher and better. The last traditional value, *future-time orientation,* is summed up in the attitude of "save today for tomorrow." The stereotyped image of the teacher as a stern drillmaster who encourages children to respect their elders, work hard for tomorrow's success, and always reach for higher and higher grades reflects these traditional values.

In 1990, Spindler and Spindler added the following to the five values of American mainstream society: equality of opportunity, the value of honesty (as an expedient best policy), a belief in the openness of the American socioeconomic structure that can be penetrated by personal commitment and hard work, and a sociable, get-along-well-with-others orientation (p. 37). These values are only broad categories that can be further elaborated on to indicate numerous implications for daily living. But, of course, it is enough to point out that the most fundamental trait of these traditional values is that they are regarded as absolute and fixed. Hence, they are believed to constitute the idealized norm of behavior for all Americans and perhaps for all humanity. It is for this reason that we may say that the holders of these values are ethnocentric.

Challenges to the Core Values

Mid-1950s to Early 1960s

As a result of complex and rapid socioeconomic, political, and technological changes in our society, various forces challenging the validity of these core values have arisen. According to a study of several hundred students enrolled in professional education courses and representing lower-middle-class to upper-middle-class socioeconomic status in the early 1960s, the core values of college students had shifted considerably from those of their parents. Unlike their parents, the subjects held as their core values (1) sociability, (2) a relativistic moral attitude, (3) consideration for others, (4) a hedonistic, present-time orientation, and (5) conformity to the group (Spindler, 1963, pp. 132–147).

Sociability means liking people and being able to get along well with them. A *relativistic moral attitude* is the belief that what is moral is relative to the group to which one belongs. To be *considerate* of others means being sensitive to and having tolerance for other people's feelings so that the harmony of the group is not disturbed. *Hedonistic, present-time orientation* is the opposite of the traditional future-time orientation of Puritan morality. It is said to come from the notion that because no one can be certain about tomorrow, we should enjoy the present, a sort of "eat, drink, and be merry, for tomorrow we die" attitude. Yet even this fourth value was to be carried out within the limits of the norm set by the group. The last value, *conformity to the group,* emphasizes the importance of group harmony as the ultimate goal of individual members.

In the 1960s, conflicts between parents and school officials steeped in the Puritan morality and youth were unavoidable because their value orientations were so contradictory. Yet no serious confrontations occurred between those two generations because the young were more concerned with balance, adjustment, and harmony than with individualism, spontaneity, and autonomy. Since the completion of Spindler's study, increasing evidence has suggested that the value orientation of youth has continued to move even further from the value systems of their parents. Today even a casual conversation with upper grade school and junior high school children reveals their strong belief in the individual's right to privacy and freedom. The significant change in the value commitments of young people may have been partially due to the student activism and counter-culture movement of the mid-1960s. And although today's adolescents and college youths tend to conform more to adult demands and norms, the flame of their doubts about the legitimacy of the traditional core values of American society continues to burn. It is to this condition that we may attribute some fundamental changes in certain areas of young people's value orientation.

Mid-1960s to 1970

The proponents of the counterculture movement in the mid-1960s argued that although the United States had achieved unprecedented economic affluence through the work–success and achievement ethics, it continued to emphasize economic success and productivity. As a result of this endless search for greater and greater affluence, even the worth of an individual was said to have been determined according to success and productivity as defined by corporations and industry. But to growing numbers of young people, the long-sought economic affluence and security became simple facts of life. They were no longer legitimate objects to be achieved. Consequently, the young were convinced that the core values of the older generation—that is, the cultural values of the industrial ethic—were outdated and irrelevant to their lives.

Once the society is able to demonstrate that it can produce enough for all its members, its primary concern should not be to produce more and consume more. The supporters of the counterculture movement insisted that we develop a more just and equal means of distributing the nation's wealth so that more people's lives could be meaningful and leisurely. The young people of the mid-1960s were not against technology but rather against the worship of it, because a technology-worshiping culture tends to treat people as products of a technological system and to subordinate human needs to industrial and technological needs. To the advocates of the counterculture movement, the moral imperatives and urgency behind production, acquisition, materialism, and greater economic affluence had lost their validity. At the same time, the authorities (adults) who subscribed to the traditional values had lost their legitimacy. These and other similar warnings against the dehumanization of individuals were increasingly heard in the 1970s.

For the young to believe that they had been oppressed by their elders was nothing new and perhaps is to be expected in almost any period in history. But for youth to view authority as illegitimate was something new. One of the consequences of this phenomenon was that with the declining legitimacy of authorities there was a rise in coercive violence launched by terrified authorities to maintain their threatened power. Moreover, because the young were convinced of the illegitimacy of the Establishment and its values, they struggled against institutional conformity, centralized power, and uniformity of any kind.

The young's demand for radical cultural revolution in the mid- to late-1960s appeared in the form of increased requests for the governed to become actively involved in political, economic, and social processes. Students also sought opportunities to participate in their own educational experience and planning. Idiosyncratic lifestyles and personal grooming were said to symbolize their revolt against uniformity, and marijuana smoking was believed to be a ritual action by which they asserted a new moral position.

The counterculture movement is no longer a potent force among the youth of the United States. But young people's desires for privacy, autonomy, and greater involvement in participatory democracy have not changed. The younger generation today still questions the legitimacy of the traditional values, even though many are willing to conform more to the adult norm because of current insecurities related to finding and keeping jobs and because of anxieties related to the general political, social, and economic uncertainties of the time.

Early 1970s to Early 1980s

According to a 1971 survey of 1,244 students in fifty college and university campuses, conducted by the firm of Daniel Yankelovich, Inc., more than 75 percent mentioned that they were chiefly concerned with friendship, privacy, freedom of opinion, and nature (*Kansas City Star,* 1972, p. 4). Only about 25 percent still regarded changing society and combating hypocrisy as their primary interests. These data seem to suggest that college students had moved away from emotional involvement in social and political causes. They appeared to be channeling their efforts to those aspects of their lives over which they could have more control. The findings also showed that these students were less willing than those in the 1960s to fight wars for any reason; 50 percent of the participants saw war as justified only if it were for counteracting aggression. Perhaps the greatest single erosion of relations to authority was in the "boss" relationship: Only 36 percent of the young people did not mind being "bossed around" on the job. Moreover, in 1971 only 39 percent held the belief that "hard work always pays off," whereas a 1968 survey by Yankelovich shows that 69 percent believed that "hard work will always pay off" (Yankelovich, 1981, p. 7). This shift from the traditional work–success ideal was indeed radical. In regard to sex, the 1971 group generally sought a much greater degree of sexual freedom and its acceptance by their elders. In summing up the study, a majority of the participants believed that American democracy or justice did not function evenhandedly, and that a considerable degree of inconsistency existed between American ideals and practices.

A survey conducted by the University of California at Los Angeles and the American Council on Education suggested that college freshmen in 1973 tended to be more liberal and were more inclined to support greater freedom for students than their predecessors. This study polled more than 318,000 students at 579 institutions; from this population 190,000 were statistically adjusted to represent the nation's 1.65 million freshmen (*Kansas City Star*, 1974, p. 15). In general, the findings of this study did not indicate any significant changes in the young people's attitudes from those found in the Yankelovich survey.

Although it is true that the studies conducted by both Yankelovich and UCLA and the American Council on Education dealt primarily with college students, their cumulative data since 1968 indicate a major shift in the core values of a sizable segment of American youth. Data from two major national studies by Joseph Veroff, Elizabeth Douvan, and Richard A. Kulka (1981) and Daniel Yankelovich (1981) also show a significant erosion in the general public's belief in the intrinsic worth of hard work. These studies also support earlier findings showing that a large segment of Americans sought greater personal freedom and fulfillment of personal inner desires. More indirectly, the extraordinary number of "pop psychology" books on self-improvement reflected people's preoccupation with self-fulfillment in the late 1970s into the early 1980s.

Mid-1980s to Late 1990s

Surveys of freshmen in two- and four-year colleges and universities in 1988 and 1999 revealed an interesting combination of attitudes and values. The findings from the 1988 study, which were culled from 209,627 responses, indicated that "being very well-off financially" was one of the top goals of 75.6 percent of those polled, up from 73.2 percent in 1986 and 70.9 percent in 1985, and nearly twice the 1970 figure of 39.1 percent (*Chronicle of Higher Education*, 1988, p. 34). In the similar 1999 survey, which reported the responses of 275,811 freshmen, 74 percent of the respondents indicated that "being very well-off financially" was a very important goal (*Chronicle of Higher Education*, 1999, p. A40). This inclination toward financial well-being is also reflected in the finding that more than 69 percent in 1988 and 74.6 percent in 1999 said they would "agree strongly or somewhat" that the chief benefit of attending college is increased earnings. It is worth noting that "becoming a business executive" was the career occupation most often preferred by respondents in the 1988 survey (13.1 percent). In the 1999 survey, however, becoming an engineer was the most frequently cited occupation choice (7.0 percent), while those expressing interest in becoming business executives had declined to 7.9 percent. In the 1999 survey, 11.8 percent of the respondents were "undecided" about their probable careers.

Politically, most students in both surveys described themselves as "middle of the road." In 1999, 56.5 percent of the students polled described themselves as "moderate," as compared with 56 percent in 1988. Only 18.6 percent of the 1999 respondents considered themselves as "far right." These are small percentages given that the mid-1990s were a period when conservatives made considerable electoral gains. However, only 26 percent of the survey participants in 1999 said that "keeping up with political affairs" was a very important goal. This figure was the lowest recorded since the beginning of the annual survey of freshmen in 1966. Despite this expressed apathy toward politics and the political climate in the nation, 82.5 percent said "the federal government should do more to control the sale of handguns"; 50.9 percent of the 1999 freshmen polled said they believed that "abortion should be legal"; and 58.7 percent agreed that "wealthy people should pay a larger share of the taxes than they do now." On the other hand, 78.5 percent agreed that "there is too much concern in the courts for the rights of criminals," and 80.6 percent agreed that "employers should be allowed to require drug testing of employees or job applicants" (Howe & Strauss, 1993).

Several other studies of youth values (*Chronicle of Higher Education*, 1999; Gabriel, 1995; Lawton, 1994) reveal that young people continued to regard "being well-off" and "making money" as well as marriage and parenthood as very important in their lives. But the young worried about increasing violence, sexually transmitted diseases, increasing personal indebtedness, control by others, and an uncertain future (Frazier, 1994; Gabriel, 1995; Lipsky & Abrams, 1994; Morin, 1994). On the other hand, they seemed to place greater emphasis on such issues as more tolerance toward homosexuality, alternative lifestyles, divorce, and environmental protection than more traditional matters such as economic growth, strong national defense, and maintenance of an orderly society. It would appear that the views of college students by the late 1990s reflected a mix of liberal and traditional values. However, those who hold a pessimistic view of the period's youth described them as cynical and apolitical, self-centered and withdrawn, overly preoccupied by material acquisition, and undermotivated for creative expression.

In the 1990s, the behaviors of adolescents continued to represent challenges to traditional core values. According to a 1995 report issued by the Carnegie Council on Adolescent Development (Carnegie Council, 1995), one-third of eighth graders and nearly one-half of twelfth graders used illicit drugs, and binge drinking was a serious problem in the eighth grade, with almost 28 percent of twelfth graders engaged in it. Regarding the issue of adolescent mothers giving birth, more than a half a million babies were born to girls fifteen to nineteen years old. Young girls reported that the first act of intercourse was usually forced, and 60 percent of girls thirteen years and younger had had coerced sexual experiences (e.g., rape, incest, molestation). Between 1985 and 1992, the firearm homicide rate for ten- to fourteen-year-olds more than doubled (from 0.8 to 1.9 per 100,000). These and such other incidences as suicide, reckless driving, substance abuse, unsafe sex, and AIDS indicate that today's adolescents face challenges not experienced by their parents. Yet, youth are tolerated or endured but seldom viewed as possible partners or contributors to the society (Bernard, 1996, p. 31).

From 2000 to Present

The year 2000 was the beginning of a new era in which our traumatic encounters with the 9/11 attacks and the subsequent "War on Terror" have and will continue to affect every aspect of life in the United States. It is neither surprising nor unreasonable to expect the values and attitudes of our youth to have been influenced by these distressing events.

According to the 2003 survey of 282,549 first-year students at 437 four-year colleges and universities conducted by UCLA (*Chronicle of Higher Education,* 2003, pp. A35–38), 45 percent of the students supported an increased federal spending on the military and a decreasing proportion of the group—27.8 percent, compared with 29.9 percent in 2001—reported themselves as "liberal." In other areas of ideological shifts, "conservatives" increased from 19.1 percent in 2001 to 20.0 percent in 2002. Not surprisingly, 3.0 percent of the freshmen in 2001 as compared to 2.5 percent in 2002 identified themselves as "far left." Those who reported as "middle of the road" increased from 49.5 percent in 2001 to 50.8 percent in 2002, while "far right" decreased to 1.3 percent in 2002 from 1.8 percent in 2001. Notwithstanding this move away from "liberals" to "conservatives," the freshmen's attitudes regarding some issues seem to betray the "conservative" shift. For example, the percentage of those who favored the right of gay couples to marry increased to 59.3 percent from 57.9 percent in 2001 and only 24.8 percent supported laws prohibiting gay relationship. Also, 53.6 percent and 39.7 percent of the youth "agreed strongly or somewhat" that abortion and marijuana, respectively, should be legalized.

Like terrorism, economy too seems to have affected the study population. In 2002, 66.5 percent of the freshmen, as compared to 64.6 percent in 2001, were concerned about the possibility of not having enough money to pay for college. Not unlike their counterparts in the mid-1980s to the late 1990s, 73.2 percent of the current youth believe that "very well-off financially" was an important objective of life. Similarly, "to be able to get a better job" and "to be able to make more money" were indicated as "top reasons" for deciding to go to college by 71.6 percent and 70.5 percent, respectively. Only 40.6 percent reported that developing a "meaningful philosophy of life" was very important to them. The percentages of the study respondents in various academic fields were business 16.2 percent, professional fields 12.3 percent, education 10.6 percent, social sciences 10.4 percent, engineering 9.5 percent, biological sciences 7.2 percent, and physical sciences 2.7 percent. These future career choices seem to reflect the young people's economic concerns.

In other areas, 77.8 percent of the respondents "agree strongly or somewhat" that the federal government should do more to control the sale of handguns, 75.1 percent and 64.0 percent, respectively, held that the federal government should do more to discourage energy consumption and that there is too much concern in the courts for rights of criminals. Sixty percent and 50.1 percent of the freshmen, respectively, "agreed strongly or somewhat" that college should prohibit racist and sexist language on campus and wealthy people should pay a larger share of taxes than do now.

As compared to the youth values and attitudes in the period from mid-1980s to the late 1990s, the above findings seem to support the conclusion that, though modest, today's college freshmen did have an ideological shift from "liberals" to "conservatives." Perhaps the unprecedented fear of terrorists' assaults from without, the disastrous downturn in the stock market, as well as the calamitous unemployment following the 9/11 catastrophe may have contributed to the attitudinal change.

In characterizing today's youth, the authors of *Millennials Go to College,* Neil Howe and William Straus (Howe and Straus, 2003) describe the Millennials, those born in the early to mid-1980s, as being different from their counterparts in the preceding two decades in that they are sheltered/protected, self-confident, close to their parents, team oriented, comfortable with their parents' values, academically pressured, and achievement oriented (Howe & Straus, 2000; 2003, pp. 51–129). Howe and Straus go on to point out that the Millennials are beginning to correct what they see as "the excess of today's middle-aged Boomers" by

> [opting] for the good of the group, patience, conformism, and a new focus on deeds over words. When they argue, it is less among themselves, and more with older generations whose members stand in the way of civic progress. With adults of all philosophical stripes yearning for "community," the Millennial solution is to set high standards, get organized, team up, and actually create a community. (p. 22)

While additional data may be needed to support the authors' claim that today's teens are "an updated version of the upbeat, high achieving, team playing, and civic minded [post-World War II] G.I. Generation," (pp. 22–23) findings of the UCLA survey and Howe and Straus's work do suggest that the relationship between the young and their adults appears to be less conflict ridden and more congenial than anytime in the last three to four decades. Yet, the differences in their views regarding such critical issues as racism, human sexuality, abortion, death penalty, environmental conservation, legalization of drugs, and the "War on Terror" are not likely to disappear. Values and attitudes of the rising generation and changing socioeconomic, political, and technological changes continue to challenge the soundness of the traditional core values. But the major institutions in this country, including the schools, persist in adhering to the traditional conceptions of the American way. Even the affirmative action and equal employment opportunity programs for women and minorities did not seem to have had profound impact on the traditional core values of the mainstream society. However, it seems that the concepts of hard work and success have been defined more in terms of productivity and efficiency as seen by corporations and industries than by individual workers. Even contemporary educational institutions frequently view effective education in terms of cost efficiency, to which educational accountability is closely tied. Notwithstanding the rapid shifts in values of our young people, few school board members, administrators, and teachers critically analyze the grounds for the officially prescribed norms of behavior and learning activities in relation to the changes taking place in the young people's worldviews and belief patterns. Too many educators refuse to understand the young from their own "cultural" perspective. And even when they study the young, it is usually to induce them to abandon their "barbarism" and "irrationality" so that they can assimilate or acculturate them into the idealized norms of the grown-up world.

It would appear that as the white middle class is ignorant about minority cultures, so too are adults ignorant about the cultures of childhood, adolescence, and youth. Although understanding young people's cultural perspectives will not eliminate generational disagreements, it may help to make the conflicts less disruptive and alienating. If we are to treat conflicts in school and in the classroom as cultural conflicts, both school officials and students must abandon their ethnocentrism—that is, the attitude that youngsters are "senseless" and the attitude that "old fogies just don't understand." Educationally, this means that board members, administrators, and teachers must act not as royalty but as equal members of a society in which individuals with varied cultural backgrounds (both ethnic and generational) live together. School personnel and students should act as members of a community that creates rules as a means of effective group functioning and resolves conflict through inquiry.

Administrators and teachers should act more as moderators than as judges.

Transmission of Values

Historically, the primary function of the U.S. school system has been seen as the transmission of the core values of the society at large. The process of schooling is closely tied to the linguistic codes, behavioral expectations, and value systems of the mainstream middle and upper middle classes. For this reason, children from lower socioeconomic classes are often seen negatively (Hurn, 1993; Knapp & Woolverton, 1995, p. 559). There is an inextricable relationship between social class and how schools operate and what they teach. More specifically, except in large urban magnet schools and complex transitional school districts, the predominant social class of the community shapes the social makeup of the student population. The community social class also influences its expectations of the schools and students (Knapp & Woolverton, 1995, p. 593). In a very real sense, values are transmitted to children by social class culture of the family and community and reinforced or modified by schools. Even so, most school personnel, as well as the public, save some ethnic minorities, accept the transmission of mainstream core values as the most important role of the school. But in a society where rapid scientific and technological developments occur, there are equally swift changes in the patterns of institutional and individual behaviors. Both the number and the complexity of social and moral problems resulting from such changes outstrip our ability to cope with them effectively. As an example, although our technology can manufacture automobiles that can move 125 miles per hour, we have not yet found effective means of controlling drunk driving or various types of environmental pollution stemming from industrial wastes. In addition, the impact of rapid technological changes on culture often leads to serious discrepancies between the society's established core values and the actual ways that people think and behave. Major institutions such as schools and churches extol the inherent virtue of being honest at all times. But the young may value honesty only in relation to what it can bring them, because their attitudes and values are significantly influenced by the contents of mass media, which mirror economic and industrial interests more than traditional core values. What all this suggests is that cultures have functionally different ways of dealing with essentially similar human problems, but not all cultures are equally functional. The degrees to which various elements of a culture are consistent and integrated with each other vary from society to society. In short, some cultures contain more contradictory norms than others, and more such discrepancies seem to be found in highly technological societies. Many aspects of American culture conflict with one another. For example, our country is said to guarantee equal rights and opportunities to all; however, full civil rights have yet to be granted to many people. Further, although long-range socioeconomic planning is often regarded as unAmerican and socialistic, Americans seem to be conflicted about whether governmental planning and intervention are necessary to ensure wage, energy, and media controls. In addition, most members of the dominant American culture believe that moral principles are absolute and unchangeable, but they also insist that one has to be flexible in making value decisions, particularly in relation to business practices affecting other individuals. The educational consequence is that unless we are aware of these and other inconsistencies and their influence on children's learning, we may transmit and cultivate self-defeating qualities. For example, the school may intend to develop self-reliance, creativity, and democratic leadership, but students may become docile and submissive if school activities and climate are inconsistent with the intended objectives. Specifically, a course in social studies should not be taught in an authoritarian manner, nor should school rules be merely repressive measures.

In this time of rapid technological development, it is easy for educators to become preoccupied with the efficiency with which we can accomplish our goals and measure the outcomes. More often than not, preoccupation with efficiency leads to quantification of both the ends and the means of education. Notwithstanding the importance of technology as a tool, educators need to be especially sensitive to and critical of how our use of technology enhances or detracts from the quality of what we hope to accomplish through education.

DIFFERENCES ARE NOT DEFICITS

We become individuals through our culture. Because our culture is so much a part of what we are and what we do, we often view it as if it were an innate or absolute dictum by which all individuals must guide their lives. Ethnocentrism, the belief in the superiority of our own culture, leads us to judge others in terms of our own cultural norms and inclines us to conclude that those who do not conform to our norms must be stupid, depraved, irresponsible, psychopathic, inferior, or sinful to a point beyond all redemption. When the dominant group in a society adopts the posture that its own set of values constitutes the only idealized norm in that society, the ethnic practices or traits of minority cultures are likely to be seen as deficient patterns that must be corrected either through education or coercion. In other words, the dominant culture tends to treat the minority cultures as sick forms of the normal or "right" culture and to define differences as deficits. This attitude makes it difficult for us to see that other cultures also provide effective means of dealing with the needs and problems of their respective societies. The deficit perspective, or social pathology, model of viewing minority groups contributes to the perpetuation of institutional racism and robs our society of richness (Baratz & Baratz, 1970). At the personal level, minority individuals are made to be ashamed of their ethnicity and cultural heritage.

Although the **deficit view** of minorities usually refers to ethnic or racial groups, this perspective is frequently but subtly adopted in dealing with such other groups as women, the aged, the handicapped, and even children. The deficit model is used in schools and other areas of our society to justify the subordinate status of minority groups of all kinds. For example, in recent times, there has been a trend toward encouraging people to choose their own roles according to talents and abilities across gender or sex role categories. But the traditional view of sex roles includes two distinct sets of culturally assigned characteristics for men and women. More specifically, "male culture consists of the knowledge necessary to operate in the marketplace and political arena whereas female culture focuses on home and family" (Goetz, 1981, p. 58). Although the gender-specific characteristics are culturally assigned, the mainstream society frequently views the traits specifically linked to females as inferior to those belonging to males (Lee & Gropper, 1974; Shapiro, Sewell, & Ducette, 1995, p. 14). The distinctively female characteristics are considered deficits, because "the dominant male culture is used as an arbitrary yardstick of success and both cultures are evaluated in terms of the model achievement of one, its so-called deficits are articulated in global rather than situation-specific terms, and the logical extension of globally stated deficits is an indictment of the whole female culture as pathological" (Lee & Gropper, 1974, p. 382). As Lee and Gropper cogently conclude, the deficit view

> fails to impart a highly prized cluster of abilities: production, achievement, problem solving, and environmental mastery. But a person raised according to the code of femininity should not be judged by the standards of masculinity. If the situation were reversed, males would find themselves as unfairly indicted. Each culture should be evaluated in terms of the degree to which it has prepared its members to adapt to the conditions of their lives. By this standard the two cultures would appear to be equally adequate. (p. 385)

Another example of the deficit view concerns American Sign Language. Although ASL is the single most widely used and effective means of communication among the hearing impaired, many do not view it as a legitimate language because it does not have the same structure as Signed English or Manually Coded English (MCE) (Reagan, 1985). Yet both ASL and MCE are equally functional to the people who use them. As another example, the elderly are often characterized as being similar to an ethnic minority, for their behaviors, values, and lifestyles are not considered worthy alternatives to the dominant ways of our society (Strange, Teitelbaum, et al., 1987).

Finally, in our society, the young are assumed to be incapable of dealing with their problems without adult intervention. They are also thought of as imperfect grown-ups who should be pushed to abandon childhood as early as possible so that they can reach the normal and ideal state of adulthood (Kimball, 1968). Anthropologist Mary Ellen Goodman (1970) suggests that in America, the culture of childhood is defined in terms of deficiencies requiring compensatory measures (pp. 2–3). Thus, children are perceived as "adults-in-the-making" (Thorne, 1987). This view of the young is based on the questionable assumption that human beings grow sequentially toward a supposed ideal and inescapable state (adulthood) (Kagan, 1978).

The deficit view has deleterious effects on the personal development of minority individuals because this perspective usually leads to cultural imperialism, which compels minority groups to adopt only the dominant norms by rejecting the culturally distinctive practices that may have served them well. Abandoning personal cultural ways denigrates the individual's dignity and impugns the integrity of the group to which the person belongs. As we have already stressed, cultural practices that deviate from our own should not be considered deficits, because cultures represent different but legitimate ways of dealing with essentially similar human problems and needs.

Some Differences Are Not Mere Differences

The notion that a difference is not a deficit is useful in exposing ethnocentric assumptions underlying various social and educational programs in our society. But it is not without difficulty, for we are not always clear about just how far the notion should be carried. For example, are we willing to grant that, because the practices of all cultural groups are said to be different but equally valid, we should make no judgment about them? If we answer yes, are we then willing to insist that the racist practices of the KKK or the Nazis are nothing more than culturally different practices? In point of fact, those who affirm the ideals of participatory democracy do not view religious bigotry and racial or sex discrimination as merely culturally different practices carried on by certain special-interest groups in the United States. Rather, we judge such practices to be unethical, undemocratic, and even unlawful. The fact that different cultures have different norms does not necessarily imply that values ought to be relative or that there cannot be some objective way of justifying value judgments.

The slogan "differences are not deficits" does not suggest that any and all cultural differences, regardless of their harmful effects on others, should be treated as mere differences. Nor does it imply that there are no objective and rational bases for justifying basic ethical conduct. Rather, its purpose is to remind us that cultural differences should be respected and considered enriching to human experience. Implicit in this belief is the notion that we should consider the possible consequences of our actions on others, for their deeds will eventually affect our own well-being. If taken literally, this slogan can lead to the view that any inhumane and unjust actions may be condoned and justified. To avoid this kind of extreme relativism, we must subscribe to a set of ideals such as the Universal Declaration of Human Rights (United Nations, 1948), which affirms everyone's inherent dignity and rights to freedom, expression, association, equal opportunity, justice, security, education, and worship without any distinction of color, race, sex, language, religion, or national or social origin.

Are All Cultures Equally Functional?

No matter how strange and irrational other cultural patterns may appear to us, the very existence of the practices implies that all cultures do their job. However, this does not imply that they are all equally functional. That is, some cultures may be more effective and less maladaptive than others, and cultures may be compared with each other in terms of the degree to which they are functional. The cultural patterns producing the least number of self-defeating consequences may be considered the most functional. Cultural changes may be suggested on the basis of the effectiveness or ineffectiveness with which the prevailing patterns help the group deal with its problems. This is one objective way of judging a culture.

As an example, in an ancient Korean custom, two competing villages held annual rock battles in which the men expressed their masculinity and demonstrated their fighting skills. These annual events usually identified some promising warriors, but many men were fatally wounded. Because more and more men would have been killed off if such battles had continued for many generations, the maladaptive, self-defeating practice would have been a serious barrier in perpetuating the village populations. Alternative ways of expressing masculinity and identifying promising warriors could have been suggested. Similarly, the fact that sunbathing is widely practiced for the sake of health and good looks in this country does not necessarily suggest that it is the best way of promoting health and maintaining beautiful skin. To the contrary, available scientific evidence suggests that sunbathing is likely to cause skin cancer. Again, simply because certain belief and behavior patterns have been worked out by a given culture as a means of dealing with its concerns, we should not conclude that such patterns are necessarily the best possible ways of meeting human needs in that society. Nor should we even insist that a particular practice that has worked well in one cultural setting will be equally effective in a different cultural setting.

Ample evidence exists to suggest that some cultural practices, particularly in highly technological societies, despite fulfilling immediate needs, often have counterproductive long-term consequences. The culture of a society that selects its means of problem solving chiefly in terms of its immediate utility may face many complex and unsuspected outcomes that may be self-defeating to its fundamental goals. Clearly, tenacious adherence to one's own cultural practices in a radically different cultural context may be maladaptive. We should not consider the use of self-defeating patterns as merely a matter of applying different but equally valid cultural norms. In a similar sense, the adopting of cultural practices that are contradictory to the fundamental ideals of a given society—say, participatory democracy—ought not to be viewed as a matter of just following different patterns.

As Harry Broudy (1981) points out, "the social organization necessitates varying degrees of interdependence, whereas cultural diversity that claims complete autonomy for each cultural group can only result in an aggregate of groups with a minimum dependence on each other. Taken seriously and interpreted strictly, it leads to cultural separatism or atomism" (p. 232). As members of a society, we must be concerned about the consequences of acting to achieve personal objectives. The merit of our actions should be tested in terms of our personal goals, which in turn should be examined according to the fundamental principles upon which one's society is founded. In the final analysis, personal or cultural practices that are contradictory to the ideals of the society will affect everyone's life. For example, in a democratic society, if one's own cultural norms sanction exploitation of others and limit their freedom and equality, such practices cannot be justified in the name of cultural pluralism, because they are self-defeating at both the personal and the societal levels. To the degree to which our actions violate the rights and freedom of others, our own freedom and rights are diminished. It is in this sense that certain practices of various cultural groups may not always be viewed as simply cultural differences and that this belief should become the basis of democratic education.

STEREOTYPES VS. GENERALIZATIONS

Human beings tend to seek to understand and simplify their experiences by sorting out and categorizing their experiences. This process leads us to draw conclusions based on observations of a limited sample of things, events, or people. For example, by polling one to two thousand high school teachers about the pros and cons of Health Maintenance Organizations (HMOs), we may gain reliable and accurate information about how high school teachers as a group view the advantages and disadvantages of HMOs. The degree of reliability and accuracy depends, of course, on how adequate and representative the sample population is. **Generalizations** are useful in understanding typical characteristics of a group as a whole without ascribing them to every member. However, in addition to the traits individuals commonly share as members of various groups such as parents, teachers, artists, Asians, Hispanics, and Europeans, each person has certain particular characteristics that are not shared with anyone else. Members of a group then can be seen as unique individuals. For this reason, by avoiding **stereotyping**, we *can* speak about each individual's distinctive traits as well as the general characteristics of their groups without being contradictory.

Unlike generalizations, stereotypes can be damaging. Stereotyping occurs when certain, allegedly typical, characteristics of some members of a group are treated as belonging to all members. A stereotype is a fixed idea, a standardized mental picture that allows for no individuality or variation. A stereotype is more rigidly held than a generalization and is less prone to change. Unlike a generalization, based on experience, a stereotype is often based on misconceptions and lack of information. Stereotypes may include positive ideas about other groups—for example, that all Asian Americans are good at math or that all Jews are highly intelligent. Whether positive or negative, however, stereotypes are harmful in that they lead to inaccurate expectations and judgments. An Asian American child who is not good at math, for example, may find that he or she does not get the help and support from the teacher that other, non-Asian, children get because the teacher simply does not recognize that this child, in fact, is having problems with math.

Often there is enough supporting evidence for stereotypes to make them *seem* true—there are dumb blondes, rich Jews, and lazy Mexicans. Furthermore, some stereotypes have arisen because of historical circumstances. For example, throughout much of European history, Jews in Europe were forced to live in ghettoes. It is ironic, then, that one stereotype that developed about Jews is that they are clannish. Similarly, George Bernard Shaw once remarked that Americans are a funny people in that they make the Negroes [sic] lick their boots and then call them bootlickers.

It is the rigidity and uncritical acceptance of stereotypes that make them dangerous. Generalizations are more tentatively held and open to change and individual variation. Stereotypes are more difficult to confront and change. Because they are based on ignorance and limited experience, they can be broken down with experience and information. This is particularly true with young children, whose stereotypes are not likely to be as firmly set. Teachers can begin to confront stereotypes by probing for misconceptions and by providing accurate information. For example, a teacher might ask her students to draw pictures of "boy toys" and "girl toys" and then follow this with a discussion of why they classified the toys as they did. In their discussion they might think about examples of children playing with toys not typical of their gender and consider why they might do that. Depending on the age of the children, the class could investigate how advertising influences our ideas about what toys we want. They might also move into a more in-depth examination of sex roles at home and in school. Helping young people examine the complexity of the real world can help them move away from stereotypical thinking.

EDUCATION AND SCHOOLING AS A CULTURAL PROCESS

As was pointed out earlier, every culture attempts to perpetuate itself through deliberate transmission of what is considered the most worthwhile knowledge, belief, skills, behaviors, and attitudes. This deliberate transmission of culture is called **education**. In non-literate societies, the educative process is carried out in a more or less informal manner. The young learn various skills, beliefs, and attitudes from their elders as well as from their peers without having a specific time or place designated for this purpose. This informal process sometimes involves certain formal rituals—for example, puberty rites. In non-literate societies even folkways and mores serve as instructional media. However, in a complex, literate, and technological society, most cultural transmission takes place within the confines of specially arranged environments. There the young are expected to learn certain amounts and kinds of knowledge and skills within a specified period of time from those who are specialists in these areas. This formal and more restrictive process of cultural transmission may be called **schooling**.

Education is a form of **enculturation**, the process of learning one's own culture. When this process occurs formally in an institutional setting, it is called *schooling*. Thus, the process of enculturation is much broader than education, because the former includes both deliberate and non-deliberate learning, such as teaching and learning through imitation, whereas the latter includes only deliberate teaching and learning activities. Schooling is a much narrower concept than education, for it necessarily involves specialists teaching within the institutions designed specifically for this purpose. Education, although deliberate, need not take place in a formal institutional setting.

In spite of the differences among enculturation, education, and schooling, all three should be viewed as a single process whereby an individual learns and manipulates his or her own culture. Enculturation and education, at least in their informal sense, are present in all cultures. Education is only one means of enculturation. Similarly, schooling is one of many ways in which a person can become educated. All this suggests that although there is no society without enculturation and education, some societies are without schooling.

SCHOOLING AS AN ENCULTURATIVE AND ACCULTURATIVE PROCESS

Education in a socially and culturally diverse society such as the United States is not only *enculturative;* it is also *acculturative.* That is, while many students in our schools are learning their own culture (enculturation), minority children are attempting to grasp a new and different—that is, dominant—culture (**acculturation**). In a real sense, the ghetto child learning white, middle-class values from a white, middle-class teacher is learning an alien culture. In a culturally diverse society, it is important for school administrators, teachers, and counselors to realize that different behavioral, attitudinal, and belief patterns of minority children stemming from their ethnic backgrounds should not be viewed as either social or cognitive deficits. For example, teachers generally expect students to speak up only after they have been duly recognized, and students who express their thoughts and feelings spontaneously are frequently considered disruptive or troublemakers. Yet many of our schoolchildren come from cultures in which spontaneous expressions of their thoughts and feelings are encouraged. Other young people have been taught to respond to a teacher's reprimand by lowering their heads in silence. This behavior is considered quite appropriate in relating to unhappy adults in the youth's culture, but it is generally viewed as a sign of non-responsiveness or even rebellion by our teachers. The point is not that minority children be allowed to behave only according to the norms of their own culture; it is to suggest that unless these children are taught about the differences between the dominant and their own cultures and what standards of behavior are appropriate in school, they are likely to be treated as problem cases requiring disciplinary or other special measures used for children with emotional and behavioral disorders. In fact, to many minority children, schooling in the United States represents a difficult and agonizing process of learning to function in an alien (dominant) culture that either rejects their ethnic heritage or gives it a low status.

Education as an acculturative process can also be viewed as the modification of one culture through continuous contact with another. Antagonism often results when one culture is dominant, and this antagonism becomes exacerbated by the dominant culture's attempt to speed up the process. When the dominant group sees minority group characteristics as deficits, the antagonisms are aggravated. Harry F. Wolcott (1994) believes that the teacher might deal more effectively with conflict and in capitalizing on his instructional efforts if he were to recognize and to analyze his role as enemy rather than by attempting to ignore or deny the conflict (pp. 280–283). He goes on to illustrate that in the enemy relationship, specific demands are made of enemy prisoners. But these demands are not based on common values about fair play, human rights, or the dignity of office. The relationship is based on fundamental differences rather than on the recognition of similarities. This perspective of thinking about teachers and their culturally different pupils as enemies may invite teachers to examine the kinds of differences cherished by enemies just as they have in the past addressed themselves, at least ritually, to what they and their pupils share in common. Another helpful approach may be to have both teachers and culturally different students treat each other as visitors from extraterrestrial worlds. In this way, they cannot understand each other without asking each other the "why" questions.

To recognize that the process of schooling in the United States is both enculturative and acculturative is to accept that many of the young in our schools are there to learn the dominant but alien culture. This implies that many learning and behavioral difficulties may come from the differences between the norms the school considers desirable and those that minority children view as appropriate. The culturally different young people in our society must learn to function according to the dominant as well as their own cultural norms, depending on their purpose and the circumstances in which they find themselves. At the same time, educators need to understand that human actions do not have inherent meanings and significance. Understanding that various cultures assign different meanings to the same action can help educators interpret seemingly strange or disruptive behaviors from appropriate cultural perspectives and, consequently, minimize learning and behavioral difficulties. It is when educators believe that all children in our schools are there to learn their own culture that the patterns that deviate from the dominant norms are treated as deficits to be eliminated. However, the notion that schooling is both encultural and acculturative does not necessarily imply that ethnic minority children in our schools will be completely assimilated (acculturated) into the dominant culture for they may learn to function appropriately in the mainstream and their own ethnic communities. They may also develop a new and unique identity by combining certain elements of the dominant and their own cultures.

PRIVATE CULTURE, OPERATING CULTURE, AND SYNCRETISM

For a person to be competent in multiple cultural settings, the individual should not only have knowledge about disparate cultures. We all have several different positions (identities) in the dominant culture and the particular ethnic group to which we belong. So, it is important that we should also be able to make intelligent decisions about the most appropriate modes of thinking, acting, and communicating in any given situation. It is for this reason that critical and reflective thinking must play a key role in education. The following brief discussion of Goodenough's (1963) notions of **private culture** and **operating culture** as well as **syncretism** will help clarify how personal cultures are formed and changed.

Private Culture

As every society has its own unique and predominant culture, so may we speak of each person as having his or her own private culture, which includes the generalized view of the culture of the individual's community, that is, public culture, as well as the awareness of several distinct cultures of other individuals (Goodenough, 1963, pp. 261, 264). This cultural awareness within a person's private culture represents the individual's perceptions of how others have organized their experiences based on the standards by which they perceive, predict, judge, and act. It is through our knowledge of the private cultures of our associates that we learn to accomplish those goals that are best achieved through working together. Hence, a person's private culture may include knowledge of several language patterns, norms of conduct and valuation, and procedures for getting things done (Goodenough, 1963, pp. 260–261). Depending on the nature of one's purpose and its context, the individual often moves from one set of cultural norms to another. For example, when we go from our classroom to a Hispanic community center, our spoken language, communication style, and etiquette may change to fit the new situation. Such a change is possible only if certain aspects of the Hispanic culture are part of the repertoire of our private culture.

Operating Culture

In interacting with others in various social and cultural contexts, a person shifts from one culture to another within his or her repertoire but tends to use the cultures in which he or she is already proficient. "The particular other culture [he/she] selects is . . . [his/her] operating culture" (Goodenough, 1963, p. 261). Most individuals have several or more operating cultures, but they tend to use only one or two of them. As individuals become more skilled in using a limited number of operating cultures, they tend to use them as guides to their behavior in all contexts. Consequently, in unfamiliar situations, these individuals tend to be clumsy and awkward. Their behaviors are often inflexible and maladaptive because their operating cultures are inappropriate for the new situations. For example, individuals who operate only in terms of the middle-class culture may not be able to interact effectively with those who are in lower socioeconomic minority groups. Similarly, people whose lives are confined to the central city environment are not likely to be competent in interacting with suburbanites. The inability of many of our teachers to relate effectively with culturally or socioeconomically different children may be attributable to the fact that teachers as a group are mono-cultural in their experience and education. Only when individuals increase the repertoires of their private and operating cultures and make use of them can they function proficiently in culturally divergent situations.

If a person operates rigidly in terms of a single culture (e.g., using Standard English only in a multiethnic and multilingual community), that person will be less effective in accomplishing his or her purposes. This suggests that the greater a person's breadth of cultural competencies and the more flexible he or she is in shifting from one appropriate cultural context to another, the more successful that person will be in achieving desired outcomes. As Goodenough (1963) points out, an increase in interethnic contacts is educationally important because such an increase enlarges "the number of other cultures in the private [and operating] cultures of the individuals [from which they can select]" (p. 262).

Typically, a person uses only a limited number of cultural orientations. If the dominant culture views other cultural patterns as deficits, the number of alternative cultural orientations that an individual could use would be limited to those the mainstream culture regards as legitimate. Minority children, for example, may be pressured, implicitly or explicitly, to reject their own language and use only Standard English. Rejection of their language pattern as a low-status form reinforces the negative image minority children have of their own culture and personal identity. One problem of the deficit view for minorities of all kinds is that the more one conforms exclusively to the dominant (the "right") norm, the more one crushes self-esteem and pride in one's own identity. The deficit view not only robs richness from both the dominant and minority cultures but also increases alienation and sociopsychological conflicts.

Changes in Private and Operating Cultures

A fundamental purpose of education in a culturally diverse society is to modify the ways in which individuals see themselves and others so that they can function in a progressively more effective way in an increasingly complex world. Changes in a person's perceptions of and attitude toward other people and their culture may properly be seen as the results of changes in the individual's private and operating cultures. According to Goodenough (1963), changes in private culture occur through the adding or refining of the existing organization of experiences (pp. 272–274). In other words, a person's private culture may be changed by acquiring completely new experiences or restructuring the organization of past experiences. For example, learning a new foreign language enlarges one's cultural repertoire, and intense personal encounters with ethnic minorities may modify the individual's pattern of interaction with minority students. "Whatever form change takes, its results represent additions to one's private culture, not replacement within it" (p. 272).

The impetus for changes in private culture comes from a person's desire to seek a more effective way of dealing with new situations that he or she could not handle successfully within the existing private culture. But the quest for alternative approaches to problem solving may not arise if the individual is ethnocentric and views all differences as deficits. Thus, whereas some immigrants become engrossed in learning the ways of their new country, others choose to live in the confines of their ethnic community.[1] Similarly, some members of the mainstream culture are deeply interested in learning about other cultures at home and abroad because they are concerned about becoming more successful in their

---

[1]Recently, some sociologists and other social scientists suggest (Huntington, S., 2004, Jose, can you see?, *Foreign Policy*, March/April, pp. 30–45) that if the massive influx of Mexican immigrants continues, such trend "could consolidate the Mexican-dominant areas of the United States into an autonomous, culturally and linguistically distinct, and economically self-reliant bloc within the United States" (p. 42). They note that in such areas "the Anglo had three choices. They could accept their subordinate and outside position. They could attempt to adopt the manners, customs, and language of the Hispanics and assimilate into the Hispanic community—"acculturation in reverse"—or they could leave the area (p. 43). Further, "as their numbers increase, Mexican Americans feel increasingly comfortable with their own culture and often contemptuous of American culture." As this trend persists, the incentive for cultural assimilation becomes reduced. "Mexican Americans no longer think of themselves as members of a small minority who must accommodate the dominant group and adopt its culture. . . . They become more committed to their own ethnic identity and culture" (p. 44).

work. On the other hand, there are those who have no desire to expand their private culture because they are convinced that only their cultural norms are valid. An operating culture may also be changed by acquiring new experiences or refining or reorganizing certain aspects of one's private culture. But a change in the person's identification with a particular group can also lead to a change in the individual's operating culture.

Syncretism

There is yet another way in which changes in an operating culture may occur. A person may change his or her operating culture through syncretistic incorporation of elements from a different culture into the private culture (Goodenough, 1963, p. 275). That is, ethnic minorities may develop distinctive ways of interacting with other people by maintaining certain aspects of their own ethnic norms and integrating them with mainstream standards. For example, an Asian American girl may discard her unquestioning obedience to elders and become more self-assertive while retaining that part of Asian culture that requires her to be responsive to the needs and expectations of others. This is tantamount to saying that in a culturally pluralistic and democratic society, ethnic minorities should preserve and extend their culture through the syncretistic process. Here, the notion of "preservation and extension" should not be seen as a reactionary, "back-to-the-blanket" move. Rather, "syncretism is the reconciliation of two or more cultural systems or elements with the modification of both" (Burger, 1966, p. 103). This concept is not the same as the "melting" of distinctive cultures into one allegedly superior one. Syncretism refers to the development of a new and unique culture and a new personal identity by interweaving different cultural elements. The syncretistic process is important to the members of both minority and dominant cultures, for everyone's private and operating cultures can always be expanded for effective handling of varied contingencies in life.

What we learn about other cultures is not classified neatly into different cultural pigeonholes in our mind so that the right pattern is pulled out of an appropriate category when a situation calls for a particular way of acting. Our knowledge of and experiences in other cultures become integrated into the complex terrains of our private and operating cultures. Hence, acting appropriately in different situations or having multicultural competencies requires not only knowledge of divergent patterns but also an ability to evaluate the situation. Equally important is the ability to formulate available options in relation to one's goals and then to critically choose the option that will help achieve the present objective as a means to accomplishing future goals. Thus, education in a culturally diverse society should be seen as the process by which each individual can learn to live in a progressively effective and enriching way by increasing the individual's cultural repertoire and reconciling divergent patterns so that a new and unique approach to life may emerge.

LEARNING OR TEACHING?

According to Margaret Mead (1963), one of the important effects of the mingling of different races, religions, and levels of cultural complexity on our concept of education is the "shift from the need for an individual to learn something which everyone agrees he would wish to know, to the will of some individual to teach something which it is not agreed that anyone has any desire to know" (pp. 310–311). Melville J. Herskovits (1968) agrees that in nonliterate societies much more emphasis is placed on learning than on teaching. But he attributes this shift to the fact that in simpler societies the skills and techniques the young learn have practical application. What is learned is used in everyday life; hence, the motivation to learn comes from the immediate utility of the techniques to be acquired. On the other hand, in highly technological and culturally complex societies, individuals cannot hope to learn "just everything" needed in that society. Quite the contrary, intense specialization is necessary to make a living. In a modern society, we cannot rely on our own personal resources to learn what is required even in our own area of specialization. Nor is it reasonable to expect young learners to know what skills are needed to become a specialist in a desired area (e.g., a psychiatrist). It has become almost mandatory that we rely on experienced and recognized specialists to give us accurate and comprehensive information about what ought to be learned in a given field. Experts must tell others what they ought to learn. Modern societies are so complex that even among experts we do not always find agreement about what ought to be taught.

While teaching is a social practice aimed at causing learning (Atran & Sperber, 1992, p. 41), it does not always or necessarily lead to learning. On the contrary, there are other, non-teaching, activities (e.g., rituals) that contribute to learning. For example, children often learn the norms of their culture through observing and imitating their parents or other adults. It is for this reason that "learning" should not be thought of as equivalent to "being taught" (p. 41). However, in the context of education wherein learning needs to be systematic and cumulative, teaching and learning should be seen as having a close and dynamic relationship. There is no simple answer to the question of why modern education has shifted its emphasis from learning to teaching. But an important lesson lies in the slogan "learning is more important than teaching." When our attention is focused on learning, we are likely to become more concerned about providing conditions under which learning can occur. Because conditions for learning are varied, we may grow more flexible in whatever we do to facilitate learning. On the other hand, when a greater emphasis is placed on teaching, we are more likely to become preoccupied with what the teacher must do. Teaching, then, should not be viewed as a set of acts or routines rather than a process of facilitating learning conditions. Indeed, teaching and learning are not mutually exclusive ideas, nor can we say that one is more important than the other in any absolute sense. Further, it is doubtful that, as Mead (1963) argues, it is the shift from learning to teaching that "moved us from spontaneity to coercion, from freedom to power . . . and the development of techniques of power, dry pedagogy, regimentation, indoctrination, manipulation, and propaganda" (p. 320).

Finally, society uses education for many more purposes than the transmission of culture. In some societies, both formal and informal education serve as agents of genuine change. By providing greater educational opportunities to wider and wider segments of the population, liberating social and economic as well as political changes can be created to eliminate illiteracy and poverty and to restore human freedom and dignity. On the other hand, education can also be used by those who possess wealth and power to perpetuate the status quo. Domination over minority groups of all kinds is often achieved through proselytizing the oppressed to believe that they do indeed "belong" to the positions and classes that they occupy. In such societies, educational opportunities are so restricted that the likelihood of any significant social, economic, or political change occurring would certainly be remote. This has long been the way colonies have been maintained. The following two chapters will examine how schooling in America functioned in relation to the two uses of education just discussed and will give a broad historical overview of how the dominant society's attitude toward minority cultures has influenced schooling in the United States.

 ## Cases for Reflection

Although the following excerpts are descriptions of educational practices from the mid-1930s and 1940s, they are presented here because they so clearly illustrate how schools attempted to transmit the norms of the mainstream culture as the only idealized standards from which no one should deviate. No doubt, some will point out that such practices are no longer in use. However, a review of current educational issues related to school policies and practices regarding student discipline, curricular contents, and minority students will reveal that while specific forms may have changed, more often than not the spirit still remains. The primary purpose of this narrative is to facilitate a discussion of how the values, attitudes, and beliefs of the dominant culture may have influenced the classroom teacher's work and the latent transmission of certain values and attitudes through school policies and instructional activities.

EFFECTIVE CITIZENSHIP

The Arizona state superintendent's office advised teachers that "every phase of school life" of the Mexican child "should take part in promoting the meaningful use of English." Without the English language, warned the superintendent, Mexican people would not realize "effective citizenship." [In this] schooling atmosphere . . . school authorities organized the system of rewards and punishments accordingly. The child achieved "success" when he learned English and became Americanized; a child "failed" when he remained a non-English speaker. The Arizona State

Course of Study for Bilingual Children arrived at a standard for successful behavior and learning on the part of the Mexican child when it posed the following questions: "Does he try to accommodate himself to American culture as represented by the school setting; does he try to learn to speak English?" If the child made an "honest effort" and if he "responded with genuine interest to the school situation," then the Course of Study concluded that the child had met minimal standards for Americanization. "He should feel pride," continued the Course of Study, "in making progress in the accepted task of learning a new language." . . .

School officials often combined English instruction with direct attempts to manipulate the "aliens'" cultural standards. For example, many segregated schools in the Southwest contained showering facilities where children were obliged, after a morning inspection, to shower. In the East Donna, Texas, Mexican school, a twelve-room building served five hundred students in which "morning inspections in each classroom [were] regularly conducted," and children who failed to pass inspection were "required to wash before they [were] permitted to begin the day's activities." If their clothes were dirty, they were required to change into clean clothes loaned by the school "in emergency cases." . . .

[In California,] the objective of the English instruction program for non-English speaking children included creating a way of life characterized by initiative, cooperation, courtesy, cleanliness, and a desirable home life. "Help them to want to be clean," urged the California Guide for Teaching Non-English-Speaking Children, "and provide opportunities for making cleanliness possible." The Guide also suggested a method of teaching "habits and attitudes that make home life clean, comfortable and happy." Consequently, English drills incorporated practice in setting the dinner table and arranging bedrooms and living rooms. Such instruction also included "constant and careful work . . . to promote correct enunciation and pronunciation." Through the program, which combined language and culture, the state expected a cultural transformation. [The Guide goes on to say that] constant contact with an environment that ministers to the love of the beautiful and orderly creates an abhorrence of anything that is not well-ordered and clean. Through this subtle, indirect influence the standards of foreign homes may be raised, for when these children grow up they will not be happy in an environment widely different from that to which they have been habituated.

Source: Gilbert G. Gonzalez, "Culture, Language, and the Americanization of Mexican Children." Copyright © 1997. From *Latinos and Education,* ed. by Antonia Darder, Rodolfo Torres, and Henry Gutierrez. Reproduced by permission of Taylor & Francis/Routledge, Inc.

DISCUSSION QUESTIONS

1. What values of the dominant culture are reflected in the programs described above? Discuss why schooling in the above context should be seen as being both enculturative and acculturative in nature?
2. What values and attitudes might be transmitted to the English-speaking, as well as non-English-speaking children in the above school settings?
3. In what sense do the above settings reflect the deficit view? Can you think of some current school and classroom practices that are likely to convey the deficit views of other cultural, racial, ethnic, linguistic, gender, and age groups to children?
4. What are some values and attitudes that are latently transmitted to school children? Is latent transmission of values bad? Why? Why not?

What are some possible ways of preventing or at least minimizing such latent transmission?

5. How many different operating cultures do you find within your own private culture? Be specific. Identify those aspects of your private and/or operating cultures which have resulted from incorporating certain aspects of two or more cultural norms or practices. How effective have they been in dealing with cultural conflicts? Should schools promote syncretism? Why or why not?

■   ■   ■   ■

LISA

The following is a brief account of an actual case involving a young Southeast Asian girl who was adopted by a white middle-class couple. Many details have been left out intentionally, leaving enough information so that readers can think about and discuss the general approach they might take in dealing with a similar situation by critically analyzing the assumptions implicit in the ways we observe and evaluate individuals from another culture. Although the case deals with the difficulties a Southeast Asian girl had in an upper-middle-class suburban school in the United States, a young white girl from a lower socioeconomic class in the same school would have had somewhat different but equally difficult problems.

After living for three years in an orphanage, Lisa, a young Southeast Asian girl, was adopted by a white middle-class family in a Midwestern city. Since the orphanage did not provide Lisa's adoptive parents with her birth certificate, nobody knew exactly how old she was. According to a nearby medical center, she was either nine or ten years old. In spite of Lisa's claim that she had had two years of schooling in the orphanage, she was placed in a first-grade classroom because she had neither an adequate command of the English language nor official documents certifying her earlier schooling.

Lisa's adoptive parents were very warm and caring people who provided her with most of the things that a nine-year-old girl would want and should have—including piano lessons. Lisa was very good in music. In fact, in less than six months after beginning piano lessons she was able to play new pieces at first reading. In addition to these "privileges," she was given a number of household chores to do. Lisa was to let the family puppy out and feed her as soon as she came home from school. She was also responsible for checking all the windows and watering house plants. In addition, Lisa was to stay in the house with all the doors locked until one of the parents came home from work. She carried out the chores well, and Lisa and her parents were very happy with one another.

At school, Lisa did not do as well. According to her teacher, Lisa was always the first child to hand in the assigned work in the class. But she did very poor work, because she could not follow the teacher's instructions. Whenever the teacher told Lisa to pay more attention to her instructions and reprimanded her for handing in poor work, Lisa consistently lowered her head in silence. She responded similarly to other adults when she was admonished by them. According to Lisa's classroom teacher, she had a disruptive influence on other children because "she bothered them a lot." For these academic and behavioral problems, Lisa had been sent to the principal's office several times.

As a result of a number of reports from Lisa's teacher, a reading specialist and a teacher of English as a second language, the principal recommended that there be a comprehensive evaluation of Lisa's performance, behavior, problems, needs, and potentials so that an individualized instruction plan could be developed. This process is usually referred to as "staffing." Lisa's staffing meeting was attended by several specialists, a teacher of English as a second language, Lisa's teacher, and her parents with an "advocate." An advocate is a person who helps the child's parents make sound and appropriate judgments about their child's education program.

Following a series of reports on social, psychological, intellectual, and behavioral aspects of Lisa, the group, except the parents and the advocate, agreed that Lisa had serious emotional problems and that she ought to be referred to a professional counselor or a clinical psychologist. The school psychologist reported that her IQ score was below the norm of her age group, and the social worker indicated that Lisa had problems getting along with other children. The group also recommended that she be sent to a school providing special education programs for children with learning and behavioral difficulties. After a lengthy discussion of how her cultural background may have influenced Lisa's academic performance and interpersonal relationships, the decision was made not to send her to special education classes. [The details of how this decision was reached have been omitted intentionally so that readers may explore various options for Lisa and choose the most appropriate instructional plan for her with the information provided herein.]

Lisa is now an above-average high school senior with many friends. She is looking forward to attending a nearby university. She has continued to study music and art, and she works part-time like many of her peers.

DISCUSSION QUESTIONS

1. What is your estimate of the ways in which Lisa's problems were determined? Does the concept of "deficit view" apply here?
2. What are some assumptions the school personnel had implicitly used in evaluating Lisa?
3. How would you explain Lisa's problems?
4. How might Lisa have been affected had she been sent to special education classes?
5. On the basis of what has been discussed in chapter 2, what information or knowledge, as well as attitudes, would you need to make intelligent decisions about Lisa's situation?

6. What might be done in teacher education programs to prepare prospective teachers to be able to deal effectively with children from culturally, as well as socially and economically different, backgrounds?

◼   ◼   ◼   ◼

LEARNING COMPETITION

The following describes the experience of an early adolescent African American girl attending a predominantly white school for the first time.

I was sent to an integrated high school that was not in my neighborhood. I describe it as "integrated" rather than "desegregated" because no court mandates placed black children there. I was there because my mother was concerned about the quality of our neighborhood school.

There were a handful of African American students in my seventh-grade class, but I knew none of them. They lived in a more affluent neighborhood than I did. Their parents had stable blue-collar or white-collar jobs. They had gone to better-equipped elementary schools than I had. The white students were even more privileged. Their fathers had impressive jobs as doctors, lawyers—one was a photo-journalist. Most of their mothers were homemakers. In contrast, my mother and father both worked full-time. My father often even worked two jobs, yet we still lived more modestly than most of my classmates did.

In seventh grade I learned what it means to be competitive. In elementary school my teachers did not seem to make a big deal out of my academic achievements. They encouraged me but did not hold me up as an example that might intimidate slower students. Although I suspect I was a recipient of a kind of sponsored mobility—perhaps because my mother always sent me to school neat and clean and with my hair combed—I don't think this preferential treatment was obvious to other students. But in my new surroundings the competition was very obvious. Many of my white classmates made a point of showing off their academic skills. Further, their parents actively lent a hand in important class assignments and projects. For example, one boy had horrible penmanship. You could barely read what he scrawled in class, but he always brought in neatly typed homework. I asked him once if he did the typing and he told me that his mother typed everything for him. She also did the typing for his cousin, who was also in our class and had beautiful penmanship. The teachers often commented on the high quality of these typed papers.

I had come from a school where children learned and produced together. This competitiveness, further encouraged by the parents, was new to me. I could attempt to keep up with this unfair competition and "act white" or could continue to work my hardest and hope that I could still achieve.

Source: G. Ladson-Billings, *The dreamkeepers: Successful teachers of African American children*, pp. 9–12. Copyright © 1994. Reprinted with permission of John Wiley & Sons, Inc.

DISCUSSION QUESTIONS

1. What "core values" were being conveyed in this classroom and how were they being transmitted?
2. In what ways were the values and attitudes in this classroom in contradiction with those that the writer had encountered previously in her home and in school? How would you account for these differences in cultural terms?
3. What recommendations would you give this student? To the teacher? Why?

REFERENCES

Atran, S., & Sperber, D. (1992). Learning without teaching: Its place in culture. In L. T. Landsmann (Ed.), *Culture, schooling and psychological development: Vol. 1. Human development*. Norwood, NJ: Ablex.

Baratz, S. S., & Baratz, J. C. (1970). Early childhood intervention: The social science base for institutional racism. *Harvard Educational Review, 40*(1), 29–50. See also Nell Keddie (Ed.), (1973), *The myth of cultural deprivation*, Baltimore: Penguin Books, for more discussion of this topic.

Benedict, R. (1934). *Patterns of culture*. Boston: Houghton Mifflin.

Bernard, T. (1996). What stays the same in history? In D. G. Rojek & G. F. Jensen (Eds.), *Exploring delinquency: Causes and consequences* (pp. 3–9). Los Angeles: Roxbury Publishing.

Broudy, H. S. (1981). Cultural pluralism: New wine in old bottles. In J. M. Rich (Ed.), *Innovations in education* (pp. 230–233). Boston: Allyn and Bacon.

Bruner, J. (1996). *The culture of education*. Cambridge: Harvard University Press.

Burger, H. (1966). Syncretism, an acculturative accelerator. *Human Organization, 25,* 103.

Carnegie Council on Adolescent Development. (1995). *Great transition: Preparing adolescents for the new century*. Concluding Report. New York: Carnegie Corporation of New York.

The Chronicle of Higher Education. (1988, January 20).

The Chronicle of Higher Education. (1999, January 29).

The Chronicle of Higher Education. (2003, January 31).

Erickson, F. (1997). Culture in society and in educational practices. In J. A. Banks & C. M. Banks (Eds.), *Multicultural education: Issues and perspectives* (3rd ed.). Needham Heights, MA: Allyn and Bacon.

Frazier, S. H. (1994) *Psychotrends*. Boston: Houghton Mifflin.

Gabriel, T. (1995, February 12). A generation's heritage. *New York Times,* pp. 27, 158–159.

Geertz, C. (1973). *The interpretation of cultures*. New York: Basic Books.

Goetz, J. P. (1981). Sex-role systems in Rose Elementary School: Change and tradition in the rural-transitional South. In R. T. Sieber & A. J. Gordon (Eds.), *Children and their organizations: Investigations in American culture* (pp. 58–73). Boston: G. K. Hall.

Goodenough, W. H. (1963). *Cooperation in change*. New York: Russell Sage Foundation.

Goodenough, W. H. (1976). Multiculturalism as the normal human experience. *Anthropology and Education Quarterly, 7*(4), 4–7.

Goodman, M. E. (1970). *The culture of childhood: Child's-eye views of society and culture*. New York: Teachers College Press.

Herskovits, M. J. (1968). Education and the sanctions of custom. In J. H. Chilcott, N. C. Greenberg, & H. B. Wilson (Eds.), *Readings in the socio-cultural foundations of education* (pp. 98–101). Belmont, IL: Wadsworth.

Hollins, E. R. (1996). *Culture in school learning: Revealing the deep meaning*. Mahwah, NJ: Erlbaum.

Howe, N., & Strauss, B. (1993). *13th generation*. New York: Vintage Books.

Howe, N., & Straus, B. (2000). *Millennials rising*. New York: Vintage Books.

Howe, N., & Straus, B. (2003). *Millennials go to college*. Washington, DC: American Association of Collegiate Registrars and Admissions Officers.

Huntington, S. (2004, March/April). José, can you see? *Foreign Policy, 140:* 30–45.

Hurn, C. (1993). *The limits and possibilities of schooling* (3rd ed.). Boston: Allyn and Bacon.

Kagan, J. (1978). *Infancy: Its place in human development*. Cambridge: Harvard University Press.

Kansas City Star. (1972, April 13).

Kansas City Star. (1974, February 10).

Kimball, S. T. (1968). Cultural influences shaping the role of the child. In J. H. Chilcott, N. C. Greenberg, & H. B. Wilson (Eds.), *Readings in the socio-cultural foundations of education* (pp. 124–133). Belmont, IL: Wadsworth.

Kluckhohn, C. (1968). Queer customs. In J. H. Chilcott, N. C. Greenberg, & H. B. Wilson (Eds.), *Readings in the socio-cultural foundations of education* (pp. 29–38). Belmont, IL: Wadsworth.

Knapp, M. S., & Woolverton, S. (1995). Social class and schooling. In J. A. Banks & C. M. Banks (Eds.), *Handbook for research on multicultural education.* New York: Simon and Schuster.

Lawton, M. (1994). More students aspiring to advanced degrees. *Education Week, 13*(19), 6, 158–159.

Lee, P. C., & Gropper, N. B. (1974). Sex-role culture and educational practice. *Harvard Educational Review, 44*(3), 381–388.

Lipsky, D., & Abrams, A. (1994). *The declining prospects of the twentysomething generation* (p. 162). New York: Random House.

Luria, A. R. (1976). *Cognitive development: Its cultural and social foundations* (M. Lopez-Morillas & L. Solotaroff, Trans.; M. Cole, Ed.). Cambridge: Harvard University Press. (Original work published 1974)

Mead, M. (1963). Our educational emphasis in primitive perspective. In G. D. Spindler (Ed.), *Education and culture* (pp. 309–320). New York: Holt, Rinehart & Winston.

Morin, R. (1994, January 31–February 6). Much ado about twentysomethingers. *The Washington Post,* National Weekly Edition, p. 162.

Reagan, T. (1985). The deaf as a linguistic minority: Educational considerations. *Harvard Educational Review, 55*(3), 265–277.

Shapiro, J. P., Sewell, T. E., & Ducette, J. P. (1995). *Reframing diversity in education.* Lancaster, PA: Technomic Publishing.

Spindler, G. D. (1963). Education in a transforming America. In G. D. Spindler (Ed.), *Education and culture* (pp. 132–147). New York: Holt, Rinehart & Winston.

Spindler, G., & Spindler, L. (1990). *The American cultural dialogue and its transmission.* New York: Falmer Press.

Strange, H., Teitelbaum, M., & Contributors. (1987). *Aging and cultural diversity: New directions and annotated bibliography.* South Hadley, MA: Bergin & Garvey.

Thorne, B. (1987). Re-visioning women and social change: Where are the children? *Gender and Society, 1*(1), 93.

United Nations. (1948). Universal declaration of human rights. General Assembly Resolutions 217A (III).

Veroff, J., Douvan, E., & Kulka, R. A. (1981). *The inner American.* New York: Basic Books.

White, L. A., & Dillingham, B. (1973). *The concept of culture.* Minneapolis: Burgess.

Wiles, J., & Bondi, J. (1993). *The essential middle school* (2nd ed.). Upper Saddle River, NJ: Merrill/Prentice Hall.

Wolcott, H. F. (1994). *Transforming qualitative data: Description, analysis, and interpretation.* Thousand Oaks, CA: Sage.

Yankelovich, D. (1981). *New rules: searching for self-fulfillment in the world turned upside down.* New York: Random House.

PART TWO

Culture and the American School

3

Schooling as Americanization: 1600s–1970s[1]

KEY *Concepts:*

- Americanization
- Bilingual education
- Compensatory education
- Cultural capital
- Cultural deprivation
- Melting pot ideal

It is through the study of history that we understand how people and institutions have changed or not changed over time. Understanding historical change and continuity helps us to better understand today's social and cultural institutions. History can give us insight into what caused changes in the past and what may create change today. Knowing history helps us to understand "why." Why are particular practices prominent in some schools and not others? Why, for example, are many high school class periods about 50 minutes long? Why is a child's grade level determined by age rather than by developmental readiness? Why are schools organized as they are? And why are there tensions about issues of race, class, and gender in schools, and in society, today?

History is also about interpretation. Some elements of the past are easy to identify. Certain dates and names may be clear and unarguable. For example, we know that the American Civil War began in April 1861. But when we ask "why?" and "what were the consequences?", we are getting into areas of historical interpretation. Of course, historical interpretation is not simply about one opinion or another. Historians must rely on evidence to support their interpretations, but historical evidence is by its nature incomplete and uncertain. We can

---

[1]Some ideas and concepts expressed in this chapter appeared in similar form in Van Cleve Morris and Young Pai, *Philosophy and the American School* (2nd ed.), Boston: Houghton-Mifflin, 1976.

read newspaper reports of the start of the Civil War. We can delve into personal diaries and government documents. But when we explore such primary source documents, that is, eyewitness and personal accounts from the period, we often find conflicting and contradictory information. Ask three of your friends to independently describe an event they all witnessed, and you will likely get three different first-hand accounts!

The same differing interpretations occur when historians examine schooling in the United States. In general, for example, there are at least two competing views concerning the purpose of public schools (Altenbaugh, 2003). The first is the view that public schools represent a vision of equal opportunity for all. It has been frequently said that no nation has had more faith in education than the United States. As a people, we have always believed that through education not only could we produce literate, enlightened, responsible, and productive citizens, but we could also establish a society where freedom, equality, and fraternity could be guaranteed for all regardless of sociocultural, religious, and racial heritages. It was through free public schools that the United States hoped to achieve these goals. This persisting faith in U.S. schools goes back to the earliest days of the nation. The public school was seen as the prime agent through which native sons and daughters, as well as immigrants, could achieve economic affluence, higher social status, and political and religious freedom. This, it was believed, would serve to create patriotic and responsible citizens.

A second view is that public schools limit opportunity and maintain the status quo, thereby limiting freedom and opportunity. While this is not a new viewpoint, it has become more dominant in the last fifty years. Since the early 1960s various minority groups have been insisting that their own cultural patterns should not only be allowed to exist but also encouraged to develop in their own way. They have asked that full civil rights be guaranteed and that social, economic, political, and educational equality be provided for all, regardless of race, ethnicity, class, gender, disability, or religious background. These demands are rooted in the belief that the United States has consistently attempted to assimilate minority cultures into the dominant WASP culture (see "The Core Values of American Culture," in chapter 2). Moreover, these groups believe that the awarding of socioeconomic rewards, such as social status and income, has been based on the extent to which minorities conformed to the WASP norm. To members of minority groups, perpetuating this cultural imperialism, which regards cultural difference as a deficit, is clearly contradictory to democratic ideals. Minorities have also contended that the American school, as a special agent of the society at large, has promoted Anglo superiority by teaching children that to be American is to be white, if not also Anglo-Saxon and Protestant. In spite of the criticism that significant reforms in socioeconomic, political, and educational institutions have not been fully achieved, the American school and its personnel have come a long way in becoming sensitive to the rights and needs of minority groups since the days of the seventeenth-century Puritans.

SCHOOL AS AN AGENT OF CULTURAL TRANSMISSION

In this and subsequent chapters we will critically examine the ways in which American society and schools have dealt with questions regarding cultural diversity and issues related to the education of the culturally different during several broad historical periods. This chapter is not an extensive history of schooling in America. Rather, it explores the cultural past of U.S. schools. We argue that education in the United States has moved from one of cultural imperialism, in which the majority white male culture dominated both the cultural expectations of schools and the path to success, to one in which cultural understanding has come to be more highly valued. We certainly do not argue that tensions around cultural diversity have ceased to exist—rather, that there has been change and that change has been in the direction of valuing diversity. Furthermore, we hope to make clear that such changes have occurred because of men and women, together and individually, who have worked to make change happen. The tensions and struggles continue. An understanding of history can enhance our understanding of the change or condition of schools today.

A discussion of the Puritan perspective will cover the years from 1647 (when the first major school law, known as the Old Deluder Satan Act, was passed) to about 1870, the beginning of an influx of immigrants with non-Anglo-Teutonic backgrounds. Americanization as Anglo conformity and the melting pot ideal will be examined as related to the periods from 1870 to the 1920s and the 1920s to 1965. The early 1920s are significant because during these years several legislative measures sought to limit or eliminate the immigration of nonwhite and non-European people into the United States. It was not until 1965 that the laws were changed and quotas in favor of European countries were abolished to provide equal immigration opportunities to all races and nationalities. The impact of President Lyndon B. Johnson's Great Society program on the American school (1965–1970s) and the issues concerning cultural pluralism and multicultural education (early 1970s–2000s) will be discussed in this chapter as well as in chapter 4.

QUEST FOR HOMOGENEITY: THE PURITAN PERSPECTIVE (1647–1870)

Because school was viewed as a primary facilitator of Americanization, its major mission was to enculturate the children of the WASP community and to acculturate the children of those who did not have the same heritage. This involved changing not only their behavioral and language patterns but also their beliefs and the way of thinking to conform to WASP norms. Schooling as **Americanization** meant helping children learn to think, believe, and behave according to the white Anglo-Saxon Protestant ways while divesting non-WASP children of cultural practices that differed from the mainstream. The view of education and schooling as an Americanization process, explicitly fostering conformity to the dominant culture and hostility toward cultural diversity, can be traced to the Puritans' view of their destiny and mission in life. This Puritan perspective has had a lasting impact on the educational policies and practices as well as the social, political, economic, and religious lives of people in the United States. For this reason, it is important to understand how the Puritans saw themselves and their work.

The Puritans of Massachusetts Bay Colony viewed themselves neither as ordinary immigrants from Europe nor fortune-seeking adventurers. Rather, they were convinced that they were given a special mission in God's grand plan for the world. The Puritans were committed missionaries who believed their purpose was to carry out God's will by converting everyone to their own religious perspective. The Puritan worldview rested on the belief that there was only one set of idealized norms to which all had to conform. Deviations from such norms were to be regarded as deficits, abnormal conditions to be eliminated.

The Puritans believed that humans were, by their very nature, depraved, having fallen in the sin of Adam. This evil nature was to be controlled, lest the devil become the master. Schools were established to prevent idleness and to overcome evil (Pulliam & Van Patton, 2003, p. 93). Religious orthodoxy, in schools and in society generally, would be a beacon for the world, the way toward salvation for all humanity. They were convinced that these goals could be accomplished by maintaining the purity of their beliefs and way of life. Cultural diversity was seen as harmful to national unity. The Puritans steadfastly believed that the purity of their ways could be assured and cultural heterogeneity be overcome through education. Schools were intended to enforce conformity, and communities were expected to take care of schooling. In 1647 the General Court passed the Old Deluder Satan Act. This act required every town to establish a school or to pay a larger town for the support of education. The curriculum of these schools was heavily steeped in Puritan theology as well as social expectations. Children could be flogged for breaking the rules, "since Puritan theology called for literally beating the devil out of the child" (Cremin, 1977, p. 95).

The Puritan legacy has been a powerful one in American education. The tradition of local establishment and control of schooling can be traced back to early New England. Puritan values also left their imprint on American schooling. Values such as obedience, hard work, competition, and respect for authority continue to be seen as key American values to be transmitted by schools. The Puritans laid the foundation for what were to become middle-class values in the United States: hard work, thrift, saving for the future. They also put down the groundwork for the expectation of conformity to a single set of values. Intolerance toward diversity and the quest for uniformity continued to be a theme in American education even after independence. This intolerance affected nonwhite minorities more than any other non-Anglo-Teutonic people. White skin was thought of as a necessary condition for becoming a "normal" and acceptable member of the dominant society.

In spite of some cultural, linguistic, and religious differences, the Americanization of immigrants through education did not pose a serious problem in the Puritan era because most immigrants came from the British Isles or other

European countries with Anglo-Teutonic backgrounds. Because the Puritans were so unquestionably convinced that cultural diversity would lead to national disunity and divisiveness in people's beliefs and values, much of their educational efforts focused on the centrality of conformity and uniformity in the growth and security of the nation.

Puritan schools did contribute significantly in building a society of a single culture, the WASP culture, but their approach to education also fostered intolerance and hostility toward diversity and the rejection of distinctive cultural heritages. People who spoke, thought, believed, and acted differently than the dominant group were viewed with suspicion and their integrity was demeaned, for they were said to pose a potential threat to national unity and prosperity. Clearly, a primary purpose of the American school was to establish cultural homogeneity through conformity to the WASP norms. Any deviation from these norms was considered inimical to the fulfillment of America's God-given mission of establishing the best society, the best religion, and the best form of government.

The years following the American Revolution set the stage for the development of common schools, known today as public schools (Spring, 2001, p. 58). Prior to the common school movement, many children did go to school. Like the Puritans, many of the American colonies, and later the states, valued education. Often, however, poor children were likely to attend "charity schools" established by the state, while wealthier children attended private schools. Common school reformers argued that all children should be educated in a common, or like, manner. Common school leaders, the most prominent of whom was Horace Mann (1796–1859), championed the cause of equal education, which they believed would lead to the creation of a one-class/middle-class society without social or economic disparities. The establishment of the common school was part of the process of establishing political stability and loyalty toward the new nation. Fear of instability and disunion were a great concern and most "post-Revolutionary leaders rejected the idea of a multicultural society and advocated the creation of a unified American culture" (Spring, 2001, p. 58). Neither the worth of cultural diversity in national development nor the importance of a person's unique cultural heritage to personal growth is found in the educational thought of influential leaders who lay the foundation for the common school.

KEEPING AMERICA AMERICAN (1870–1920s)

The late nineteenth and early twentieth centuries were a time of massive immigration to the United States. The immigrants who reached American shores after 1870, however, differed markedly from their predecessors, for they came mainly from southern and eastern Europe, Asia, and South America. These newcomers, without the Anglo-Saxon or Teutonic heritage, had more than a little difficulty adjusting to the English language and Protestant orthodoxy that dominated public schools. Establishment of ethnic settlements by these new immigrants and their attempts to maintain the manners, customs, observances, and languages of the old countries presented a new problem and a challenge to educators and government officials. Rather than rethinking their Americanization policy and the goal of education in an increasingly culturally diverse society, the nation's educators simply reaffirmed their belief in Americanization as Anglo conformity. Thus, an educational historian, Ellwood P. Cubberly (1909), remarked:

> Our task is to break up these groups or settlements, to assimilate and amalgamate these people as a part of our American race, and to implant in their children, so far as can be done, the Anglo-Saxon conception of righteousness, law and order, and popular government, and to awaken in them a reverence for our democratic institutions and for those things in our national life which we as a people hold to be abiding worth. (pp. 15–16)

As in the Puritan era, being American and democratic was equated with conforming to the Anglo-Saxon pattern of language, morality, and behavior, and the immigrants were to give up their own cultural forms.

An implicit assumption underlying this view was that if minority group members conformed to the WASP norm, prejudice and discrimination would disappear. The clear implication was that members of minority groups should do all the changing. The sooner they divested themselves of their own ethnic traits, the better. This view of Americanism as Anglo conformity was held not only by those who came from WASP backgrounds but also by some non-Anglo-Saxon immigrants. Thus, both the dominant culture and some minority groups adopted the deficit view. Of course rejection, segregation, and prejudice did not disappear for those nonwhite ethnics, even if they did succeed in adopting the Anglo-Saxon pattern. Being nonwhite, it was implied, meant having a permanent deficit condition. Enactment of such legislation as the Chinese Exclusion Act of 1882, California's anti-miscegenation law of 1878 prohibiting intermarriages of whites with blacks or "Mongols," and the National Origin Act of 1924, which effectively halted the immigration of nonwhites, reflected the view that to be American was to be white. This racist view of being American is best summed up in President Calvin Coolidge's remark to Congress in 1923 that "America must be kept American."

The new immigrants, however, were not always eager to give up their cultural heritage. Prior to World War I, immigrant groups often demanded and received the right for their children to be taught in their native languages (Rothstein, 1998, p. 675). Both public and private schools in which German was the dominant language were established in Pennsylvania, Wisconsin, St. Louis, and other cities in which there was an influx of German immigrants. Other immigrant groups also succeeded in establishing variations of bilingual education programs:

> In Texas, in the late 19th century, there were seven Czech-language schools supported by the state school fund. In California, a desire by the dominant culture to segregate Chinese children seemed to play more of a role than demands

by the Chinese community for separate education. . . . San Francisco's German, Italian, and French immigrants, on the other hand, were taught in their native languages in regular public schools. Here bilingual education was a strategy designed to lure immigrant children into public schools from parochial schools where they learned no English at all. (Rothstein, 1998, p. 176)

Immigrant groups frequently sought to establish their own schools as a response to the belief held by the dominant culture that minority cultures represented deficit conditions to be eradicated by the schooling process.

At the same time, schools were undergoing major changes. Increasingly, all children were expected to receive at least an eighth-grade education. By 1900, compulsory attendance laws had been passed in thirty-two states (Parkay & Stanford, 1998, p. 79). Comprehensive high schools—schools that would serve all adolescents, both college bound and non-college-bound—developed in the early twentieth century. New and competing approaches to curriculum were emerging, from a focus on curriculum that was based on scientific knowledge of child development to a curriculum that would efficiently prepare children for their anticipated roles in life (Kleibard, 1995). Among the major forces responsible for these changes were industrialization and urbanization of America's cities as well as rapid developments in the mass media of communication.

Almost as profound as the impact of technological changes and the sociopolitical pressures of the times was the influence of new educational thought. As early as 1902 John Dewey insisted that every school be a microcosm of society, that is, containing the same sorts of elements and activities (enterprises) as found in the society at large. Dewey believed that the school could become a force for social reform by enabling individuals and the society to make their lives increasingly efficient and effective. Hence, children were to learn through experiences and grow progressively to higher and higher levels under the careful guidance of the teacher. In general, Dewey was concerned with eliminating social, class, racial, and cultural differences as barriers to building a democratic community in which all could enjoy freedom and equality and in which every individual was valued for his or her intrinsic worth. Dewey thought that schooling was to have a harmonizing effect on different groups, but he did not deal specifically with the value and the role that cultural background has in enhancing a person's life and identity.

As pointed out in the preceding chapter, all societies attempt to transmit and perpetuate their culture through both formal and informal education. In this sense, it is not only reasonable but proper for American society to expect its schools to Americanize the young. Americanization should be an important mission of the American school. However, when the concept of being American is so narrowly defined that certain individuals and groups are excluded from becoming full-fledged citizens because of their racial, cultural, and religious backgrounds, then schooling as Americanization becomes inconsistent with and contradictory to the ideals of participatory democracy for which this nation stands.

THE MELTING POT IDEAL (1920s–1965)

Following the massive influx of immigrants from all over the world between 1870 and the 1920s, both native-born Americans and newcomers to the country realized that simple Anglo conformity was not feasible. Hence, around the early twentieth century, Americanization as Anglo conformity took on a more liberalized form as the **melting pot ideal**. According to this view, ethnic differences that were "melted" into a single "pot" would produce a synthesis—a new homogeneous culture that was not Anglo-Saxon, Jewish, Italian, or Asian. Advocates who offered the melting pot ideal as an alternative means of establishing a viable nation challenged the belief that anything that weakened the Anglo-Saxon pattern would result in national disaster, arguing that

> A nation is great, not on account of the number of individuals contained within its boundaries, but through the strength begotten of common ideals and aspirations. No nation can exist and be powerful that is not homogeneous in this sense. And the great ethnic problem we have before us is to fuse these elements into one common nationality, having one language, one political practice, one patriotism and one ideal of social development. (Mayo-Smith, 1904, p. 78)

In a more dramatic vein, Israel Zangwill (1909) glorified the ideal in his play *The Melting Pot:*

> It is in the fire of God round His Crucible. There she lies, the great Melting-Pot—listen! Can't you hear the roaring and the bubbling? There gapes her mouth—her harbor where a thousand mammoth feeders come from the ends of the world to pour in their human freight. Ah, what a stirring and seething! Celt and Latin, Slav and Teuton, Greek and Syrian—black and yellow—Jew and Gentile.
>
> Yet, East and West, and North and South, the palm and the pine, the people and the equator, the crescent and the cross—how the great Alchemist melts and fuses them with his purging flame! Here shall they all unite to build the Republic of Man and the Kingdom of God. Ah, Vera, what is the glory of Rome and Jerusalem where all nations come to worship and look back, compared with the glory of America, where all races and nations come to labour and look forward!
>
> Peace, peace to all ye millions, fated to fill this continent—the God of our children give you peace. (pp. 184–185)

Many poor and illiterate immigrants acquiring fame and fortune supported the melting pot ideal. When we consider the number of non-Anglo-Saxon individuals who contributed to American civilization as scholars, scientists, industrialists, philanthropists, and artists, it would appear that the melting pot has produced a new and unique culture. When we consider the ways in which pizza and bagels, jazz and salsa, have permeated American society, it would appear as though we have become an amalgam of many cultures. However, the melting pot ideal of diversity "was predicated on a firm understanding that, in the habits that counted, diversity would quickly yield to a single American standard" (Grant & Gomez, 1996, p. 19).

From the 1920s to the early 1960s, neither school policies nor instructional materials deviated from the Anglo-American ideal upon which the American educational goals, principles, and practices of the preceding era were founded. In reality, what happened in the melting pot conception of Americanization was that all varieties of ethnicities were melted into one pot, but the brew turned out to be Anglo-Saxon again. The ingredients of this melting pot were, in fact, to be assimilated to an idealized Anglo-Saxon model.

The process of melting into the Anglo-Saxon model was not only difficult for nonwhite ethnic minorities; it was impossible. They may have adopted the Anglo norm, but people of color could never become white. Racial discrimination made it extremely difficult, if not impossible, for these groups to participate meaningfully in the democratic process or even to assimilate into the mainstream culture through intermarriage. It is indeed ironic that Americanization as Anglo conformity and its more liberalized melting pot ideal resulted in the same end, that of forcing ethnic minorities to divest themselves of the cultural elements central to their identity. In sum, the promise of a new synthesis—a unique and homogeneous American culture from the melting pot—was a myth. In fact, the new arrivals were expected to accept and embrace the Anglo-Saxon ideal. What the melting pot myth did was reinforce the ethnocentrism of the majority and convince ethnic minorities that their ethnicity and cultural heritage were illegitimate and hence needed to be abandoned. Educationally, children of the dominant group were robbed of the opportunity to enrich their lives by learning about and appreciating other cultures as different but effective alternative ways of dealing with essentially similar human problems. On the other hand, masses of ethnic minority children learned to be ashamed of their cultural heritage. Nonwhite children had to live with the awareness that at best they were second-class citizens. But a more pervasive and pernicious effect of the melting pot myth was that children of all groups were given a picture of American society that was neither realistic nor consonant with the fundamental ideals found in the U.S. Constitution.

The 1920s and 1930s were a time of educational reform and new ideas, often in the name of social reform and expanded democracy. However, concepts such as the "social reconstructionist school" of Harold Rugg or William Heard Kilpatrick's "project method" in the 1920s and the 1930s addressed issues other than how cultural variables affect how and what children learn. In principle, nothing in Rugg's concern for the learner's freedom, self-expression, and creativity or in Kilpatrick's interest in learning as inquiry would have been inconsistent with or contradictory to the notion that cultural factors do play an important role in teaching–learning processes. But the Anglo-Saxon model—that is, the deficit view—was so pervasively and deeply ingrained in the larger society and in education as a discipline that the need for a focused critical cultural analysis of education and the schooling process in the United States was not apparent at that time.

Not surprisingly, a similar educational perspective continued into the late 1950s. Even in *The Pursuit of Excellence,* a report prepared by the Rockefeller Brothers Foundation in 1958 as a response to *Sputnik* addressed only upgrading science and math education and did not deal with the relationship between American education and ethnic minorities. James B. Conant's 1959 report, *The American High School Today,* which was seen by the public and educators as a means of implementing what was recommended in *The Pursuit of Excellence,* suggested a comprehensive curriculum. Conant's "comprehensive high school" was to include a good general education program (English, American literature, composition, and social studies) for everyone. Electives in vocational and commercial or other work-related studies were to be provided for non-college-bound young people, while advanced work in foreign languages, mathematics, and science was to be made available to the academically gifted. Conant did recommend improving the quality of education for African Americans so that they could become integrated into the socioeconomic mainstream. Although this suggestion was based on providing African Americans with learning environments similar to those of white middle-class youth, his focus was not the ways in which different cognitive and learning styles and other cultural factors might have helped develop alternative ways of helping African Americans to do better educationally. The possibility that studies of other cultural patterns, both at home and abroad, could have added richness to the learner's life and self-image did not occupy a significant place in the report.

Following *The Pursuit of Excellence* and Conant's report, public school personnel, scholars, and private foundations sought to achieve educational excellence through innovative approaches to teaching and academic subjects such as the physical and biological sciences, mathematics, and the social sciences. By the beginning of 1960, the schools were doing more things for more people than ever before, for

> the schools . . . were transformed significantly. . . . Vocational training was introduced as a principal component of the junior and senior high-school curriculum; social studies programs sought to connect the school's substance to local community activities; physical education and the arts made their way into the curriculum; a substantial extracurriculum developed, organized largely around student athletics, student journalism, student government, and student clubs; and the materials of study and instruction changed to reflect a greater concern for the individual child and his progress through the various academic subjects. (Cremin, 1977, pp. 100–101)

Efforts to meet the needs of individual children, however, did not include taking into account the diverse cultural backgrounds and experiences of children. In the 1954 Supreme Court decision *Brown v. Board of Education,* the court mandated desegregation of public schools within a "reasonable time" because "separate but equal" education was considered inherently unequal. Most of the literature on educational reforms, curriculum and instructional theories, and pedagogy up to the late 1950s was based on the implicit assumption that all effective learning occurred when the Anglo styles of thinking, learning, and communicating were used and the learners lived in a white middle-class-like environment. Indeed, the picture of American society, its norms, and its history remained overwhelmingly Anglo-Saxon. The fact that the school operated according to the majority's norms—whereby the young needed to function according to these norms for success in school and society—is beyond dispute. Educators and scholars had not even explored the possibility that other ways of thinking, learning, acting, and judging may have helped the culturally different to learn more effectively. This view was culturally ethnocentric, intellectually myopic, and educationally tunnel-visioned at best. Despite all the changes that the American school went through from 1870 to the early 1960s, schools continued to strive to eliminate all real differences in the name of national unity and educational excellence.

By the early 1960s, however, there was the perception that an "urban crisis" was developing, based in large part on the growing population of minorities in cities. About 56 percent of the African American population (12.1 million people) had moved to major urban areas in search of better economic, social, and educational opportunities. Although some were successful in improving their lot, many found their lives in large cities to be filled with as much or even more poverty, unemployment, poor education, and racial discrimination as they had encountered in southern rural areas. As Ravitch (1983) notes, "The 'urban crisis' atmosphere had political implications, for it galvanized the impulse to take action against poverty and to respond to black grievances and make possible a breakthrough on the long-stalled issue of federal aid to education" (p. 148).

The movement of southern African Americans into major northern cities, coupled with a dramatic and massive influx of immigrants from Asian and Latin American nations after 1965, drastically altered the racial and cultural makeup of the population of the country and its schools. As described in chapter 1, the demographics of the United States began changing significantly in the last third of the twentieth century. Increasingly, young people in our schools arrived with diverse racial and ethnic origins, religions, and linguistic competencies.

In keeping with the increasing concern for the elimination of poverty in the early 1960s and the acceleration of the civil rights movement, President Lyndon B. Johnson introduced his Great Society programs, including educational measures. Special provisions, such as the 1964 Economic Opportunity Act and the Elementary and Secondary Education Act of 1965, allocated federal funds for education on the basis of the number of poor children in school. This new legislation was viewed as the avenue through which full civil rights and economic, social, political, and educational equality were to be assured for the poor and ethnic minorities. Numerous projects and programs were also designed to promote better understanding of the significant roles played by various minority racial and cultural groups in the development of this country.

However, the massive War on Poverty did not fully achieve the promise of the United States becoming a Great Society without poverty or injustice, save some instances of modest socioeconomic gains made by limited sectors of society. There is little evidence to demonstrate that these special efforts have had significant impact on the cognitive growth of minority children, on their image of their own ethnic identity, or on the ways the schools meet the educational needs of the ethnic minorities in the contemporary United States.

THE GREAT SOCIETY PROGRAMS AND BEYOND

In principle, the notion of the Great Society was founded on the implicit assumption that the United States was to be a society in which parity of power prevailed among all groups. This was to be achieved through providing social and economic equality, which was to be accomplished by ensuring equal access to education for all races and ethnicities and both genders. But such a society is not possible without a system in which both the dominant and minority cultural groups share common national concerns, values, and attitudes and that allows minority cultures to maintain themselves and grow in their own unique ways while not endangering others.

Yet the Great Society concentrated primarily on educational programs to help poor and minority individuals improve their cognitive skills so that they could find better jobs. Few politicians or educators addressed the significance of the inextricable relationship between the parity of political and economic powers and the principle of cultural democracy. That is, there is an important connection between political and economic equity and the right of every ethnic, racial, and social group to maintain its own cultural forms, even as they participate in the broader society.

Thus, **compensatory education**, an important part of the Great Society programs, was conceived primarily in economic terms. It was considered a means of helping the educationally disadvantaged children of the poor and ethnic minorities to acquire the necessary cognitive skills (reading, writing, and computational skills) that would eventually lift them out of their low socioeconomic status through finding and keeping better-paying jobs. For this reason, many of the compensatory education programs came from legislation related to economic opportunity.

Though numerous programs were made available to children in preschool to secondary school, our discussion of compensatory education will focus on Project Head Start, which by 2002 had an annual budget of more than $6 billion (Administration for Children and Families, 2002). Examining Head Start and its outcomes is particularly important because the project contained a number of elements that have influenced and will continue to influence the ways in which American children, particularly those in minority groups, are educated. From the cultural foundations perspective, the elements deserving careful scrutiny are (1) the deficit model of viewing minority groups and the concept of cultural deprivation, (2) the use of non-Standard English, and (3) the use of standardized tests in psychoeducational assessment and placement of schoolchildren, especially those who come from poor and minority families. As we will see, there are those who are deeply convinced that the presence of these factors in compensatory education has worked against the establishment of cultural democracy by reinforcing the ethnocentric and culturally imperialistic aspects of schooling in America.

Project Head Start: Boon or Bane?

As has already been pointed out, Project Head Start, which began in the summer of 1965, was an important aspect of the War on Poverty. Its primary goal was to provide preschool education for "culturally deprived" children. By 2002, it had served more than 21.2 million children (Administration for Children and Families, 2002). The project established "child development centers" where children of four, five, and six years of age were provided with sensory, cognitive, and social experiences that would help them develop adequate language and the perceptual and attentional skills and motivations needed to succeed in school. These experiences involved field trips and the use of a wide variety of objects and books, as well as work with individual teachers and volunteers. In addition, the centers provided physical examinations, dental care, and free meals. Although a high proportion of the children in the program were African American, the project was integrated in both the North and the South in conformity with the Civil Rights Act. The entire project was based on the implicit assumption that massive intervention in the lives of "culturally deprived" children and their families would help the young to succeed educationally and socioeconomically. Accordingly, the primary purpose of the project was to help poor children grow intellectually, socially, and emotionally. However, much greater stress was placed on children's cognitive growth than on other areas. In keeping with this emphasis, project success was viewed in relation to increases in the children's proficiency in the use of Standard English and in their IQ scores.

As worthy as the project's goal was, a 1970 evaluation of Project Head Start by the Westinghouse Learning Corporation and Ohio University ("Illiteracy in America," 1970) and other subsequent studies (e.g., Bronfenbrenner, 1974; Caruso & Detterman, 1981) suggested that once the program was discontinued, many of the cognitive (IQ) gains achieved by the Head Start children were "washed out" by the end of the second or the third grade. A general conclusion of these evaluation studies was that equivalent non–Head Start children performed equally well on IQ tests and in school by the end of second or third grade. To some, this implied that Project Head Start as an early intervention had very little, if any, lasting effect on children's intellectual or emotional growth. In a controversial article, psychologist Arthur Jensen (1969) went so far as to insist that the early intervention programs failed because they were unable to raise the IQ scores of Head Start children. As he continued to argue, "In the general mental ability that a person manifests over an extended period, the genetic part of the variance of that ability in the population is consistently greater than the environment part" (p. 108). Some advocates of Project Head Start held that Jensen's article gave the federal government an excuse for reducing its support of the early intervention programs.

In spite of these strong criticisms, other researchers reported that the Head Start children not only retained significantly higher IQ gains than non–Head Start children of comparable backgrounds, but also that the former as a group performed substantially better in school than the latter (Schweinhart & Weikart, 1977). Still others insisted that the program yielded certain intangible, nonquantifiable emotional and social benefits for the Head Start children and that these children, as compared with others, tended to be more assertive and sociable. Further, Head Start had positive impacts on families and communities by encouraging parental involvement, providing jobs and services, and coordinating community social services (U.S. Department of Health and Human Services, 1984).

In 1998, Congress mandated that the overarching goal of Head Start was school readiness, and the Clinton administration developed outcomes-based assessments for Head Start Centers to assure they were progressing toward that goal. In 2002, President G.W. Bush announced an initiative he argued would improve the accountability of Head Start. Under this proposal, the Department of Health and Human Services would develop a new accountability system "to ensure that Head Start centers assess standards of learning in early literacy, language and numerical skills . . ." (Koffler & Fulton, 2002). To receive federal funding, Head Start would have to meet certain accountability requirements. In 2003, the President called for legislation that would require Head Start "to teach language, reading and writing skills as well as early math skills. . . ." The President went on to say that "those programs that are used must be proven by scientific research. The legislation would hold Head Start accountable for getting the job done" (Bush, 2003). One of the most controversial aspects of the new legislation that was ultimately passed was the provision allowing a limited number of states to receive block grants to coordinate Head Start with state early childhood programs (Moss, 2003). Edward Zigler, often noted as the "father of Head Start" for his pioneering efforts in developing the program, argued that a funding stream going from the federal government, with clear standards, to local Head Start agencies would better assure high standards than sending the money to states that would in turn fund the local agencies. Zigler argued that the federally run Head Start is superior to all state programs and feared that a change in funding and oversight would result in a decline in quality (Zigler, 2003). Others were concerned that the accountability measures being implemented were inappropriate to the developmental level of children and too simplistic to adequately assess the results of Head Start.

Was compensatory education, including Project Head Start, part of a boon or a bane? A dilemma in attempting to answer this question is that various evidence both confirms and denies the claim that Head Start or other compensatory education programs have had lasting impacts on the educational development of poor and minority children. Of course, considering the massiveness of the Head Start program, it may seem reasonable to think that the jury is still out on the project's success or failure. It is doubtful that we will ever obtain definitive evidence to show how effective or ineffective the project has been. Two major reasons account for this predicament. One is the fact that the programs varied widely in their purpose, scope, format, and content, as well as in the competence of the teachers involved. Consequently, as Levine and Levine (1996) suggest, the goals of compensatory education were not only poorly defined but also often shifted, because it was "a major national issue involving fundamental values in society . . . and everyone [could] agree on the goal of equal educational opportunity stated at this level of generality, but disagreement occur[red] as soon as the goal [was] stated in operational terms" (p. 254). The other major reason was the lack of standardized evaluation schemes that should have been an integral part of the project from the beginning. Poor sampling and data collection techniques, along with a failure to establish comparable experimental and control groups, allow us to call these earlier critical studies into question. The difficulties of assessing Head Start were worsened during the 1980s when funding for the project was greatly reduced, resulting in a significant decline of on-site monitoring (Zigler & Muenchow, 1992, p. 223).

As equivocal as the evidence for or against the success of compensatory education programs was, some have denounced the programs by arguing that the entire notion of compensatory education was founded on the deficit view of minorities, which regarded cultural, linguistic, cognitive, and affective, as well as behavioral differences, as pathological conditions to be eliminated. Consequently, compensatory education was seen by some critics as a culturally imperialistic attempt to make all poor and minority children emulate white middle-class children and, as such, was incapable of producing cultural democracy.

Because of the deficit model, even attempts to present a balanced picture of minority cultures in the United States through ethnic and non-Western studies did not lead to substantial changes in the ways in which non-Anglo cultures were depicted in instructional materials. For example, in a late-1970s study of textbooks, Fitzgerald (1979) decried the distorted portrayal of African Americans, Asian Americans, Hispanics, and Native Americans in 111 history textbooks. These same texts also presented the United States "as an ideal construct . . . a place without conflicts, without malice or stupidity, where Dick (black or white) comes home with a smiling Jane to a nice house in the suburbs" (p. 218). Fitzgerald warned:

> To the extent that young people actually believe them, these bland fictions, propagated for the purpose of creating good citizens, may actually achieve the opposite; they give young people no warning of the real dangers ahead, and later they may well make these young people feel that their own experience of conflict or suffering is unique in history and perhaps un-American. To the extent that children can see the contrast between these fictions and the world around them, this kind of instruction can only make them cynical. (p. 218)

In another study of six textbooks in American history, Glazer and Ueda (1983) found that these books devoted only a small percentage of pages to minority cultures (p. 17). Glazer and Ueda also discovered that the texts portrayed ethnic minorities as victims of "tragic" circumstances such as "ignorance of other cultures, fear of strange appearance, prejudice, and unavoidable 'cultural clash' between a free-enterprise, industrializing society and populations with pre-industrial forms of social and culture life" (p. 19). This meant that very little, if any, attention was given to the political role and the cultural contributions of ethnic minorities in the development of America as a nation. The history of ethnic groups may then be seen as a constant struggle between the oppressed and the oppressors. Glazer and Ueda argued that this view of history not only trivializes "the central processes that integrated American society" but also "fails to show how their [dominant and minority groups'] joint participation in historical movements created a fluid and pluralistic social system" (p. 61).

Compensatory education efforts had little material effect on the ways in which minority cultures were presented to children in schools. Our efforts to help the poor and culturally different were founded on the traditional concept of Anglo-Americanism, which defines being normal, educable, and American as conforming to the social, cognitive, and moral norms of only the dominant culture. We, as citizens, have failed to recognize and correct these ethnocentric assumptions underlying the compensatory education projects.

Compensatory Education and the Myth of Cultural Deprivation

Advocates of compensatory education insisted that the most effective means of liberating the disadvantaged from poverty and low social status was to give them the kinds of educational, social, and even sensory experiences that enabled middle-class white children to acquire the skills and attitudes believed to be necessary for a successful life in American society. Advocates further held that because the deleterious effects of early cognitive deficits could not be "remedied" or compensated for in a few weeks or months or by educational programs alone, intervention programs should be extended to alter the children's own sociocultural environments (e.g., by child-rearing practices). For this reason, Project Head Start was required by law to include parental and community participation and to promote the physical, social, emotional, and intellectual growth of the children. Thus, intervention in all aspects of the child's life was regarded as necessary, and the earlier the intervention, the greater the benefit. Nothing short of total effort was thought to be adequate for successful compensatory education.

If we interpret the expression *culturally deprived children* in its literal sense, it suggests that some children are without any culture. However, advocates of this concept, who attributed minority children's inadequate educability to cultural deprivation, were not claiming that these children did not have a culture of their own. Rather, children were seen as deprived of the "expected" or mainstream culture. Because "normal" was defined by a white, middle-class norm, those who behaved and spoke in other ways were characterized as "deprived."

In this sense compensatory education was said to have perpetuated institutional racism (perhaps unintentionally) by teaching children to assimilate into the mainstream culture and abandon their own unique ethnic traits.

The critics of the concept of cultural deprivation did not deny that there was a close relationship between social class and school success, nor did they reject the fact that sensory and cultural experiences of middle-class children were key requisites for doing well in school—they were a form of cultural capital. Moreover, they recognized the need for poor and minority children to acquire the kinds of cognitive and social skills to perform better academically through the kinds of sensory and cultural experiences usually available in white middle-class-like environments. However, the critics did object to the suggestion that the sorts of experiences had by minority children were either pathologically deviant or socially and morally illegitimate. For example, the critics found that the cultural deprivation view implicitly assumed the child-rearing practices of poor African American mothers to have been inadequate (often referred to as the *inadequate mothering hypothesis*) and the sensory or perceptual experiences of poor and minority children to have been deficient for the development of intelligence.

Indeed, the social and cognitive skills that allowed these children to function well in their cultural environment probably did not provide an optimal basis for developing the attitudes and skills necessary for academic achievement and getting ahead in the mainstream society. On the other hand, the kinds of mental and behavioral norms valued by the dominant culture and its institutions were not necessarily useful in helping minority individuals participate effectively in their community lives. The patterns of cognitive skills and affective dispositions that would enable an individual to function effectively in a given situation are relative to the person's social, cultural, and intellectual contexts. Demands of people's ways of life determine their styles of social interaction and thinking, which in turn influence their ways of learning. Thus, different cultures encourage the performance of certain tasks and the development of related talents and abilities to be fostered in their members.

The concept of **cultural capital** is useful for critiquing the assumptions of "cultural deprivation" while at the same time acknowledging that some children do come to school less prepared to meet the school's expectations. *Cultural capital* refers to the ability to understand and practice the norms, discourse patterns, language styles, and language modes of the dominant culture. That is, given that the cultural forms of our society are dominated by white middle-class norms, behaviors, and language, individuals who lack the knowledge and skills associated with these norms and behaviors may have limited access to success. As Lisa Delpit (1998) puts it, "While having access to the politically mandated language form will not, by any means, guarantee success (witness the growing numbers of unemployed African Americans holding doctorates), not having access will almost certainly guarantee failure." However, gaining access to cultural capital does not mean rejecting children's home culture. Rather than think of children as deprived, we can acknowledge a rich home culture and heritage and help children appreciate their heritage and still function in middle-class white-dominated society. As Delpit (1995) writes:

> I prefer to be honest with my students. I tell them that their language and cultural style is unique and wonderful but that there is a political power game that is being played, and if they want to be in on that game they too must play. (p. 39)

A central point in this view is that rather than attempting to proselytize these children into the middle-class culture, the schools should respect their culture and values and try to meet the special needs of poor and ethnic minority children. Because the behaviors, beliefs, and values of minority cultures were seen as deficits, those who believed in the cultural deprivation concept failed to recognize the possibility of helping minority children learn more effectively by utilizing the richness and strengths of their cultures. With its social pathology view of ethnic groups, compensatory education—particularly Project Head Start—denied the strengths within an ethnic community. The belief that to deviate from whites is to be inferior was reinforced.

As intense debates over the soundness of the cultural deprivation perspective continued, the term *culturally deprived* was modified to *culturally disadvantaged*, which eventually took the current form of *culturally different* in an attempt to erase ethnocentric and racist connotations. Teachers were reminded that cultural factors affected the teaching–learning processes, and various other specialists were encouraged to convey a more positive image of minority cultures through revising instructional methods and materials. Unfortunately, many of these attempts were based on rather general views about the relationship between culture and education without specific information about it or strategies for educating the culturally different. The disputes about whether the poor had a distinct culture of their own or whether they "suffered" the same sort of cultural deprivation as the children of ethnic groups complicated the issues regarding the educational needs of minority children. Even today, there is a serious and conspicuous absence of knowledge regarding how cultural variables affect the teaching–learning processes and the cognitive and affective development of children. This indeed is a consequence of educators' inability or unwillingness to understand the dynamic relationship between culture and education.

More specific educational implications of the notion of cultural deprivation and its implicit assumptions about minority cultures will be discussed in greater detail in chapters 6 and 7. One important point should be made here. The central issue in the cultural deprivation debate is not about whether poor and minority children should learn the ways of the dominant culture to the exclusion of their own cultural norms; nor is it about the desirability of allowing these children to keep their own ways without learning the mainstream culture. U.S. schools and society should be concerned with helping all children, regardless of race, ethnicity, and gender, to function effectively in a wide range of sociocultural and intellectual environments and divergent contexts without doing violence to the worth of their own culture and self-esteem. To accomplish this, it is not enough to be generally aware that cultures influence how children learn and grow. We must have specific knowledge about the varied ways of thinking, believing, learning, and communicating and how they impinge upon what schools and other institutions do. Cross-cultural research studies need to be conducted to develop concrete instructional strategies and curricular materials to assist our children, particularly those who come from lower socioeconomic classes and minority cultures, in developing social and intellectual skills that will allow them to deal successfully with a myriad of life concerns.

Minority Languages in the Classroom

Standard English vs. African American Vernacular English

One manifestation of the social pathology perspective is the way in which the dominant group views the use of such nonstandard English as African American Vernacular English (AAVE; also called Black English or Ebonics). Even today, most school administrators and teachers regard Standard English as the only "correct" form of English. Consequently, they treat the linguistic patterns of African American children as "broken English," "sloppy speech," "slang," or "some bizarre lingo spoken by baggy-pants-wearing Black kids" (Smitherman, 1998, p. 30). Children using African American Vernacular English are labeled as verbally deficient, and their use of non-Standard English is viewed as a serious barrier to their cognitive development and classroom success. However, systematic studies (Rose, 1994; Smitherman, 1986; Van Dijk, Ting-Toomey, Smitherman, & Troutman, 1997) indicate that the so-called errors actually conform to discernible grammatical rules based on West African languages (Hoover, 1998; Smith, 1998; Smitherman, 1998). Statements such as "He be lookin good" and "Ask yo momma" follow a clear and consistent set of rules. For example, when using these rules, the words *is* and *are* can be deleted in many contexts, the possessive *s* is optional, and the third-person singular or present-tense verb has no distributive *s* ending. The language is no less systematic in its rules and structure and no more ambiguous in its expression than Standard English. This implies that African American Vernacular English is a legitimate linguistic form both structurally and functionally. Hence, we ought not regard it as a "corrupt" version of the "right," or standard, English. This is not to suggest that children from African American or any other ethnic communities should not be taught to use Standard English, but it does mean that the standard form should be taught as a second language in addition to their own linguistic pattern. In other words,

> [W]e must keep in mind that education, at its best, hones and develops the knowledge and skills each student already possesses, while at the same time adding new knowledge and skills to that base. All students have the right to develop the linguistic skills they bring to the classroom and to add others to their repertoire. (Delpit, 1995, p. 67)

The perspective on teaching Standard English to ethnic minority children is particularly important when we consider that "by the time they enter kindergarten, African American children are likely to have formed a sense of identity and self-efficacy strongly linked to their ability to use oral language in highly sophisticated and stylized ways" (Meier, 1998, p. 121). For this reason, the dominant group's view of Black English is likely to have a significant impact on how black children see themselves and their culture.

Just as it is a handicap for African American children to be able to speak only their own language in the "standard-speaking" community, it is equally disadvantageous for them to speak only Standard English on the streets of Harlem. Again, as Kochman (1985) points out, "black social workers, news reporters, and others find that knowledge of black dialect is an invaluable asset in communicating with indigenous community people, a factor that puts white workers in these and other professions at a clear disadvantage" (p. 230). This suggests that speakers of Black English need opportunities to participate in authentic conversations in their own languages and they also must be helped to learn the cultural conventions expected in the dominant community (Delpit, 1995). The pernicious effect of attempting to assimilate minority children into a single linguistic, behavioral, and value orientation is that children who bring other languages to school, including Black English, are forced to make a choice between their home and community or the school. Caught in such a dilemma, children may either feel alienated from school, teachers, and the dominant society in general or learn to regard themselves and their ethnic community as bad, ugly, and inferior.

How best to teach children whose home language is Black English is a political, as well as an educational, question. In 1997 the Oakland, California, school board approved the recommendations of the Task Force on Educating African-American Students. (For the full text of the school board resolution and task force recommendations, see Perry and Delpit, 1998, pp. 143–153). This task force had been formed to develop strategies to combat the low achievement of African American students in the Oakland public schools. The task force report strongly supported the premise that all African American students must become proficient in reading, speaking, and writing Standard English. In addition, they recommended that "teachers and administrators shall respect and acknowledge the history, culture, and language the African-American student brings to the school." In the school board's resolution, the superintendent and teachers were urged to "devise and implement the best possible academic program for imparting instruction to African American students in their primary language for the combined purposes of maintaining the legitimacy and richness of such languages . . . and to facilitate their acquisition and mastery of English language skills" (p. 143). This resolution and the task force recommendations were based on the assumption that teachers who were knowledgeable about their students' culture and appreciative of the linguistic skills of African American children could better enable students to become readers and writers.

These recommendations, however, were picked up by mainstream media and portrayed as a decision to abandon the teaching of Standard English and to replace it with Ebonics. The resolutions were cited out of context and the school board's explanations were drowned in the sea of opposition. Observers on all sides of the political spectrum came together to attack this apparent abandonment of conventional English by a major school district. African American parents who were unfamiliar with the full resolution saw it as another means to narrow the choices of their children. Eventually, the school board resolution was modified; however, the intent remained the same—to enable students to maintain their heritage language and to become skilled in Standard English.

The nationwide controversy that arose over the Oakland resolution demonstrates how easily educational matters, especially those related to cultural values, can be politicized and, in the process, distorted. While we stress the importance of respecting the primary language of students, including Black English, many Americans, especially white Americans, still see using Black English as an inferior, incorrect, and low-status way of communicating. We should not regard ethnic minorities as worthy of our respect only to the extent that we can "melt" them into the mainstream culture. We must see their culturally based characteristics, such as their use of language, as legitimate and functional patterns worthy of respect and growth. To achieve this goal, the schools should offer a curriculum "which is not only immediately functional within the student's present life experience but also preparatory toward developing skills that are necessary for future use" (Kochman, 1985, p. 252). For this to happen, the school personnel involved in teaching culturally different children as well as all of middle-class America must free themselves from their narrow "Anglo ethnocentric bag" (p. 254).

Cultural pluralism based on multicultural education is, then, essential as a broader cultural foundation of American education. Remember, however, that in criticizing the assumptions underlying compensatory education, no attempt is made to suggest that minority groups need not, or do not wish to, acquire those skills and attitudes that the dominant society requires for socioeconomic success. Rather, we should see that the unexamined assumptions of compensatory education—namely, the deficit view—may have defeated the very purposes for which the Great Society programs were initiated. Today, we cannot ignore that ethnic minorities seek to achieve higher social and economic status by "making it" in mainstream society. To "make it" they must learn those cognitive and social skills, behaviors, and attitudes that the dominant society regards as necessary for economic, social, and political success. Granted that some individuals may wish to remain in their own ethnic enclave permanently, most members of minority cultures should become multicultural so that they can function optimally both in the dominant and in their own cultures.

Bilingual Education

Bilingual education involves more than teaching schoolchildren in two languages, for it is closely bound with the issues related to educational equality, assimilation of minority children, and the development and maintenance of the ethnic identity of the culturally different young people in our society. Indeed, these matters are intimately connected with the concerns discussed in the preceding section. Although there are many different types of bilingual education programs, they can be grouped into the following general categories: (1) transitional programs, (2) immersion programs, (3) submersion programs, (4) programs for English as a second language (ESL), and (5) bilingual/bicultural programs.

In transitional programs, children's native or primary languages and the English language are used as a means of helping them learn English. The immersion approach involves teaching the new (English) language to non-English-speaking (NES) and limited-English-speaking (LES) children by a teacher who is proficient in the learners' primary language. However, the teacher uses English only. In transitional as well as immersion programs, children are usually moved into regular English-speaking classes as soon as they acquire sufficient command of the English language to do their academic work. Accordingly, maintaining a learner's primary language is not an objective of either approach. Unlike the immersion approach, in submersion programs NES and LES children are placed directly in all-English-speaking classes without special help. Figuratively speaking, submersion classes may be called the "sink or swim" type programs. Submersion experiences cannot be called bilingual, in the strict sense of the term, because neither the children nor their teacher use more than one language. However, some contend that this is the most rapid and effective way to help children master English. As one may infer, the primary purpose of the transitional, immersion, and submersion approaches is not only to teach English to NES and LES children but also to help them learn the norms of the dominant culture so that they can function effectively in mainstream society. Hence, critics accuse these programs of assimilating language-minority children into the dominant group without promoting the development of pride in their own ethnic heritage.

Unlike the programs just described, teaching English as a second language involves placing NES and LES children in all-English-speaking classes, but they are assigned to separate classes or tutors who are trained to teach English as a second language. Although most ESL instructors are prepared to use special methods and techniques in their work, they may or may not have proficiency in a language other than English. ESL programs are usually used for transitional purposes, but they may also be used to teach English while maintaining the primary languages of NES and LES children.

Finally, bilingual/bicultural programs, otherwise known as maintenance programs, are based on the belief that linguistically and culturally different children have distinctive educational needs, for they must live in bilingual and bicultural environments. To linguistically different children, maintaining their primary languages and developing pride in their cultural heritages are thought to be as important as mastering the English language in becoming productive and responsible citizens. Bilingual/bicultural programs teach English as well as studies in ethnic heritages, at the same time promoting maintenance of the native languages of NES and LES children.

Those involved with the implementation of bilingual/bicultural programs and immersion programs have had problems and will continue to encounter serious difficulties because few bilingual teachers can conduct these classes effectively. Even in teaching English as a second language there appears to be a shortage of qualified personnel. Ironically, those using the submersion and even the immersion approaches may encounter problems in large metropolitan areas where the majority of children in many classes are from linguistic and cultural minority groups. Hence, in cities such as Los Angeles, New York, and Chicago the language in which the children are to be immersed or submerged could be a language other than English.

Controversies About Bilingual Education

Bilingual education has been one of the most controversial issues in American education because its purposes have deep ideological roots. In the late 1960s to about 1970, when the controversy first took hold, many viewed the goal of bilingual education as that of assimilating minority children into the dominant culture. They argued that the sooner these children became an integral part of the mainstream society, the more likely they would be to attain socioeconomic success. Advocates of this perspective supported transitional, immersion, or submersion programs. Others were convinced that bilingual education should help minority children develop positive self-images by maintaining their primary language and perpetuating their unique cultural patterns while teaching English so they could function in the larger society. Thus, bilingual education also needed to be bicultural. These opposing views were, and still are, held not only by educators and legislators but also by members of minority groups themselves.

In 1967, prior to the passage of the Bilingual Education Act of 1968, a congressional hearing on bilingual education was held. The hearing focused on meeting the unique educational needs of Hispanic children who had either no or limited command of the English language. At the time, not much was known about the cause–effect relationship among Hispanic children's negative self-image, their school failure, and the use of English rather than Spanish as the language of instruction. However, many educators believed that bilingual/bicultural education (including the use of Black English) would improve the self-concept of language-minority children and that their positive self-concept would help them do well in school. They were persuaded that a significant connection exists among the maintenance of minority children's primary language, their sense of ethnic identity, and their academic performance. Yet, in spite of testimony to this effect given at the 1967 hearing, the intent of the Bilingual Education Act of 1968 was to provide the resources for transitional rather than "maintenance" programs to poor and non- or limited-English-speaking children.

In 1974, a suit was brought against the San Francisco Board of Education before the United States Supreme Court on behalf of 1,800 Chinese children. In this class-action suit, known as *Lau v. Nichols*, the plaintiffs argued that the San

Francisco Board of Education had failed to meet the educational needs of the non-English-speaking Chinese children by not providing programs specifically designed for them. They further held that the board therefore violated Title VI of the Civil Rights Act of 1964 as well as the Equal Protection Clause of the Fourteenth Amendment. In response to these charges, the school board insisted that all children received equal education and that children's ability to understand the English language was the responsibility of their families rather than the school district. In deciding for the plaintiffs, the Supreme Court upheld the 1970 guideline of the Office of Civil Rights, which required that a school district must provide appropriate instructional programs to children with limited proficiency in the English language.

Although the *Lau* decision did not mandate bilingual education programs, it required school districts to develop and offer special language programs for NES and LES students. The Supreme Court opinion did not favor either the transitional or the maintenance programs. However, the "Lau remedies," formulated by then Commissioner of Education Terrel Bell and a special task force, unequivocally recommended the teaching of English or the primary language as well as the cultural heritages of non-English-speaking children. Throughout the 1970s and into the early 1980s, the federal government attempted to clarify, redefine, and reshape the purpose and the future direction of bilingual education without much success. The Department of Education's own skepticism about the effectiveness of bilingual programs, as well as opposition from various citizens' groups and professional organizations in education, may have contributed significantly to the federal government's inability to set a clear direction for bilingual education.

Efforts to determine the appropriate education for language minority children have been further confused by political efforts to limit the maintenance of other languages and cultures within the United States. Efforts to legislate the use of English only and to limit bilingual/bicultural education illustrate the ways in which educational efforts are influenced by politics. English Only first appeared in 1981 as a constitutional amendment to ban all uses of languages other than English by federal, state, and local governments. To some, English had become a symbol of Americanization, the cornerstone of a collective identity (Rong & Preissle, 1998, p. 98). While the efforts toward an English Only constitutional amendment made little progress, by the mid-1990s, twenty states had adopted various forms of English Only legislation (Crawford, 1998). The legislation varied from state to state, but its general intent was to require that all state and local government communication be in English only. Information about voting, taxes, and a myriad of other issues could be given only in English in any government publication or orally by any government employee, even to limited-English speakers. A Spanish-speaking clerk at a motor vehicle bureau, for example, could not legally offer assistance in Spanish to a Spanish-speaking-only client. In 1998, Arizona's English Only law was declared unconstitutional, and the arguments used in this case highlight the problems with such legislation.

The Arizona Supreme Court found that the legislation infringed on free speech and denied Arizona citizens equal protection under the law. It essentially limited the ability of non-English-speaking persons to seek and obtain information and services from government.

Meanwhile, in California, a state experiencing high immigration and extensive demands for bilingual education, a series of propositions were passed by the electorate in the 1980s and 1990s that suggest that California voters were very wary of the effect a large number of immigrants in the state would have on the state's institutions and culture. In 1986, Californians approved Proposition 63: English as the Official Language. In 1994, Proposition 187 made illegal aliens ineligible for public social services, public health care services, and public school education. Many teachers resisted efforts to get schools and teachers to monitor which of their students might be illegal immigrants. Then, in June 1998, Proposition 227: English for Children was approved by voters. This proposition called for an "end" to bilingual education. It required all school instruction to be conducted in English with short-term (normally not more than 180 days or one school year), intensive sheltered English immersion programs for children not fluent in English. Such programs allow students to be taught in their native languages, separately from regular classes. The intention, however, was for such separation to be as brief as possible. Programs aimed at maintaining home languages and culture were not to be a part of the public school curriculum.

The disparate views regarding the purposes of bilingual education are closely tied to attitudes and beliefs about whether ethnic minority children should be assimilated into the mainstream culture or be allowed to maintain and develop their own culture while learning the dominant norms. These ideological elements have influenced not only the type of bilingual programs that have been considered worthwhile but also the results of program evaluations. Reports have presented conflicting evidence concerning the effectiveness of bilingual programs. However, evaluation studies, with appropriate comparison groups and controls for preexisting differences, are difficult to design (August & Hakuta, 1997). Ultimately, students may be too varied to make recommendations as to one ideal policy for all language-minority learners (Greene, 1998).

Moreover, because of the ideological nature of the programs, it is unlikely that we will have clear consensus about either the efficacy or the desirability of bilingual education in any form. Learning to use two or more languages in any society is not merely an intellectual activity, because "languages often represent different social networks and associated value systems, and the choice of language can come to symbolize an individual's identification with either system" (Hakuta, 1986, p. 233). In a society that views the use of a minority language or a nonstandard English language as "strange," children are not apt to be motivated to learn or maintain anything other than Standard English. It is for this reason that "bilingualism will be most stable when there are social norms that govern differential use of the two languages depending on the situation" (p. 233). This implies that significant changes in the attitudes of the larger society toward minority languages are essential for successful bilingual/bicultural education. As opponents of bilingual education might ask, is this type of education necessary in our society at all? Would it not be better for poor and ethnic minority young people to become assimilated into the dominant society as soon as possible for their socioeconomic success? Or, as the proponents of the English Only movement might argue, would bilingual/bicultural education threaten the well-being of our society by encouraging separatism? Isn't use of a common language at the base of national unity?

When we consider that the growth in the population of language minority children is not likely to decrease dramatically in the near future—in fact, it is likely to increase—the policy and programmatic decisions made at the local, state, and national levels are going to profoundly impact schooling in the United States. Insofar as language-minority children are members of this society, the extent to which their special needs are served will affect the future of the society at large.

Regardless of our own perspectives on bilingual education, the reality for culturally different young people is that they must live in environments with at least two different linguistic and cultural norms—those of their own ethnic group and those of the dominant society. For them to lead a fulfilling life and preserve their personal dignity, they need not only linguistic, social, and cognitive skills but also the respect and acceptance that should be accorded to diversities of all sorts in a democratic society. Although the relationships between diversity and democracy will be explored further in the next chapter, for now it is enough to say that the development of positive attitudes toward different cultures can be promoted not only through teaching language but also by developing the critical ways in which we understand and analyze our own culture and its underlying values.

In 1908, President Theodore Roosevelt demanded the deportation of immigrants who failed to learn English five years after their arrival on U.S. shores, and the state of Iowa prohibited the use of languages other than English in gatherings of three or more people. Today there are still a significant number of individuals in the United States who are convinced that English is an endangered language needing legal protection. A common language is a significant element in unifying a nation, along with such other elements as people's sense of historical continuity, a common purpose, individual uniqueness, and so on; sharing a language can become the foundation of a nation's unity. However, when "protecting English" is used as a central argument against bilingual education and bilingualism, it often becomes a latent expression of hostility against ethnic and linguistic minority groups or immigrants as a whole. As Larmouth (1987) reminds us, educators must recognize that "the very concepts which unify a nation can divide it, if they are perceived by a disenfranchised minority . . . who feel themselves to be apart from the dominant population . . . and see themselves excluded from any realistic opportunity for advancement" (pp. 54–55). He goes on to suggest that if we were to adopt a constitutional amendment to make English our official language, we would increase a risk of disenfranchising a significant number of people, perhaps sufficiently to give rise to the very disunity that we fear. Though it may seem para-doxical, the best strategy would seem to be to continue to support a full range of opportunities for participation in the social and economic opportunities of the dominant culture, including opportunities to learn English, without disenfranchis-ing or threatening ethnocultural minorities and their languages. Furthermore, because it seems clear that minority languages pose no threat to national unity in the United States, there is little basis for opposition to efforts to recover or main-tain them (p. 55).

Intelligence, IQ, and the Achievement Gap

The compensatory education programs of the 1970s were founded on the assumption that poor minority children could be helped to develop their cogni-tive and social skills by compensating for their environmental (sensory and cul-tural) deprivation. Hence, IQ gains were used as an important criterion in eval-uating the effectiveness of Project Head Start and other compensatory programs that characterized the Great Society. However, a disparity between IQ scores of white students and black students has persisted to this day. Furthermore, while the use of IQ scores as a meaningful measure of intelligence has been called into question, African Americans, Latinos, Native Americans, and those for whom English is not the first language lag behind white, English-speaking students by all common measures. What's come to be known as the "achievement gap" has been found in school graduation rates, in the demographics of those enrolled in top academic classes, in the characteristics of those admitted to higher status col-leges and graduate programs, and in standardized test scores (Berlak, 2001). Indeed, despite optimism in the 1970s and 1980s, the achievement gap between minority and dominant culture students, including test scores, has shown little evidence of narrowing (Thernstrom & Thernstrom, 2002). Measures have fluc-tuated but, overall, have not declined significantly. This has left researchers and policymakers struggling to understand how to account for this persistent gap.

One argument is that by focusing on IQ scores, we are simply using the wrong measure. The argument over the nature and definition of intelligence is a complex one, influenced not only by science but by cultural beliefs and attitudes as well. There are those who subscribe to the argument that IQ is measurable, and to some extent, inheritable. IQ tests are said to measure a general intelli-gence factor, which is referred to as g. It is this g factor that Hans Eysenck (1998), Herrnstein and Murray (1994), Arthur Jensen (1981), and others believe is, in some part, inherited. In their controversial book *The Bell Curve* (1994), Herrnstein and Murray argued that efforts at compensatory programs were a failure because they were focused on a futile cause. Public policy, they argued, cannot correct IQ inequality.

Both the issue of the role of genetic factors versus environment (nature ver-sus nurture) and the definition of what constitutes intelligence continue to be debated. Many psychologists and anthropologists argue that intelligence is not a single unitary power a person has. Rather, it represents a complex of abilities that enable a person to recognize and solve problems. "A growing number of researchers have argued that while IQ tests provide a measure of certain linguistic and mathematical forms of thinking, other equally important kinds of intelligence, such as spatial, musical, or personal are ignored" (Gardner, 1995, p. 67). For poor minority children, or for that matter, for any children, growth in their ability to solve life problems (i.e., intelligence) requires the development of many more kinds of cognitive and affective as well as sociocultural skills than can be measured by standardized tests (Gardner, 1985). This suggests that intelligence may be meaningfully considered as more than the kinds of skills and abilities measured by a paper-and-pencil test. IQ, as opposed to intelligence, is an index of a narrow set of abilities measured by a standardized test. An IQ score represents a child's standing in relation to other children of the same age who took the same test—that is, the norm group. Those who argue that environment accounts for the disparity on the IQ scores between African American and white students attribute the lower IQ score of African Americans to the *cultural loading* of IQ tests. In other words, the items in the tests favor the white middle-class population. Defenders of the meaningfulness of the IQ test argue that statistical techniques correct for any cultural bias.

Various studies seeking to account for the gap, not only in IQ scores between African Americans and whites in the United States but in school achievement as well, suggest how complex this issue actually is. Even the argument that socioeconomic disparities and continued oppression account for educational differences may be too simple an explanation for the dynamics that influence success in our society (Singham, 1998). Some recent studies suggest the subtle ways in which culture influences school achievement. Claude Steele's work demonstrates how the threat of stereotyping can depress test scores. When African American and white students were given tests that they were told measured academic ability, the African American students did poorer than the white students. However, when told that the test was of no significance, that it was just a laboratory tool, the differences disappeared (Steele, 1992; Steele & Aronson, 1995). "Steele concluded that the fear that a poor performance on a test will confirm a stereotype in the mind of the examiner imposes an anxiety on the test-taker that is difficult to overcome" (Singham, 1998). Signithia Fordham (1996) found that academically talented African Americans expressed ambivalence toward schooling and lacked confidence that they would reap the rewards of school. Fordham concluded that experience with racism in society had led many youth to doubt that traditional routes to success were open to them.

John Ogbu's (1991) research had similar findings, indicating that the relationship between effort in school and social rewards is not a certain relationship if you are African American. Further, voluntary immigrants, a term Ogbu used to distinguish those who came to the United States willingly from those who came involuntarily, are more likely to compare their social status with those back home and to see the opportunity for a better life for their children. African Americans, who are, in Ogbu's terms, an involuntary minority group, have no home group with which to compare themselves. They are more likely to compare their status with that of white middle-class Americans and may be less likely than voluntary immigrant groups to see greater opportunities for their children. Uri Treisman's (1992) work demonstrates the power of peer group influence on school achievement. Treisman found that the African American students in his math classes at Berkeley were not doing as well as other students in his class. However, when he formed heterogeneous work groups and presented these groups with challenging problems, African American student performance improved significantly. It is significant to note that these groups focused on challenging problem solving in a group context. In short, we may be mistaken about the ways we conceptualize the problem of disparities in school achievement. In schools today we emphasize independent and often passive work. White achievement is seen as the "norm," and the performance of African American students in general is seen as a deficit. Perhaps the problem rests in how we teach all children and how we measure their success.

There are schools and school districts that have demonstrated that the achievement gap is not inevitable (see, for example, the work of the Education Trust at www2.edtrust.org). That is, there are schools, and even school districts, in which most students are minority students from homes that are at or below the poverty line, yet the students in these schools score, on average, at or above the state or national norm on standardized tests. Such successful schools share a number of characteristics: There are high expectations for students; teachers create the scaffolding, or support, to assure that students can achieve those expectations; young people are actively engaged in activities they find meaningful; expectations are clear and consistent; and learners consistently receive positive messages about the possibilities of success (Thernstrom & Thernstrom, 2002).

Beginning with the Great Society programs of the 1960s, educators and policymakers have sought ways to close the achievement gap between minority and white students. Compensatory education programs were designed to provide "deprived" children with the skills and knowledge to succeed in school and in life, yet despite such compensatory efforts, the gaps remain. Perhaps it is the very assumption of "deprivation" itself that has been a problem. Today we realize that when teachers respect and understand the cultures of their learners, when they find ways to connect school learning with children's experience, and when they maintain and work toward high expectations, such achievement gaps have the potential to narrow and even close.

This chapter examined the ways in which the dominant culture and its deficit model of viewing other cultures affected the process of schooling, along with its policies and practices, in the United States from the seventeenth century to the twentieth century. Our nation has gone through many varied approaches in dealing with minority groups. In the 1960s and 1970s, many individuals, groups, and agencies seriously attempted to eradicate prejudice, discrimination, and inequality in our society. As a result of these efforts, we are perhaps more sensitive to matters concerning human rights, equality, and freedom for all individuals, regardless of race, culture, religion, gender, or age. On the other hand, the very nature of disputes regarding such issues as cultural deprivation, compensatory education, bilingualism and bilingual education, and the English Only movement strongly suggests that the perspective of viewing schooling as Americanization rooted in the deficit view persists in many subtle ways.

Several interpretations of cultural pluralism and the educational implications of these interpretations will be discussed in the following chapter. These perspectives are considered the basis for establishing cultural democracy and multicultural education in United States.

 Cases for Reflection

In reading the following cases, keep in mind these discussion questions pertaining to educational reform: Have some aspects of American culture and its institutions changed as a result of the educational reform measures in the post-*Sputnik* era (after 1957)? If education and schooling reflect the culture of the society in which they occur, did some aspects of American culture contribute to the fact that educational reform movements in the late 1950s into the 1960s were less effective than educators might have expected? If there were such aspects, do they still exist in our society today? And how might they affect the current movements for reforms in education and teacher education?

SHAKER HEIGHTS

Shaker Heights is not your typical community. It is a small inner-ring bedroom suburb of Cleveland, covering an area of about five square miles and having a population of 30,000. It is a carefully planned city with tree-lined streets winding past well-maintained homes and manicured lawns, lakes, parks, and red-brick schools nestled in campus-like grounds. The city is about one-third African American and two-thirds white, with a sprinkling of other minorities. . . . It is also a highly educated community, with more than 60 percent of all residents over the age of 25 holding at least a bachelor's degree—a figure three times the national average. . . .

Shaker Heights prides itself on the excellence of its school system, taxing itself voluntarily with one of the highest rates in the state of Ohio in order to maintain the wide range of academic and extracurricular programs that provide the students who take advantage of them with an education that would be the envy of any child in America. . . .

But all is not well, and the problem is immediately apparent when you walk inside classrooms. Although the school population has equal numbers of black students and white ones, in the highest-achievement tracks (the Advanced Placement sections) you find only a handful of blacks (about 10 percent), while the lowest-achievement tracks (called "general education") are populated almost exclusively by blacks (about 95 percent). When educational statistics are disaggregated by ethnicity, it is found that black Shaker Heights students on average do better than black students elsewhere, just as white Shaker Heights students do better than their counterparts in other school systems. The real puzzle is why, although both communities have equal access to all the school district's educational opportunities, the academic performance of black Shaker Heights students lags significantly behind that of their white peers. For example, the average black SAT score in 1996 was 956 (compared to a national black average of 856), while the average for white students was 1198 (compared to a national white average of 1049).

Source: M. Singham (1998, September), The canary in the mine: The achievement gap between black and white students. *Phi Delta Kappan, 80*(1), 9–10.

DISCUSSION QUESTIONS

1. What reasons can you think of to explain this gap between the performance of African American and white students in Shaker Heights? Try to brainstorm as many reasons as possible before considering which you think is the best reason.
2. What do you think explains this achievement gap? In other words, of all the reasons you brainstormed for question 1, which makes the most sense to you and why?
3. What do you think the school district, schools, and teachers might do to close the gap between African American and white students' achievement?

■   ■   ■   ■

BLACK ENGLISH

Following is an excerpt from a paper written by an African American teacher education student whose personal experiences had caused her to rethink her attitude toward Black English.

Recently, while riding a city bus to campus, I overheard a conversation between two young women. One of them was upset with her boyfriend. She exclaimed loudly, "He be acting so crazy." A year ago her speech would have made me cringe. I would have dismissed her as illiterate and her speech pattern as bad English. I would have been thankful that I did not sound like that when I opened my mouth. It's amazing how much my perspective has changed over the past year. I did not realize that linguists have considered her speech pattern . . . to be a legitimate language system. . . .

The roots of my bias were planted very early in my childhood. My mother was a high school English teacher. For the first twelve years of my life, we lived in Cairo, Illinois. Cairo was a very small and economically depressed area. Blacks comprised over 60 percent of the population and most of them relied on some form of public assistance in order to survive. Alcohol and drug-abuse were becoming big problems. My mother was sickened by what was happening in her hometown but she also wanted to stay and try to make a difference in the lives of the children who lived there. She also wanted to give her three children a chance at a good life. Thus, my siblings and I were required to speak "good English" at all times. If we slipped and used "bad English" my mother would correct us immediately—she did not care where we were or who was present.

Although my mother achieved her goal of helping her children acquire "good English" skills, there were some negative consequences. Because we spoke so differently from most of our peers, my siblings and I were accused of "actin' white" or "soundin' white." We were frequently beat up by other children.

Source: Yvette Michele Harvey (1998, December). From Rejection to Acceptance: The Eradication of a Preservice Teacher's Bias toward the African-American Vernacular Dialect. Unpublished paper.

DISCUSSION QUESTIONS

1. Should African American students be corrected and forced to speak Standard American English in schools?

2. As you think about the experience of this one young woman, what do you think are the possible losses and gains of Standard American English being reinforced at all times at home and in school? Is there a middle ground that you might support?

REFERENCES

Administration for Children and Families (ACF) (2002). *Administration of children, youth and families: Head Start: Program Fact Sheet.* Available: http://www.acf.hhs.gov/programs/hsb/research/2003.htm

Altenbough, R. J. (2003). *The American people and their education: A social history.* Upper Saddle River, NJ: Merrill.

August, D., & Hakuta, K. (Eds.). (1997). *Improving schooling for language minority children: A research agenda.* Washington, DC: National Academy Press.

Berlak, H. (2001). Race and the achievement gap. *Rethinking Schools Online, 15*(4). Available: http://www.rethinkingschools.org/archive/15_04/race154.shmtl

Bronfenbrenner, U. (1974). *Is early intervention effective? A report on longitudinal evaluations of preschool programs.* (DHEW-OHD-74-25). Washington, DC: U.S. Department of Health, Education and Welfare.

Bush, G. W. (July, 2003). Remarks by the President on Early Childhood Development, Highland Park Elementary School, Head Start Center, Landover, Maryland. Available: http://www.whitehouse.gov/news/releases/2003/07/20030707-2.html

Caruso, D. R., & Detterman, K. K. (1981). Intelligence research and social policy. *Phi Delta Kappan, 63*(3), 183–187.

Conant, J. B. (1959). *American high school today: A first report to interested citizens.* New York: McGraw-Hill.

Crawford, J. W. (1998). English only. Available: http://www.ourworld.compuserve.com/homepages/JWCRAWFORD/engonly.htm

Cremin, L. A. (1977). *Traditions of American education.* New York: Basic Books.

Cubberly, E. P. (1909). *Changing conceptions of education.* Boston: Houghton Mifflin.

Delpit, L. (1995). *Other people's children.* New York: New Press.

Delpit, L. (1998). What should teachers do? Ebonics and culturally responsive teaching. In T. Perry & L. Delpit (Eds.), *The real Ebonic debate: Power, language and the education of African-American children* (pp. 17–28). Boston: Beacon Press.

Eysenck, H. J. (1998). *Intelligence.* New Brunswick, NJ: Transaction Publishers.

Fitzgerald, F. (1979). *America revised.* Boston: Little, Brown.

Fordham, S. (1996). *Blacked out: Dilemmas of race, identity and success at Capital High.* Chicago: University of Chicago Press.

Gardner, H. (1985). *Frames of mind: The theory of multiple intelligences.* New York: Basic Books.

Gardner, H. (1995). Scholarly brinkmanship. In R. Jacoby and N. Glauberman (Eds.), *The bell curve debate* (pp. 61–72). New York: Times Books.

Glazer, N., & Ueda, R. (1983). *Ethnic groups history textbooks.* Washington, DC: Ethics and Public Policy Center.

Grant, C. A., & Gomez, M. L. (Eds.). (1996). *Making school multicultural: Campus and classroom.* Englewood Cliffs, NJ: Merrill.

Greene, J. P. (1998). *A meta-analysis of the effectiveness of bilingual education.* Clarement, CA: Tomás Rivera Center.

Hakuta, K. (1986). *Mirror of language: The debate on bilingualism.* New York: Basic Books.

Herrnstein, R. J., & Murray, C. (1994). *The bell curve: Intelligence and class structure in American life.* New York: Free Press.

Hoover, M. R. (1998). Ebonics: Myths and realities. In T. Perry & L. Delpit (Eds.), *The real Ebonics debate: Power, language, and the education of African-American children* (pp. 71–76). Boston: Beacon Press.

Illiteracy in America [Special issue]. (1970). *Harvard Educational Review, 40*(1).

Jensen, A. R. (1969). How much can we boost IQ and scholastic achievement? *Harvard Educational Review, 39*(4), 1–123.

Jensen, A. R. (1981). *Straight talk about mental tests.* New York: Free Press.

Kleibard, H. (1995). *The struggle for the American curriculum: 1893–1958.* New York: Routledge.

Kochman, T. (1985). Black American speech events and a language program for the classroom. In C. B. Cazden, V. P. John, & D. Hymes (Eds.), *Functions of language in the classroom* (pp. 211–266). Prospect Heights, IL: Waveland Press.

Koffler, K., & Fulton, A. (2002, April 2). Bush announces accountability for Head Start. *Congress, Daily.* Available: http://www.govexec.com/dailyfed/0402/040202cd2.htm

Larmouth, D. W. (1987). Does linguistic heterogeneity erode national unity? In W. S. Vanhorne & T. V. Tonnesen (Eds.), *Ethnicity and language* (pp. 37–57). Milwaukee: University of Wisconsin Institute on Race and Ethnicity.

Lau v. Nichols, 414 U.S. 563 (1974).

Levine, D. U., & Levine, R. F. (1996). *Society and education* (4th ed.). Boston: Allyn & Bacon.

Mayo-Smith, R. (1904). *Emigration and immigration.* New York: Scribner.

Meier, T. (1998). Teaching teachers about Black communication. In T. Perry & L. Delpit (Eds.), *The real Ebonics debate: Power, language, and the education of African-American children* (pp. 117–125). Boston: Beacon Press.

Moss, D. (2003, June 20). *House panel passes Head Start bill over democratic opposition. Congress Daily.* Available: http://www.govexec.com/dailyfed/0603/062003njnsl.htm

Ogbu, J. (1991). *Minority status and schooling: A comparative study of immigrant and involuntary minorities.* New York: Garland.

Parkay, F. W., & Stanford, B. H. (1998). *Becoming a teacher* (4th ed.). Needham Heights, MA: Allyn & Bacon.

Perry, T., & Delpit, L. (Eds.). (1998). *The real Ebonics debate: Power, language, and the education of African-American children*. Boston: Beacon Press.

Pulliam, J. D., & Van Patton, J. J. (2003). *History of education in America* (8th ed.). Upper Saddle River, NJ: Merrill/Prentice Hall.

Ravitch, D. (1983). *The troubled crusade*. New York: Basic Books.

Rockefeller Brothers Foundation. (1958). *The pursuit of excellence*. New York: Doubleday.

Rong, X. L., & Preissle, J. (1998). *Educating immigrant students*. Thousand Oaks, CA: Corwin Press.

Rose, T. (1994). *Black noise: Rap music and Black culture in contemporary America*. Hanover, NH: University Press of New England.

Rothstein, R. (1998). Bilingual education: The controversy. *Phi Delta Kappan, 79*(9), 672–678.

Schweinhart, L. J., & Weikart, D. P. (1977). Research report: Can preschool education make a lasting difference? *Bulletin of the High Scope Foundation, 4*, 231.

Singham, M. (1998). The canary in the mine: The achievement gap between black and white students. *Phi Delta Kappan, 80*(1), 9–15.

Smith, E. (1998). What is Black English? What is Ebonics? In T. Perry & L. Delpit (Eds.), *The real Ebonics debate: Power, language, and the education of African-American children* (pp. 49–58). Boston: Beacon Press.

Smitherman, G. (1986). *Talkin and testifyin: The language of Black America*. Detroit: Wayne State University Press.

Smitherman, G. (1998). *Black English/Ebonics: What it be like?* In T. Perry & L. Delpit (Eds.), *The real Ebonics debate: Power, language, and the education of African-American children* (pp. 29–37). Boston: Beacon Press.

Spring, J. (2001). *The American School 1642–2000*. New York: McGraw-Hill.

Steele, C. M. (1992, April). Race and the schooling of Black Americans. *Atlantic*, 68–78.

Steele, C. M., & Aronson, J. (1995). Stereotype threat and the intellectual test performance of African Americans. *Journal of Personality and Social Psychology, 69*, 797–811.

Thernstrom, A., & Thernstrom, S. (2002). *Schools that work. Bridging the achievement gap*. Washington, DC: Brookings Institution Press.

Treisman, P. U. (1992). Studying students studying calculus. *College Mathematics Journal, 23*, 362–372.

van Dijk, T. A., Ting-Toomey, S., Smitherman, G., & Troutman, D. (1997). Discourse, ethnicity, culture and racism. In T. A. Van Dijk (Ed.), *Discourse as social interaction* (pp. 144–180). London: Sage.

U.S. Census Bureau. (2004). *Population projections*. Available: http://www.census.gov/population/projections/nation/summary/np-t5-c.pdf

U.S. Department of Health and Human Services. (1984). *The Head Start synthesis, evaluation, and utilization project* (HSSEU-HHS-84). Washington, DC: C.S.R.

Zangwill, I. (1909). *The melting pot*. New York: Macmillan.

Zigler, E., & Muenchow, S. (1992). *Head Start: The inside story of America's most successful educational experiment*. New York: Basic Books.

Zigler, E. (2003). Father of Head Start warns of weakness in Bush plan. *Seattle Post-Intelligence*. Available: http://seattlepi.nwsource.com/opinion/126870_focus22.html

4

Cultural Pluralism, Democracy, and Multicultural Education: 1970s–2000s

KEY *Concepts:*

- Ageism
- Charter schools
- Cultural pluralism
- Exceptional learners

- Multicultural education
- School vouchers
- Sexism

There are several different conceptions of cultural pluralism and their connection with democracy. These views as well as those about education were debated in the 1970s into the new millennium. The critical examination of these conceptions will focus on (1) setting concerns for cultural pluralism within the contexts of the educational reforms of the time, (2) comparing several different views of cultural pluralism and multicultural education, (3) analyzing the relationship between democracy and cultural pluralism, (4) formulating broader conceptions of cultural pluralism and multicultural education, and (5) exploring some possible implications of multicultural education for special education, sexism, ageism, and global, or international, education.

CULTURAL PLURALISM AND THE AMERICAN SCHOOL

The Context of Reform

A plethora of major educational reform proposals appeared in the 1980s and continued into the new century, and these had implications, sometimes by omission, concerning education in a culturally diverse society. To better understand what occurred in schools during this period, it is important to understand the context of reform in which education was set.

As a result of the publication of *A Nation at Risk* in 1983 by the National Commission on Excellence in Education, the American public's attention turned once again to the alleged failure of the American school to adequately educate young people. The report was followed by numerous additional evaluations of public education in the United States. The United States was going through another educational soul-searching experience similar to the one it underwent in the post-*Sputnik* era. In the late 1950s, educational reforms were spurred by America's desire to surpass the USSR in the aerospace race. In 1983, the impetus for educational reforms came from this nation's aspiration to outstrip other nations in economic competition. Not surprisingly, most of the educational reform proposals stemming from *A Nation at Risk* and other studies recommended additional work in English, science, mathematics, and foreign languages.

In 1989 the nation's governors and the president met in Charlottesville, Virginia, for an education summit. At this meeting, a process for establishing national goals in education was put into place. In 1990 the president and the governors announced their commitment to a set of National Education Goals. In 1991, President George Bush released *America 2000: An Educational Strategy*, which included the six goals that had been agreed to at the governors' conference. These goals, intended to be reached by the year 2000, called for:

- all children to be prepared to start school ready to learn,
- a high school graduation rate of at least 90 percent,
- high level competence in challenging subject matter,
- scoring first in the world in science and mathematics achievement,
- adult literacy necessary to compete in a global economy and to exercise the rights and responsibilities of citizenship, and
- drug and violence free schools.

Throughout the 1990s, many state governments began to initiate reform efforts that generally included the establishment of standards in core subjects and a reexamination of ways to assess whether those expectations had been met.

In January 2002, President George W. Bush signed into law the reauthorization of the Elementary and Secondary School Act known as *No Child Left Behind* (NCLB). The law was intended to assure that all students, in all income, racial, ethnic, and linguistic groups, would be proficient in literacy and mathematics by the year 2013. The law requires that all students in grades 3 through 8 be tested every year to assess the development of their academic skills. NCLB further mandates that there be a qualified teacher in every classroom and that there be strict penalties for schools that fail to make annual yearly progress as demonstrated by improved test scores.

Few would argue with the law's apparent intention, and the bill passed with bipartisan support. Nonetheless, as the law came into effect, many argued with its methods (Henninger, 2004, p. 336). Yearly testing was seen as a financial burden on school districts, an "unfunded mandate" from the federal government. By 2004, some states began considering dropping out of compliance with the testing mandates of the law, thus forfeiting federal dollars. Republicans were questioning federal intrusion into local control of education, while Democrats questioned the cost and efficacy of testing. Parents in many locales were surprised to learn that the schools they supported were not making "annual yearly progress" based on their state's testing results. In many communities, parents were more likely to question the test than were their schools. Many educators, meanwhile, became increasingly skeptical of standardized testing as the primary measure of learning. There was growing concern that the pressure for children to perform on exams might, in fact, undermine good teaching and real learning. Wrote one educator, "All children can learn but all children cannot learn as much as all other children. And all children cannot learn to some preset state or federal standards, as is currently mandated by the No Child Left Behind Act . . ." (Finley, 2004).

The movement toward national standards and mandated testing is an example of school reform that focuses on curriculum. Curricular reform during this period primarily addressed issues of standards, accountability, and assessment. Although much of the rhetoric surrounding these reforms referred to high standards "for all," the focus of these reforms was on raising expectations and test scores rather than on providing an education that is multicultural or using teaching strategies appropriate to diverse learners.

Not all reform efforts focused on curriculum, however. Other reform proposals that emerged as the twentieth century drew to a close focused on the structure of schooling. Advocates of structural reform insisted that only through restructuring schools could teaching and learning really be changed.

Proposals to restructure schools are founded on the assumption that merely tinkering with conventional schooling is insufficient to make the changes necessary to improve student learning. Structural reforms included such proposals as decentralized authority, further opportunities for school choice, flexible and block scheduling, team teaching, and shared decision making. Among the most far-reaching and politically charged structural reform initiatives to emerge in the 1990s were vouchers and charter schools. Each of these initiatives sought to create significant change and to provide parents with more options for choosing their children's schools.

Charter schools are publicly funded schools that are not under the direct control of the local board of education but rather may be managed by any interested group—for example, parents, a local college, or a profit-making firm (Manno et al., 1998, p. 490). While they must comply with basic health, safety, and nondiscrimination requirements, they are freed from the policies and procedures that charter school advocates argue prohibit schools from being responsive to local needs. The first charter school law was passed in Minnesota in 1991; since that time, more than two-thirds of the states have passed some sort of charter school law. According to Manno et al. (1998), "The charter school concept is simple but powerful: *sound school choices can be provided to families under the umbrella of public education without micromanaging by government bureaucracies*" emphasis added. Charter schools are responsible for demonstrating improved student achievement; if achievement does not improve, the charter can be revoked. Advocates argue that successful charter schools will stimulate changes in the public school system itself, both through providing a competitive choice for parents and through the development of alternative structures and curriculum. Charter schools, argues Nathan (1998, p. 500), are built on core American values: responsibility, opportunity, and choice.

School vouchers, like charter schools, are intended to provide parents with choices and flexibility in selecting schools for their children. However, under a voucher system, parents are given a "voucher" by the state for the amount of public money a school district would receive to educate that child. This voucher could then be applied toward the child's tuition at a private school. Because public schools are funded on a per-pupil basis, any public money given to parents to fund private school education would not be given to the district that child would leave. Public money would follow the child out of the public school and into the private school. States that permit vouchers do so in limited numbers and have strict guidelines under which private schools would be eligible to participate. In 2002, in a 5–4 vote the Supreme Court upheld the constitutionality of the Cleveland, Ohio, voucher plan. The Cleveland plan offered low-income Cleveland families vouchers that could be used at religious as well as secular private schools. The decision that such vouchers do not violate the constitutional guarantee of separation of church and state was seen as a victory by many voucher advocates (Walsh, 2002).

Supporters of school vouchers argue that vouchers would encourage competition among schools, and thus market forces would serve to encourage improvement in schools generally. In addition, vouchers would enable poor children to attend private schools and thus contribute to equalizing educational opportunity (Berliner & Biddle, 1995, p. 175). Opponents of vouchers see this as a way to divert tax dollars to elite private schools (Berliner & Biddle, 1995, p. 177). Money would flow out of public schools and into private institutions with only a very few poor children benefiting from this move: "This sets up a two-class educational system, in which the private schools serve the talented and wealthy students and the increasingly poorly financed public schools are left to cope as best they can with the poor and the disadvantaged" (p. 176).

Advocates of restructuring the school system by allowing school choice argue that the poor and disadvantaged are better served by choice. Rather than being forced to remain in a school that is failing children, parents could choose to send their children to another school and have public funding support that choice. School-choice advocates argue that diversity and equity are better served by a market system. Opponents of vouchers and charter schools believe that only a very few poor and minority children would benefit from choice; most would suffer in schools depleted of public funds, emptied of the most talented students, and robbed of the advocacy of concerned parents. Research reports on the effectiveness of voucher plans in raising student achievement differ.

Other proposals for restructuring schools do not assume a flow of students away from public schools or away from existing schools. In the 1990s, proposals included decision making at the school level (site-based management), integrated curriculum and team teaching, flexible scheduling to allow the use of diverse teaching strategies and time for in-depth study, and the development of small learning communities within larger schools.

Certainly, there are no "silver bullets" or easy answers as to how we might improve teaching and learning. Structural changes in themselves do not guarantee that students will learn. For example, changes that focus on creating an orderly school environment as an end in itself may result in an orderly school but not necessarily in improved student learning. However, there is research to suggest that when school restructuring is undertaken with a focus on student learning, real change can take place. As Newmann and Wehlage (1995) note in their study of school restructuring, "We found that restructuring offered no panacea, but that it advanced student learning when it concentrated on the intellectual quality of student work, when it built school-wide organizational capacity to deliver authentic pedagogy, and when it received support from the external environment that was consistent with these challenges" (p. 4). Newmann and Wehlage conclude that there are six structural conditions that can promote intellectual activity of high quality:

1. Shared governance that increases teachers' influence over school policy and practice.
2. Interdependent work structures such as teaching teams, which encourage collaboration.
3. Staff development that enhances technical skills consistent with school missions for high-quality learning.
4. Deregulation that provides autonomy for schools to pursue a vision of high intellectual standards.
5. Small school size, which increases opportunities to pursue a vision of high intellectual standards.
6. Parent involvement in a broad range of school affairs. (p. 52)

Newmann and Wehlage's work suggests that when the culture of a school is focused on high-quality learning and on collaboration and interaction among teachers, students, and parents, academic achievement can be increased.

As the twentieth century drew to a close, there seemed to be no end to proposals for curriculum innovations and organizational changes. The history of school reform in the United States suggests however, that change comes slowly, if at all. Ours is a nation founded on ideals but subject to the anxieties and tensions of any civil group. Efforts at school reform in the United States have been characterized by a desire to reform not just education but society itself. As Tyack and Cuban (1995) note, "For over a century and a half, Americans have translated their cultural anxieties and hopes into dramatic demands for educational reform" (p. 1). Actual reform, however, has been gradual and incremental, "tinkering with the system," as Tyack and Cuban note. Significant change generally has come very slowly; reform initiatives seem to rise up and then fade away, leaving teachers and the public generally very cynical about the next "fad" to appear.

There are several possible reasons for the failure of widespread and deep reform to take root. First, many Americans have an expectation about what school ought to be, an image of what "real school" looks like (Tyack & Cuban, 1995, p. 9). When school reform initiatives depart too much from this image, consensus about what goes on in schools is threatened. School reform is ultimately a political process, with diverse groups seeking to influence the direction of change in ways that would respond to their needs. As Tyack and Cuban (1995) write, reform efforts reflect the values of the nation and of the diverse groups that make up the nation:

> Cycles of reform talk and action result, we believe, from the conflicts of values and interests that are intrinsic to public schooling. The rhetoric of reform has reflected the growing tensions between democratic politics, with its insistence on access and equality, and the structuring of opportunity in a competitive market economy. (p. 59)

To maintain broad general support for schooling, decisions must represent a consensus among often disparate groups. Thus, policies concerning public schooling are the results of an ongoing public debate about the nature and purpose of schooling in the United States. Conflict and debate are signs of a healthy democracy and, we would hope, will not disappear any time soon:

> In continuing this tradition of trusteeship of the public good, this engaged debate about the shape of the future, all citizens have a stake, not only the students who temporarily attend school or their parents. And this is the main reason that Americans long ago created and have continually sought to reform public education. (p. 142)

The debates about academic excellence and school improvement that were embedded in most of the calls for reform often overwhelmed concerns about equity and pluralism. Nonetheless, throughout this period there continued to be concern for and debate about the response of schools to the demands of a pluralistic nation. The desire to develop multicultural education and a truly pluralistic society persisted among many Americans, especially those, such as ethnic minority groups, who continued to feel excluded.

Religious Diversity

In the wake of the terrorist attacks on September 11, 2001, there were those who saw Muslims in the United States as a security risk, or at least a threat to our cultural heritage. In fact, the United States has never been religiously homogeneous. During the early years of the republic, most citizens would have identified themselves as members of a Protestant sect; however, they were hardly a homogeneous religious force (Williams, 2002). Class and regional differences were apparent, and these differences manifested themselves in ideological and power divisions. In the nineteenth century, Irish and German immigrants dramatically increased the numbers of Roman Catholics in the country. The late nineteenth and early twentieth centuries saw an influx of Jewish immigrants, which added to the religious mix of the nation. Catholics and Jews often encountered barriers to full membership in the American community. Both were often barred from elite social and educational institutions, for example, and prohibited from moving into certain neighborhoods.

By the late twentieth century, the legal landscape that had allowed discrimination based on religious belief had changed. With the dismantling of segregation, religious as well as racial and gender discrimination were prohibited. At this time, too, a large increase of non-Christian religious groups was becoming apparent. By the twenty-first century, the number of Muslims in the United States had surpassed the number of Jews. Along the West Coast, the number of Asian Buddhist communities increased. For some Americans, the rise of non-Christian religions in the United States posed a threat to the social fabric of the nation. To others, it was simply part of the ever-changing pluralistic nature of American society. For schools, the question of how to accommodate to varying religious practices became even more important.

Cultural Pluralism in America

One of the problems with cultural pluralism in America is that the term is often used ambiguously. Sometimes **cultural pluralism** is used simply to describe the fact that cultural diversity exists in our society. But at other times it refers to an ideological perspective that stands for a set of interrelated ideas or ideals that characterize a social group. As is the case with all ideologies, cultural pluralism contains ideals, slogans, and directions and strategies for social, political, and educational actions; it also includes some statements about the nature of reality and values, as well as the arguments in support of their validity.

Beyond Tolerance

The demand for cultural pluralism in the United States is based partly on the belief that it is intrinsic to democracy, yet its proponents have not always clearly articulated the meaning of cultural pluralism, its social, political, and educational implications, or its alleged connections with democracy. Clearly, the kind of cultural pluralism believed to be consistent with democracy is much more than the separate and independent existence of disparate ethnic groups without any contact between institutions or individuals. Rather, it is an ideal that seeks to establish and encourage not only cultural diversity but also a basis of unity from which the United States can become a cohesive society enriched by shared, widely divergent ethnic experiences. Hence, cultural pluralism is based on the belief in equality of opportunity for all people, respect for human dignity, and the conviction that no single pattern of living is appropriate for everyone. In this context, the traditional notion of tolerance for different cultural patterns is said to be patronizing, suggesting that a superior group is willing to tolerate "inferiors."

Cultural pluralism, then, must include the belief that, in situations where people with diverse cultural backgrounds coexist, to be different is not to be inferior. Although this pluralistic view necessitates the acceptance of the intrinsic worth of all human beings as unique individuals; it does not require that one's "native" cultural pattern never change. On the contrary, an individual life, or the culture of a group or a nation, may be enriched by preserving and sharing different sociocultural patterns. The possibility of changing one's lifestyle by interacting with other ethnic groups, based on mutual interest, should not be restricted. For example, one can belong to and participate in the activities of racially or ethnically mixed community groups—such as Asian American groups and Mexican American groups—and at the same time develop a unique lifestyle that incorporates various aspects of these groups.

One of the first to articulate a concept of cultural pluralism was Horace N. Kallen (1915; 1949), a Harvard-educated philosopher and an American Jew. As early as 1915, Kallen asserted that the melting pot ideal, which looked to a blending of cultures into a new United States, was not the appropriate goal for American society. He argued for the maintenance of communal life and the preservation of cultures. According to Kallen, ethnic groups should develop a positive self-image and pride in their respective group's cultural heritage and communal values but still function as partially integrated political and economic entities in American society. He was convinced that the United States would be richer as a result of cultural diversity. Kallen believed that democracy involves the interaction of semi-independent, autonomous groups and communities on important issues of life experience. He conceived of the United States as consisting of a number of nationalities making up a single nation, a "federation of nationalities."

Later in the century, another advocate of cultural pluralism, Isaac B. Berkson, supervisor of schools and extension activities of the Bureau of Jewish Education and a student of John Dewey, argued against Anglo conformity and the melting pot ideal as inconsistent with American democracy. Like Kallen, Berkson believed that a democratic society is obliged to provide equal opportunities for "the perfection and conservation of differences" in every individual (Berkson, 1969, p. 55). Because Berkson saw self-determination as the quintessence of democracy, he criticized Kallen's federation of nationalities for being too restrictive in allowing minorities to leave their ethnic enclave if they so desired. He argued that Kallen's model would lead to freedom of association for the various cultural groups but not enough freedom of contact for the individual. For example, Kallen encouraged different ethnic groups to have joint activities but discouraged ethnically mixed marriages.

Unlike Kallen, Berkson was more concerned with the integrity of ethnic groups within the larger society. His primary concern was with reducing, if not eliminating, societal forces that would pressure a minority to either dissolve or perpetuate itself. If an individual member of an ethnic community decides to leave the group and join the dominant group, such a decision should be accepted as proper and legitimate. (This view is also known as the community model.) Both Kallen and Berkson adhered to the desirability of preserving ethnic communities, but the latter argued for greater flexibility and opportunities for choice.

The New Pluralism

The civil rights movement and the Great Society of the 1960s brought a strengthened emphasis on cultural pluralism, but with a different thrust. Although the new pluralists held, as did Kallen, that diverse peoples in our society should be unified into a cohesive democratic nation, their arguments were heavily skewed in favor of allowing minority cultures, as different but equal groups, to participate in the various activities of the country on their own terms. Further, social institutions, particularly our schools, were asked to adapt both curriculum and teaching strategies to the cultural and linguistic diversity of students.

Advocates of the new pluralism insisted that participatory democracy is fundamentally pluralistic and that it entails the acceptance of the intrinsic worth of all human beings and their unique individuality. Cultural differences between groups should be viewed as differences, not deficits. The view that a difference is not a deficit is useful in highlighting the unwarranted assumptions underlying the deficit model of viewing other cultures. However, as discussed earlier, when interpreted literally it leads to an extreme form of cultural relativism that considers all human actions and practices equally adaptive and effective. Advocates of pluralism do not necessarily agree on how far to carry respect toward differences. However, most would agree that there needs to be some core of common values to which all are committed. James Banks (1999b) represented this view well in his argument that all groups should respect the basic values expressed in our major historical documents.

> Each ethnic group should have the right to practice its own religious, social, and cultural beliefs, albeit within the limits of due regard for the rights of others. There is, after all, a set of overarching values that all groups within a society or nation must endorse to maintain social cohesion. In our nation, these core values stem from our commitment to human dignity, and include justice, equality, freedom, and due process of law. (p. 301)

Building a cohesive democratic society cannot follow from an argument that (1) all cultures are equally functional, (2) there can be no objective standards with which to judge other cultures, and (3) therefore all cultural groups should be permitted to practice their own ways regardless of the consequences to the larger society. This, of course, is not what the pluralists are advocating, yet educators often view cultural pluralism and multicultural education as representing an extreme cultural relativist view that would allow anything and everything. It is not unusual to find that multicultural education is understood as being concerned exclusively with preserving and extending minority ethnic patterns. The fact that different cultures have different norms does not necessarily imply that values ought to be relative or that there cannot be some objective way of justifying value judgments. In point of fact, those who value cultural diversity and support cultural pluralism do not view religious bigotry and racial discrimination as practiced by certain groups in the United States as mere cultural differences; rather, they judge them to be unethical and undemocratic.

The central problem of cultural pluralism is how minority groups can maintain enough separation from the dominant culture to perpetuate and develop their own ethnic traditions without, at the same time, interfering with the execution of their responsibilities to the American society. That is, how can cultural diversity and unity be maintained simultaneously, particularly when conflicts arise between the dominant society and its subunits? One solution is to fight a value conflict, where it exists, at the ballot box and in the arena of public opinion. However, the goal is to keep such conflict to a minimum by emphasizing the areas of flexibility, permitted alternatives, and free choice in American life and by refraining from imposing one's own collective will as a standard of enforced behavior for other groups.

Value conflicts between groups can be minimized as much as possible by allowing groups and individuals many alternatives from which to choose their own courses of action. For example, one can choose to learn the dominant language and behavior patterns and work outside of one's ethnic group, or one can choose to remain in the ethnic enclave and carry on a trade that would serve primarily the members of that community. A constantly recurring theme of cultural pluralism is the belief that no single group should impose its own pattern as the idealized norm for every other group.

To some, cultural pluralism as a social ideal to preserve each ethnic group's cultural distinctiveness within the context of U.S. citizenship involves contradictory social practices. To maintain one's unique cultural traits, a person must maintain the most meaningful personal relationships with his or her group, but if an individual is to achieve social, political, and economic status in the larger society, he or she must also participate in the processes of the dominant culture. Whether these practices are contradictory is debatable.

Generally speaking, as the twentieth century drew to a close, two phenomena took place among ethnic minority groups in the United States. First, in large metropolitan areas such as Los Angeles, San Francisco, San Diego, Seattle, Chicago, New York, Detroit, Atlanta, Dallas, Houston, and Washington, D.C., masses of new immigrants maintained their cultural patterns by associating only with members of their own ethnic groups at the primary, or face-to-face, level. Their contact with the dominant society remained at the secondary level. Only in institutions such as schools, hospitals, and workplaces did they have significant interaction with members of the dominant culture. Second, many well-educated minority group members shed much of their cultural distinctiveness, yet interacted only minimally with other minority groups or with the dominant society.

Cultural Pluralism or an Open Society?

Although calls for cultural pluralism continue in our society, many still argue that the United States should be an open society in which individual merit and competence are the primary determinants of the worth of individuals. This position is one in which individual equality and national unity rather than cultural diversity are emphasized. From this perspective, each member of any given minority group is first a citizen of the country rather than a member of a subculture.

Although the United States may be approaching a state wherein an individual's position and merit are evaluated in terms of competence and achievement, it is little help to tell non-white minority youth that their identity should be achieved in terms of their status as citizens of this country. These young people find that their status as Americans is still affected by their color and ethnic backgrounds. At the same time, they discover that they belong to neither the dominant white culture nor the culture of their parents, and consequently, they see themselves as dislocated and alienated. This condition is common among today's younger generation of minority cultures, whose self-image is not intimately tied to their legal citizenship in the United States. Children of ethnic groups should be helped to develop pride in their own racial and cultural heritage and to achieve their identity as unique and intrinsically worthwhile human beings by rejecting the belief that to be different is to be inferior. This kind of positive self-image and cultural integrity needs to be developed not only in children of poor ethnic minorities but also in children whose parents occupy middle-class and upper-middle-class socioeconomic statuses. The so-called identity crisis is no less severe among these children.

In a culturally diverse society such as the United States, it is not enough to propose that an individual be evaluated according to merit and competence. We must also regard cultural diversity as an asset to be developed, for even a person with full civil rights cannot escape from the racial and ethnic backgrounds that inexorably govern one's view of oneself. For culturally different and economically poor children, developing a positive self-image is hard to achieve without persistent attempts by the mainstream to appreciate the worth of other cultures.

Furthermore, it is important to critically evaluate the fundamental assumptions underlying the dominant norms of our society. The primacy of individual rights found in American culture is rooted in the Protestant history and tradition of our society. This tradition goes back to the Puritan belief that salvation was personal and individual. This was later secularized as a focus on individual effort as the key to success. Furthermore, the rights and responsibilities of citizens as embedded in the core documents of our nation, such as the Declaration of Independence, are expressed as the rights and responsibilities of individuals.

However, as Campbell (1996) notes, "Admiration for strong individualism is an attribute of the dominant culture in our society, but it is only a culturally specific choice, not a human universal" (p. 37).

Implicitly or explicitly, those who advocate cultural pluralism or multiculturalism in the United States do not seek to maintain cultural diversity alone, for there needs to be a basis for national unity. However, the pluralists argue that this unity should not be founded on establishing one linguistic, ethical, or behavioral pattern as the only idealized norm for all individuals. Unity should be based on the belief that all human beings are to be regarded as ends in themselves so that no person can be exploited by other individuals or institutions. The question of whether cultural pluralism is achievable in this country hinges on the meaning of cultural pluralism in the context of American democracy. Neither Kallen's federation of nationalities nor Berkson's community model is wholly acceptable. The former is likely to result in insular pluralism in which minority groups perpetuate their own ethnic communities with minimal participation in the mainstream society of which they are an important part. Berkson's community model and the open society concept are also unsatisfactory, for they minimize the dominant culture's pressure on minority individuals to assimilate into the dominant culture by divesting themselves of their heritages. These two perspectives do not pay sufficient attention to the critical role ethnicity plays in the development of self-identity among minority people.

Cultural Pluralism: A Definition

Cultural pluralism as an ideology consonant with the principles of participatory democracy goes beyond mere cultural relativism, in which all and any cultural practices are viewed as equally functional and hence permissible. Cultural pluralism is an ideal that seeks to encourage cultural diversity and establish a basis of unity so that the United States can become a cohesive society whose culture is enriched by sharing widely divergent ethnic experiences. Cultural boundaries are seen as "porous, dynamic, and interactive, rather than the fixed property of particular ethnic groups" (Gates, 1992).

The ideology of cultural pluralism is founded on the belief that diversity is enriching. Human life becomes much more interesting, stimulating, and even exciting when there are many varied ways of thinking, feeling, expressing, acting, and viewing the world. Perhaps more important, given the range in the kinds and complexity of human needs and wants, the more alternative problem-solving approaches there are, the more we are likely to find solutions that enable us to live our lives in an increasingly effective way. Cultural differences as alternative ways of dealing with essentially similar human problems and needs present us with a wide variety of options from which we can learn to grow. The core premise of this belief is that diversity is enriching because no one has a monopoly on the truth about the good life. Diversity is further valued because it provides any society with a richer pool of leadership from which to draw in times of crisis. The worth of the culture is not based solely on the fact that it is ours; rather, our culture is worthy because its patterns and norms have enabled us to achieve our purposes.

The belief in the enriching nature of cultural diversity suggests that it is the responsibility of the dominant group to actively promote the right of minority cultures to exist and develop in their own way and to examine critically the assumptions underlying the dominant norms. As a democratic ideology, cultural pluralism implies that minority groups become actively committed to and deeply involved in the affairs that affect the growth and well-being of the larger society. Cultural pluralism is characterized by a commitment to the worth of cultural diversity and factions promoting an agenda of politics, but it goes beyond the promotion of the values of cultural subgroups to the development of a shared sense of a "public" of which all groups are a part. In the broadest sense, cultural pluralism's fundamental tenets should apply to the relationships between the dominant society and ethnic minority groups as well as groups characterized by differences in gender, age, socioeconomic status, sexual orientation, and mental or physical exceptionalities.

Cultural Pluralism and Democracy

The preceding discussion implied a close connection between cultural pluralism and democracy, but is there a sound basis for arguing that cultural pluralism is indeed intrinsic to American democracy? The fundamental principles of democracy as articulated in the Declaration of Independence and the Constitution of the United States are based on the premise that each person is endowed with human dignity. It is for this reason that exploitation of any individual or group violates a democratic maxim. Institutions in our society are to serve the individual, not vice versa.

To regard each individual as an end is to affirm the belief that there is an "intrinsic connection between the prospects of democracy and belief in the potentialities of human nature—for its own sake" (Dewey, 1939a, p. 127). In building democracy we must begin with the faith that all people have the capacity to develop and exercise their own intelligence in shaping their own future (Dewey, 1957, p. 49). It is not that these capacities are already formed and ready to be unfolded, but if given the opportunity, individuals can grow socially, emotionally, and intellectually so that they cannot only decide what is best for them but also find the most effective means of attaining it. Hence, democracy "denotes a state of affairs in which the interest of each in his work is uncoerced and intelligent: based upon its congeniality to his own aptitudes" (Dewey, 1961, p. 316). Consequently, freedom of all kinds is essential to democracy, and "the cause of democratic freedom is the cause of the fullest possible realization of human potentialities" (Dewey, 1957, p. 129).

A democratic society is necessarily pluralistic (culturally, politically, intellectually, and socially), because it is founded on a belief in the intrinsic worth of individuals and their unique capacities to become intelligent human beings. In this sense, the unique qualities of individuals or groups become assets rather than hindrances. Accordingly, "there is no physical acid which has the corrosive power possessed by intolerance directed against persons because they belong to a group that bears a certain name" (Dewey, 1939a, p. 137). In a more revolutionary vein, Freire (1997) pointed out:

> They [the oppressed or minorities] are treated as individual cases, as marginal men who deviate from the general configuration of a "good, organized, and just" society. The oppressed are regarded as the pathology of the healthy society, which must therefore adjust these "incompetent and lazy" folk to its own patterns by changing their mentality. These marginals need to be "integrated," "incorporated" into the healthy society that they have "forsaken." (p. 55)

For Freire, oppressed minorities of all sorts are not "marginals"—that is, people living "outside" society. They have always lived "inside" the sociocultural structure that made them "being for others" because they did not conform to the norms of the dominant culture. Hence, they were not treated as ends in themselves but rather as means to someone else's end—objects of exploitation and oppression. The solution, Freire concluded, is not to completely absorb or assimilate minorities into the dominant social structure but to transform that structure so that they are "being for themselves." From Dewey's perspective, this means that a society must provide equality of opportunity that will enable individuals to develop their capacities to the fullest. Hence, "all individuals are entitled to equality of treatment by law and in its administration. Each one is affected equally in quality if not in quantity by the institutions under which he lives and has an equal right to express his judgment" (1939b, p. 403). Thomas Jefferson's insistence that a system of education be open to all youth as a necessity for democracy reflects this equal opportunity principle.

The demand of ethnic minorities to preserve and develop their own cultural patterns stems from the firm belief in the democratic principle, which regards uniqueness of individuals and equal opportunity for their development as intrinsically good. However, democracy requires not only an emphasis on personal needs and interests and on various points of shared interest but also recognition of mutual interest as a means of social control. A democratic society should encourage not only free interactions among individuals and groups but also changes in social habits—that is, continuous readjustments as a result of meeting new situations in a wide variety of personal interactions. It is essential for the members of a democratic society to recognize that the needs of others are as important to those people as their own are to them. This recognition is a prerequisite for effective handling of conflicts among individuals and groups.

In a truly democratic society, no single group rules over others because of the implicit faith in the human capacity for intelligent behavior. Democracy requires a method of resolving conflicts by inquiry, discussion, and persuasion rather than by violence. Hence, education that cultivates reflective thinking and conflict resolution through discussion and persuasion is essential for realizing cultural pluralism.

CULTURAL PLURALISM AND MULTICULTURAL EDUCATION

In the early 1970s, many educators and minority groups became increasingly vocal in pointing out that schooling in the United States was ethnocentric and monocultural. Because genuine democracy was believed to be necessarily connected with cultural pluralism and multicultural education, these educators and minority groups argued that the American school was undemocratic. That is, our schools failed to provide equal educational opportunity to poor and minority children. Not surprisingly, minority groups and concerned educators demanded that our schools provide multicultural education by becoming more sensitive to the unique cultural norms, language patterns, cognitive and learning styles, and communication styles of the ethnic and socioeconomic minority groups.

The mounting interest in and concern for cultural pluralism in education were given a boost when the board of directors of the American Association of Colleges for Teacher Education (AACTE) officially sanctioned the cause in its "Not One Model American" statement of October 1972. The fact that AACTE was (and still is) one of the largest and most influential organizations involved in teacher preparation suggested the seriousness and urgency with which U.S. educators viewed the problem of making schools a major means of achieving cultural pluralism in our society.

In addition to the action taken by the AACTE board of directors, numerous conferences and workshops promoted **multicultural education** in our public schools and universities with teacher education programs. Of these efforts, the inclusion of a standard on multicultural education into the accreditation standards of the National Council for Accreditation of Teacher Education (NCATE) in 1977 was significant. According to NCATE (1977), multicultural education was to be seen as "preparation for the social, political, economic realities that individuals experience in culturally diverse and complex human encounters" (p. 4). By 1994, the NCATE standards included the expectation that evidence of attention to cultural diversity would be found throughout the standards. Although the degree to which the multicultural education components have genuinely permeated the curricula of the colleges and universities for teacher education is not known, these institutions did attempt to infuse studies of minority cultures and the role of cultural factors into the teaching–learning processes.

In spite of the attempt to broaden the multicultural concept, many educators persisted in viewing it only as a strategy for dealing with the educational concerns of minority children. Still others thought multicultural education was synonymous with ethnic studies. Unfortunately, these misconceptions about multicultural education have led many school and college personnel to insist that multicultural education components were unnecessary in their programs because their institutions either did not have many minority students or were located in ethnically homogeneous areas. In short, many educators consider multicultural education merely an add-on set of strategies for addressing the issues related to the education of minority students. Such a narrow and distorted conception of multicultural education may contribute to the rise of resentment among teachers and teacher educators stemming from the belief that the state and national accreditation standards on multicultural education should be made applicable only to urban and other institutions with substantial minority enrollments. Indeed, a broader conception is necessary if multicultural education is to serve as a means of making our schools more democratic in a culturally, racially, and socioeconomically diverse society.

Approaches to Multicultural Education

As described above, by the 1990s the neoconservatives' argument that multicultural education failed to serve the nation's common good had begun to permeate the national consciousness. Multicultural education, argued opponents such as D'Souza (1991), Ravitch (1990), and Schlesinger (1992), was an attempt on the part of special interests to fragment the curriculum and to serve their own ends. However, as Banks (1999a) points out, the opponents to multicultural education were, themselves, representing a special interest:

> A clever tactic of the neoconservative scholars is to define their own interests as universal and in the public good and the interests of women and people of color as *special interests* that are particularistic (Ravitch, 1990). When a dominant elite describes its interests as the same as the public interests, it marginalizes the experiences of structurally excluded groups, such as women and people of color. (p. 28)

The confusion of meanings of multicultural education may result from the multiple meanings used both in the field and in classrooms where multicultural education is implemented. Various multicultural educators have described what they see as the common and/or desirable approaches to multicultural education. James Banks (1999a), for example, suggests that there are four approaches teachers use as they develop multicultural curriculum. These approaches are (1) the contribution approach, (2) the additive approach, (3) the transformative approach, and (4) the social action approach. Banks suggests that it is useful to think of these approaches as different levels of multicultural education.

The first two levels, the contribution approach and the additive approach, are most common. Using the contribution approach, the curriculum includes content about holidays and celebrations of various ethnic groups, especially at the early childhood and elementary levels. Thus, children learn about Black History month, Cinco de Mayo, and Asian/Pacific Heritage Week. Using the additive approach, content about minorities is added to the curriculum without substantially changing its goals or structure. Using these two approaches, or levels, content about minorities, women, and other underrepresented groups is generally presented in a way that reflects the norms and values of the dominant culture rather than those of the groups being studied. Those who challenge the status quo as it is currently recognized are less likely to be included in the curriculum, or they are included in a way that downplays those challenges. Thus, children are likely to learn about Martin Luther King, Jr.'s efforts at gaining civil rights for African Americans, a goal generally accepted at some level by most Americans today, but they are less likely to learn about his antiwar stand during the Vietnam War or about his efforts, at the time of his death, to rally the poor and working classes to stand against dominant economic institutions. Banks advocates moving to the level of the transformative approach and the social action approach.

According to Banks, the transformative approach changes the basic assumptions of the curriculum "and enables students to view concepts, issues, themes, and problems from different perspectives and points of view" (p. 31). Curriculum is aimed at helping learners understand events and society from the perspectives of different groups. Learners come to see that knowledge is socially constructed—that is, that people create meaning based on their own experiences with and understandings of the world around them. They would see, for example, that Columbus's "discovery" of America wasn't discovery from the point of view of the indigenous people he encountered, or that the title "Westward Expansion," used on a unit of study about the migration of Euro-American settlers into the Western territories of the United States, reflects only the point of view of the white settlers, not the people being forced from their lands. In this approach, students would be challenged to understand differing perspectives and why such perspectives emerge. They would be expected to study events and institutions from various points of view and to reach their own conclusions based on such study. As Banks (1999a) writes, "Important aims of the transformative approach are to teach students to think critically and develop the skills to formulate, document, and justify their conclusions and generalizations" (p. 32).

Finally, the social action approach suggests that once learners have studied an issue and have drawn their own conclusions, they should be able to take personal, social, or civic action. Upon learning about the different perspectives toward the migration of Euro-American settlers in the nineteenth century, students might write to textbook companies urging a more balanced approach, or they might use the Internet to develop a reading list that includes various perspectives on the subject. They might volunteer to read to younger children stories that reflect diverse perspectives.

Yet another way of thinking about the various approaches to and understandings of multicultural education is presented by Christine Sleeter and Carl Grant (2003). Based upon their review of the literature and research in multicultural education and on their experiences as multicultural educators, Sleeter and Grant describe five approaches to teaching multicultural education, all of which present a somewhat different perspective than that of Banks. Sleeter's and Grant's approaches include (1) teaching the culturally different, (2) the human relations approach, (3) single group studies, (4) multicultural education, and (5) education that is multicultural and social reconstructionist.

The first approach, teaching the culturally different, emerged in the 1960s as the civil rights movement brought cultural and learning differences to the forefront of thinking about teaching. It came to include thinking about developmental differences as well as cultural ones. This approach "focuses on adapting instruction to student differences for the purpose of helping these students succeed more effectively in the mainstream" (Sleeter & Grant, 2003, p. 31). This approach differs from any developed by Banks in that it focuses on instructional strategies rather than curricular issues. However, it is similar to the first two levels presented by Banks in that it does not challenge the status quo in curriculum.

The human relations approach also emerged in the 1960s. This approach focuses on developing and supporting positive interactions between individuals and groups. The goal of this approach is to develop the skills and attitudes necessary to reduce stereotypes and discrimination and to encourage positive and productive interactions among all students. This approach is "directed toward helping students communicate with, accept, and get along with people who are different from themselves; reducing or eliminating stereotypes that students have about people; and helping students feel good about themselves and about groups of which they are members, without putting down others in the process" (Sleeter & Grant, 2003, p. 78). In the 1990s, this approach was represented by efforts in many schools to develop programs for peer mediation and conflict resolution. This approach, like the first, does not directly challenge the traditional curriculum. It is often used as an add-on; conflict resolution, for example, is often taught as something separate from the core academic curriculum. However, this approach has the potential to influence curriculum in ways suggested by Banks's transformative and social action approaches. As Banks argues, to really understand other groups, it is important to understand the world from varying perspectives. Furthermore, efforts to reduce stereotypes and eliminate discriminatory behavior suggest the possibility for serious and extended social action projects. The extent to which this approach can reflect Banks's third and fourth levels depends on the ways in which teachers and schools implement this approach.

The single group studies approach emerged during the 1970s as an effort to substantially change the curriculum rather than simply find ways to fit underrepresented groups into the curriculum. Ethnic studies, women's studies, and other studies of particular groups were aimed at expanding knowledge and understanding of a particular group. A reaction, in part, to the additive approach described by Banks, a major goal of this approach was to empower oppressed groups (Sleeter & Grant, 2003, p. 110). This approach, then, is consistent with Banks's transformative and social action approaches. Sleeter and Grant point out that "the ability to think through issues from a critical perspective and to act upon one's insights in an effort to transform unjust social conditions related to gender or race, for example, is central to the mission of any [single] group-study program" (p. 111).

The third approach described by Sleeter and Grant is labeled multicultural education. They acknowledge that it may seem odd to label one approach to multicultural education as multicultural education. However, they argue that they do so precisely because there are several different approaches that have been grouped together under the umbrella of "multicultural education." This approach is an effort to conceptualize educational change broadly and in ways that are designed to value cultural diversity. The approach reflects efforts to promote equal opportunity and social justice and to promote an equitable distribution of power among social groups. It focuses on all aspects of the school experience (Sleeter & Grant, 2003, p. 153). In the classroom, curriculum focuses on the perspectives and experiences of different groups; it is made relevant to students' experiences and backgrounds; it focuses on critical thinking and analysis of differing viewpoints. Instruction is built on students' learning styles and skill levels and engages students in cooperative learning. The classroom is decorated in ways that represent a variety of people and groups, but this approach is not confined to the classroom—it must be school-wide. Ways are found to involve lower-class and minority parents in the school. Diversity and nontraditional roles should be reflected in the composition of the staff and in the work that they do. Extracurricular activities should not reinforce stereotypes. Discipline procedures should not penalize any one group. The building should be accessible to people with disabilities. In short, this approach to multicultural education is not simply a change in curriculum; rather, it permeates the entire school culture.

Sleeter and Grant's fifth approach, education that is multicultural and social reconstructionist, extends the fourth approach into the realm of social action. The goal of this approach is to move multicultural education beyond the school to society and the elimination of the oppression of all groups. This approach "prepares future citizens to reconstruct society so that it better serves the interests of all groups of people and especially those who are of color, poor, female, gay, lesbian, transsexual, disabled, or any combination of these" (p. 189). As Sleeter and Grant say, "This approach is visionary" (p. 189). It extends the idea that a major function of school is to prepare students to participate in their society and, in the United States, to participate as citizens in a democracy. This approach assumes that part of participating in society is helping to "reconstruct" it in the direction of a more socially just and equitable society. Sleeter and Grant agree with Banks that multicultural education should transform thinking and lead to social action and social justice.

MULTICULTURAL EDUCATION: A BROAD VIEW

Since the 1960s, when ideas about multicultural education began to be more widely discussed, the idea has developed and spread. What began in many classrooms as just an add-on has become an effort to transform curriculum and schooling. Sleeter and Grant, Banks, and others have shown us the ways in which multicultural education can be conceptualized as a broad-based change in schooling and in society. To better understand this broader conception of multi-cultural education, it is important to review the relationship between schooling and culture. As Dewey (1961) pointed out, education is "the process of forming fundamental dispositions, intellectual and emotional, toward nature and fellow men" (p. 328). The specific fundamental dispositions toward nature and fellow human beings that need to be formed are culture bound. As already pointed out in chapter 2, there is no denying that education is a cultural process. From soci-ety's perspective, education is the process of transmitting its culture to the young. For the young, education becomes the process of learning societal norms. More specifically, because cultural diversity exists to some degree in every society, learning the culture of a society means learning its sub-cultural variations and learning when these variations are appropriate or inappropriate.

A person's ability to function effectively in a socioculturally diverse society depends on the individual's specific knowledge about other subcultures and the skills needed to function appropriately in varying cultural contexts. Hence, learn-ing to understand other cultures and to interact effectively with their members should be an integral part of the educational goals in any society. Furthermore, such understandings are not about knowledge alone. As Banks (1999a) notes,

> Knowledge alone will not help students develop an empathetic, caring com-mitment to humane and democratic change. An essential goal of a multicul-tural curriculum is to help students develop empathy and caring. To help our nation and the world become more culturally democratic, students must also develop a commitment to personal, social, and civic action, and the knowledge and skills needed to participate in effective civic action. (p. 33)

In addition to knowledge, learners must develop the values, attitudes, and skills needed to understand the perspectives of others and to take action for the greater good. Action and caring, while distinct, must be related if students—and citizens—are to act in ways that promote a greater good as well as the interests of particular groups.

Furthermore, in a multicultural society, the individual must not only have knowledge about and empathy toward various cultural groups but also must be able to make reasonable decisions about the most appropriate modes of think-ing, acting, and communicating in any given situation. Thus, critical and reflec-tive thinking must play a key role in multicultural education. What we learn about other cultures is not classified neatly into different cultural pigeonholes in our mind so that the right pattern is pulled out of an appropriate category when a situation calls for a particular way of acting. Our knowledge of and experi-ences in other cultures become integrated into the complex terrains of thinking and acting. Hence, acting appropriately in different situations or having multi-cultural competencies requires not only knowledge of divergent patterns but also an ability to evaluate the situation. Equally important is the ability to formu-late available options in relation to one's goals and then to critically choose the option that will help achieve the present objective as a means for accomplishing future goals. Thus, multicultural education can be seen as the process by which each individual can learn to live in a progressively effective and enriching way by increasing the individual's cultural repertoire and reconciling divergent patterns so that he or she can develop a new and unique approach to life. This should indeed be a central goal of lifelong learning. Therefore, multicultural education serves not only social goals toward increased justice and equity but also personal goals of greater growth and competence in a pluralistic society.

These two sets of goals, the personal and the social, are, of course, mutually supporting. By exposing the deficit assumptions underlying the prevailing views of ethnic minorities, women, or the aged, a person may begin to redefine his or her own role and self-identity in the larger society. Through this kind of experience, the person's further experiences and thinking can become more inclusive and integrative.

Conflicts in interest and values are bound to arise in a society with many diverse cultural elements. We are constantly in a position of having to interact with individuals who do not share our own system of norms and beliefs. Thus, we cannot depend on our own cultural ways to gain a reliable reading of what others are going to do next or how we will deal effectively with our own life problems. As members of a culturally diverse society, we may need to modify some of our ways by going beyond our own culture. To do this, we need to understand the dominant and minority cultures in terms of their points of agreements, disagreements, and conflicts with our own norms so that new and unique cultural patterns consonant with the fundamental ideals of participatory democracy may emerge. However we cannot normally go beyond our own culture without the ability to think critically about the taken-for-granted norms and values of the dominant society. Helping learners develop a critical understanding of their own culture and those of others leads them to become more effective decision makers, both in their personal lives and in their civic lives. For members of minority groups, the key question should not be about the extent to which they should or should not assimilate the dominant norms. Rather, the critical concern should be about what one must know and be able to do to function most effectively in life.

The Aims of Multicultural Education

The specific aims of multicultural education just described are (1) the cultivation of an attitude of respect for and appreciation of the worth of cultural diversity, (2) the promotion of a belief in the intrinsic worth of each person and an abiding interest in the well-being of the larger society, (3) the development of multicultural competencies to function effectively in culturally varied settings, and (4) the facilitation of educational equity for all regardless of ethnicity, race, gender, age, or other exceptionalities. Developing an appreciation of cultural diversity as enriching rather than harmful to individuals or the national unity is the first aim of multicultural education. As pointed out in chapter 1, culture represents a system of practices that enable a group of people to deal successfully with needs and problems arising out of their environment and interpersonal or inter-group relationships. In this sense, having many different cultures in our society is tantamount to having a wide range of tested alternative problem-solving approaches.

Cultural diversity is enriching because we can become progressively effective and efficient in dealing with our problems by learning from other cultural patterns. Appreciating different cultures, which should be viewed as pools of collective experiences, knowledge, wisdom, and the vision of other people, can make our own lives richer. Hence, other cultures are worthy of our respect. This implies that no one culture represents the best and the only right way of coping with human needs and problems. There cannot be a single cultural perspective from which the world and human encounters must always be seen.

Members of ethnic minority groups in this country may indeed have to learn to behave according to the dominant norms, but their own cultural patterns should not be judged as either inferior or deficits to be eliminated. Put differently, educators should not ban the student's voice "by a distorted legitimation of the standard language [dominant norms]," but they should help the young appreciate the "value of mastering the standard dominant language [culture] of the wider society" (Freire & Macedo, 1987, p. 152). In this way, we may begin to treat other cultures with the same sense of respect and appreciation we show toward our own.

The belief in the worth of cultural diversity is also based on the assumption that each person's identity is rooted in the culture to which he or she belongs. Hence, if we are to respect other cultures, we must also respect their members. Similarly, if we demean other people's cultures, we not only impugn their legitimacy, we also denigrate the dignity of other human beings. By affirming the worth of cultural diversity, we are attesting to the positive value of individuals with varied cultural heritages and perspectives.

Belief in the intrinsic worth of each person and an abiding interest in the well-being of the larger society make up the second aim of multicultural education. In a democratic society, each person should be treated as having intrinsic worth. Democratic institutions must serve the individual in becoming the best that he or she can be. Accordingly, rather than exploiting others, we should be willing to extend to others the same respect and rights that we expect and enjoy ourselves. As our actions have direct or indirect bearing on others, other people's conduct also influences our lives. Members of a democratic and pluralistic society must then have a deep and enduring interest in the affairs of the larger society. In so doing, freedoms of all sorts are possible insofar as our deeds do not violate the rights of others or harm the health and growth of the larger society.

There is indeed a symbiotic relationship between the social collective and its members. Our recognition of this inextricable relationship between individuals and society and our commitment to the belief in the intrinsic worth of each person constitute the fundamental principles to which all members of a free society should subscribe. Extolling cultural diversity without such a basis for social control and unity may lead to an extreme form of cultural relativism and separatism. If we insist that all values are completely relative to the cultures in which they are found and if we reject the possibility of having any objective criteria of evaluating cultures, then all cultures may be considered as equally good and functional. Under such relativism, all things are permissible. Further, if individuals identify themselves exclusively in terms of their membership in a particular ethnic group, their sense of loyalty to and concern for the larger society may diminish to the minimal level. There is little doubt that such a phenomenon would fragment the larger society and undermine its unity.

Allan Bloom (1987), author of *The Closing of the American Mind*, suggests that ethnic minority groups' insistence on preserving their culture may weaken our belief in God and the country that has helped to unify the American people (p. 192). Bloom goes on to say that "the blessing given the whole notion of cultural diversity in the United States by the culture movement has contributed to the intensification and legitimation of group politics, along with a corresponding decay of belief that the individual rights enunciated in the Declaration of Independence are anything more than rhetoric" (p. 193). He argues that the emphasis on cultural diversity and ethnicity, or "roots," is a "manifestation of the concern with particularity" (p. 192). For Bloom, this concern with particularity (ethnicity) is superficial because it fails to deal with the real differences among human beings, which he insists are based on the "differences in fundamental beliefs about good and evil, about what is highest, about God. Differences of dress or food are either of no interest or are secondary expressions of deeper beliefs" (p. 192). What Bloom is suggesting is that the fundamental beliefs that unite a society of people are universals or perhaps absolutes that go beyond the routine concerns of daily life.

Bloom's apprehension regarding the possible effects of preoccupation with cultural diversity is reasonable and even appropriate. However, the argument is marred by his failure to recognize that the specific contents of the fundamental beliefs about "good and evil, about what is highest, about God" are determined by the cultures in which they are found. Bloom holds that what we wear and eat are unimportant or are secondary expressions of deeper beliefs, but he does not recognize that these deeper beliefs are reflections of each culture's unique worldview. Even more questionable is Bloom's tacit assumption that the beliefs about "good and evil, about what is highest, about God" as found in the allegedly superior Western culture are cultural universals and absolutes.

As Aronowitz and Giroux (1988) point out, Bloom considers ethnic or racially based cultures as the anti-intellectual elements that threaten the "moral authority of the state," because he sees the foundation of the Western ethic as its capacity to "transcend the immediate circumstances of daily life in order to reach the good life" (p. 174). If Bloom had his way, he would have this society return perhaps to the Puritan era, in which cultural diversity was seen as harmful to the national unity. This unity was to have come from everyone conforming to the allegedly superior Anglo norms in language, behavior, government, morality, and religion, yet what the Puritan perspective accomplished was to reinforce the ethnocentric attitude of the dominant group and intensify the sense of alienation and discrimination experienced by ethnic and racial minority groups.

The third aim of multicultural education deals with multicultural competencies. We live in a world in which individuals and groups constantly influence each other. For example, an agricultural disaster in the Midwestern states would affect the food-processing industry, the trucking industry, the supermarkets, and the pocketbooks of every family in the country. Such a chain of consequences would eventually lower the sales and production of automobiles, appliances, and other durable goods as well as the rate of national employment. Similarly, prolonged bitter warfare between two major oil-producing countries could and would have a calamitous impact on the technology and politico-economic conditions of almost every nation in the world. In a world where human beings not only affect each other but also are interdependent, we cannot always resolve difficulties by relying exclusively on our own devices. Social, political, and economic realities of our time demand that we learn to work with each other, for no one person or group or nation is capable of solving complex human problems single-handedly. As Banks (1999a) argues, the ability to see issues, themes, and problems from diverse perspectives and points of view is crucial to the success of democracy (p. 89). Specific knowledge about the ways in which people in other cultures think, behave, communicate, and interpret the world is imperative for establishing an effective working relationship. Respecting other cultures as we do our own and critically understanding our own culture are equally important requisites in intercultural cooperation.

Educational equity, the fourth aim, is based on the conviction that each person be treated as an end and helped to become the best he or she can be in terms of capacities and envisioned possibilities. As Gollnick and Chinn (1998) advocate, "In a country that champions equal rights and the opportunity for an individual to improve his or her conditions, we must be concerned with helping all students achieve academically, socially, and politically" (p. 27). Accordingly, "educational and vocational options should not be limited by sex, age, ethnicity, native language, religion, socio-economic level, or exceptionality" (p. vi). Providing educational equity is then a necessary condition for aiding all learners to realize their fullest potential.

Broadly speaking, educational equity has two key elements. One is providing equal access to educational opportunities so that each person can participate in the desired programs to develop his or her interests and capacities. This goal would require all sorts of academic advising, career counseling, and other appropriate support services to help learners find the most effective means of becoming self-fulfilling and socially productive individuals. The second aspect of educational equity is the facilitation of conditions under which students can maximize their learning outcome. Clearly, all learners share certain common traits and needs, but they also possess those special characteristics and conditions that are unique to each person.

The idiosyncratic characteristics and conditions may be culture, race, gender, or age. Accordingly, educators need to have specific knowledge about the ways in which social, cultural, and even biological factors affect the teaching–learning processes. Developing instructional strategies based on such knowledge is imperative in multicultural education, for every learner has his or her own exceptionalities or hurdles to overcome and distinctive capacities to develop in achieving personal goals. Additionally, using curricular materials that contain balanced and representative accounts of the experiences and contributions of ethnic groups, women, and other minorities in the history of this nation and the world is indispensable in multicultural education.

Sexism, Ageism, and Exceptionality

The following discussion examines the specific issues and problems related to sexism, ageism, and discrimination against exceptional learners in education. However, the primary purpose of this discussion is to suggest a perspective that may be useful in developing concrete measures for providing egalitarian respect, treatment, and education to all learners. This perspective, which will be called the multicultural perspective, rests on the premises that (1) women, homosexual and transgendered individuals, the elderly, and exceptional learners constitute distinct subcultural groups in the mainstream society, and (2) the fundamental concepts and principles of the suggested view of multicultural education are applicable to these groups. More specifically, women, homosexual and transgendered individuals, the elderly, and exceptional learners should be accorded the same kind of equality of opportunity, freedom, justice, and respect to which ethnic and racial minority groups are entitled.

A multicultural perspective rejects the belief that all deviations from the norms of the dominant society or group are deficits or pathological conditions rather than differences. From the deficit perspective, minority groups are either excluded from participating in the activities of the dominant group or thought to require special compensatory measures to remedy their pathological conditions. By rejecting the deficit view, educators should encourage all learners to examine the society's racist, sexist, or otherwise discriminatory expectations.

Sexism

In spite of the strides made in attempting to eliminate sexism from our society, ample evidence suggests that men and women are not equally treated in this country. More often than not, women are considered inferior to men. The consequences of sex discrimination in our society appear in the forms of higher prestige and wages attached to so-called *men's occupations* as compared with the stereotypic feminine jobs. But more fundamentally, a primary source of **sexism** is that in our culture the traditional male roles are valued over traditionally female roles. Women's progress and success in society is therefore judged on the basis of women's success in what have traditionally been considered men's roles. We point to a woman who is a CEO in a corporation, not to the woman who has raised three wonderful children, as evidence that women have made progress. Unless men and women encounter some experience that casts a cloud of doubt over the legitimacy of their culturally assigned sex roles, they will continue to work toward fulfilling the established gender roles and positions.

Lesbian, gay, and transgendered individuals also encounter prejudice and discrimination when they move outside social norms. Culturally assigned sex roles are derived from generalized stereotypic characterizations of different genders as groups. Hence, the range of developmental opportunities and options available to those who seek their future outside the culturally determined gender expectations is severely restricted. From the multicultural perspective, educators should encourage learners to critically examine and expose the hidden assumptions underlying the sex-role expectations in the classroom and in society. The purpose of promoting such critical reflection about students' sex roles is to help them develop competencies to function effectively in our multicultural world. The appropriateness of specific competencies then is to be determined by one's capacities, one's envisioned possibilities, and the setting in which the individual must live and work.

In recent years, many plans have been proposed to make our schools gender-free by eliminating sex or gender bias; in a democratic society, such plans affirm that gender should be taken as completely irrelevant in determining people's roles, status, or social organization. Disagreeing with this ideal, Barbara Houston (1985) suggests that the so-called *gender-free* strategies are likely "(1) to create a context which continues to favor the dominant group, and (2) [to undermine] certain efforts which may be needed to realize equalization of educational opportunities" (p. 365). Houston cogently points out that there are three possible meanings of the expression *gender-free* (pp. 359–360). In the first sense, gender-free education refers to the attempts to disregard gender by eliminating all gender-related differentiations. An example of such an attempt is the elimination of activities such as wrestling and other contact sports in which gender differences in achievements are due to certain biological differences between the sexes. In the second sense, gender-free education means that gender is not taken into account in any aspect of education. Gender-related standards for admissions are not used; special programs are not offered. The elimination of gender bias from education is the third meaning of gender-free education.

According to Houston (1985), research findings do not support the belief that these gender-free strategies lead to greater participation by women either in sports or in teacher–student interactions. On the contrary, such efforts "had the effect of bringing about a greater loss of educational opportunities for girls" (p. 361). This unexpected consequence of gender-free strategies is attributable to the fact that in a male-dominated society, the patterns of male conduct, speech, and interpersonal relationship are used as the norms by which females are judged. Hence, even though the teacher may ignore gender, the students do not disregard gender-related roles. In other words, "gender may be excluded as an official criterion, but it continues to function as an unofficial factor" (p. 363).

As a basis for formulating strategies for making our schools nonsexist, Houston (1985) and Martin (1994) suggest that we take the *gender-sensitive* perspective, which recommends that attention be paid to gender when such action can prevent sex discrimination and advance sex equality. This means that gender interactions should be carefully monitored to equalize opportunities for both sexes. The gender-sensitive perspective differs from the gender-free approach in that the former "allows one to recognize that at different times and in different circumstances one might be required to adopt opposing policies in order to eliminate gender bias" (Houston, 1985, p. 368). In consonance with the multicultural perspective, the gender-sensitive perspective also encourages constant and critical analysis of the meaning and significance attached to gender.

Ageism

There are at least two major reasons for studying **ageism** and its educational implications as an important aspect of multicultural education. One is that the aged constitute another minority group that frequently encounters discrimination. The other is that, unlike racism or sexism, those who discriminate against the aged will necessarily have to confront their own membership in this minority group. Here, we should keep in mind that the term *minority* is not merely a numerical concept but also that it involves the notion of "not having power of control." Consequently, even if the number of aged surpasses the number of younger individuals in our society, the aged as a group may continue to occupy minority status, for the group is not likely to have power of control. Like racism and sexism, ageism stems from the deficit view that stereotypes elders as unproductive; outmoded in thinking, attitude, and behavior; and outdated in their views of the world and morality. The aged are also depicted as tired, less capable than younger people, forgetful, slow in thinking, and sickly. As children are often described in terms of their inabilities, the aged are also characterized by their disabilities. Ageism refers to this process of the stereotyping of individuals based upon age and the perceived deficits that accompany aging. Ageism is a view of the elderly as "senile[, r]igid in thought and manner, garrulous, and old-fashioned in morality and skills" (Gollnick & Chinn, 1998, p. 285).

As is the case with individual members of ethnic minority and gender groups, elderly individuals have their own unique values, beliefs, lifestyles, communication and cognitive styles, and problem-solving approaches. These patterns have special meanings and significance for the elderly because they have served them well, yet, because of the pervasive deficit view of the aged in this society, the elderly often live out their lives by conforming to their culturally assigned roles. They frequently become withdrawn, sickly, unproductive, and less capable. Thus, the aged become victims of the culturally ascribed deficit view. It goes without saying that the process of aging is absolutely inescapable.

There can be no compensatory programs to bring back youth. We cannot restore youthful physical traits in the aged to have them redefine their role and identity. Ideally, both the individual and the society can benefit enormously by helping the aged to become self-fulfilling, productive, and contributing human beings, but if we are to accomplish this end, we need to change (1) the deficit view of the aged and (2) the way in which the aged see themselves so that they may be empowered.

One way to eliminate the deficit view is to demythologize what Sorgman and Sorensen (1984) call the theory of disengagement, which refers to "a process whereby the aged person and the society cooperate in a process of mutual withdrawal from each other" (p. 120). The acceptance of the theory of disengagement leads to a misconception of the aging process, because it implies that the elderly withdraw from interpersonal relationships and participation in social affairs as a result of aging. Though this view is contrary to the known fact that "those who are 'joiners' in earlier years will also be social minded as they age, neither the media nor the books portray this aspect of the aged" (p. 121). Further, the theory implicitly assumes that the process of disengagement is a natural process of aging. Sorgman and Sorensen point out that although some elderly may become socially inactive, the theory reflects our society's indifference toward them. The fact that the media almost never portray the elderly in situations in which they are sought out or involved in social affairs or participating in a decision-making process reveals our society's lack of serious interest in providing meaningful alternatives for this increasingly large group of people.

An in-depth study of ageism, its hidden assumptions, key concepts, and history, as well as a balanced view of the elderly's needs and their roles by the younger generations and the aged themselves, should give a basis for better understanding the culture of the aged. As increased interethnic contacts are important in understanding other cultures, more frequent interaction between the aged and younger people in different situations should have a positive effect in modifying our attitudes. These efforts may also help us avoid the deficit view so that we can see how well the culture of the aged serves the elderly in dealing with their own unique needs and problems. Rather than being bound by their culturally ascribed role and image of themselves, the aged need to explore options in their lives by developing multicultural competencies. Multicultural education for the young and the aged equally necessitates an increased cultural repertoire and critical thinking in choosing the cultural patterns most appropriate in achieving one's ends in view.

Exceptionality

Exceptional learners, both those with disabilities and those who are gifted, may suffer alienation from mainstream society because they are viewed in terms of the extent to which they deviate from the standards of "normal" people, yet learners with disabilities tend to experience much more severe discrimination and rejection than the gifted. Gollnick and Chinn (1998) point out that the rejection of the gifted is most likely to come from "a lack of understanding or jealousy rather than from the stigma that may relate to certain handicapping conditions" (p. 170). Like ethnic minorities, women, and the aged, those with disabilities are seen through a deficit model so that they are accepted to the extent to which they conform to the idealized norms of the non-disabled. Thus, for example, the patterns of behavior, interpersonal relationships, and communication and cognitive styles of the hearing and visually impaired are evaluated according to the norms of hearing and sighted people.

There is yet another way in which learners with disabilities are similar to ethnic minorities. As the mainstream society's images of minority groups are derived from distorted and unbalanced portrayals of these groups, our views of disabilities are influenced by negative descriptions of the group. The media rarely show people with disabilities occupying leadership or prestigious positions or making other notable contributions to the society. They are often seen as marginal individuals who are tolerated only to the extent that they fit into stereotypic and culturally assigned roles and statuses.

As has been suggested earlier, every person has to cope with certain contingencies if he or she is to achieve optimal learning. In some instances these contingencies are affective, cognitive, social, or physical in nature, but we need not see them as deficits or pathological conditions that must be eradicated. Groups of individuals with various kinds of disabilities have certain cultural patterns that arise out of their unique needs and circumstances. As the mainstream culture serves its members well most of the time, so do the cultures of those with disabilities. Yet, as Reagan (1985) points out, "the deaf community has had a more difficult time overcoming inferiority stereotyping by the majority culture than other minority groups, since deaf people are viewed as medical pathology" (p. 277).

There is no justifiable reason to insist that people with disabilities must conform only to the norms of the mainstream society, for they too live in a culturally diverse world requiring multicultural competencies. Quite the contrary, there is every reason to reconceptualize the education of individuals with disabilities so that they may be able to function effectively in socially and culturally diverse environments. Again, Reagan (1985) persuasively argues that "the need for the deaf child to learn to cope with and function in both the hearing and deaf cultures would make a bicultural—as well as bilingual—approach especially desirable" (p. 276). Here he is speaking about the education not only of the deaf but also of disabled or handicapped learners as a whole. To provide bicultural or, rather, multicultural education to the handicapped, we need not only reeducate the teachers but also have them rethink the ways in which they view those with disabilities. "To do otherwise, however, would be to allow an essentially imperialistic approach to the education of a sizable minority group in the United States to continue unabated" (p. 277).

In this chapter, we have examined the conceptual similarities shared by cultural pluralism, democracy, and multicultural education. Our discussion of several different approaches to multicultural education revealed the need to define it more broadly so that culture may not be exclusively connected with ethnicity or ethnic minorities in the United States. It is critical that multicultural education is understood to include an in-depth study of other cultures and how cultural factors affect education as well as the provision of educational equity to all individuals regardless of ethnicity, race, sex, or age. In sum, the fundamental principles of multicultural education should be applicable to all groups and individuals.

 ## Cases for Reflection

CELIA AND PENELOPE

Celia and Penelope teach together in a first- and second-grade combined class in western Canada. They have come to Chicago for a conference and are visiting our school. When they mention that the children in their class speak twelve distinct languages, I know that these are teachers I must talk to, and I invite them to meet with me.

The class picture they show me includes a greater variety of skin colors and ethnic features than can be found in our entire building. There are Cambodians, Vietnamese, Koreans, Chinese, Libyans, Japanese, Ethiopians, West Indians, Poles, Yugoslavians, Native Canadians, and, like the teachers, white Canadians.

"What we are," Celia explains, "more than white Canadians, is very middle class, very Canadian-centric. We're not nearly careful enough of people's sensitivities. Here's an example: our school plans a big family potluck supper and it falls on the first day of Ramadan, the month when Moslems fast during the day. Naturally none of the Moslem families can come. We hadn't even bothered to find out about Ramadan."

Penelope shakes her head. "Those kind of things keep happening and we say, 'Oh, how could we have done that!' It reflects on how middle-class Canadian we are. But it isn't easy. There are all those holidays we celebrate, Christmas, Easter, Halloween, Valentine's Day, and so on, that most of our families do not observe in their native lands."

"What do you do about them?" I ask.

"The truth?" Both women laugh. "We ignore most of them. I mean we'll mention the event without really celebrating it," Celia says. "We're trying to have the families come to do something about their own holidays. I think we're getting better at it."

Penelope's eyebrows go up. "Shall I tell her about 'O Canada'? We sing 'O Canada' every morning. Our principal pipes it into the classroom on the loudspeaker. 'O Canada, my home and native land.' Is this meaningful to non-English speaking children? And at assemblies we all recite the pledge, 'I salute the flag, the emblem of my country, to her I pledge my love and loyalty.' This gives Celia and me trouble, it really does. But our principal thinks these things unify us. We don't see it that way."

Source: Reprinted by permission of the publisher from *Kwanzaa and Me: A Teacher's Story* by Vivian Gussin Paley, Cambridge, Mass.: Harvard University Press, Copyright © 1995 by the President and Fellows of Harvard College.

DISCUSSION QUESTIONS

1. Consider the various perspectives toward multicultural curriculum described in this chapter. In what different ways might children in the elementary school learn about various ethnic holidays depending on the perspective adopted?
2. Describe the argument the school principal might give for preserving nationalistic rituals at the school. Describe the arguments Celia and Penelope might respond with. What's your position? Why?
3. What might you do in a culturally diverse classroom to create a sense of community?

BOYS AND GIRLS

For several years, the conventional wisdom—reinforced by a steady drumbeat of stories stressing female victimhood—has been that girls are shortchanged in school, getting less attention from their teachers than boys and gradually losing their self-esteem as they enter adolescence.

By many measures though, girls rule in school. They have better grades, higher reading and writing scores, higher class ranks, and more school honors, and they are more likely than boys to take advanced placement exams in English, social studies and foreign languages.

Boys are more likely to repeat a grade, drop out, be put in special education, be diagnosed with learning disabilities and be put on behavior-modifying medication such as Ritalin. As teenagers, they are also far more likely than girls to commit suicide.

Source: T. Lewin, "How Boys Lost Out to Girl Power." *New York Times*, December 13, 1998. Copyright © 1998 by the New York Times Co. Reprinted by permission.

DISCUSSION QUESTIONS

1. Based on your experiences and observations, what are some of the ways in which boys and girls are treated differently in schools?
2. Some people would argue that even though girls succeed in school at higher rates than boys, they are actually less well-served by schools. How could this be the case?
3. What are some strategies that teachers might use to treat boys and girls in school more equitably?

REFERENCES

American Association of Colleges for Teacher Education (AACTE). (1972). *AACTE bulletin: Not one model American.* Washington, DC: Author.

Aronowitz, S., & Giroux, H. A. (1988). Schooling, culture and literacy in the age of broken dreams: A review of Bloom and Hirsch. *Harvard Educational Review, 58*(2), 172–194.

Banks, J. A. (1999a). *An introduction to multicultural education* (2nd ed.). Boston: Allyn & Bacon.

Banks, J. A. (1999b). *Multiethnic education: Theory and practice* (3rd ed.). Boston: Allyn & Bacon.

Berkson, I. B. (1969). *Theories of Americanization.* New York: Arno Press.

Berliner, D. C., & Biddle, B. J. (1995). *The manufactured crisis: Myths, frauds, and the attack on America's public schools.* Reading, MA: Addison-Wesley.

Bloom, A. (1987). *The closing of the American mind.* New York: Simon & Schuster.

Campbell, D. E. (1996). *Choosing democracy: A practical guide to multicultural education.* Upper Saddle River, NJ: Merrill/Prentice Hall.

Dewey, J. (1939a). *Freedom and culture.* New York: Capricorn Books.

Dewey, J. (1939b). The modes of societal life. In J. Ratner (Ed.), *Intelligence in the modern world* (pp. 365–404). New York: Random House.

Dewey, J. (1957). *Reconstruction in philosophy.* Boston: Beacon Press.

Dewey, J. (1961). *Democracy and education.* New York: Macmillan.

D'Souza, D. (1991). *Illiberal education: The politics of race and sex on campus.* New York: Free Press.

Finly, D. (2004, March). What an educator says about "No Child Left Behind." *The Messenger* (The Mainstream Coalition), (82), p.7.

Freire, P. (1997). *Pedagogy of the oppressed.* New York: Continuum.

Freire, P., & Macedo, D. (1987). *Literacy: Reading the word and world.* South Hadley, MA: Bergin & Garvey.

Gates, H. L. (1992). *Loose canons: Notes on the culture wars.* New York: Oxford University Press.

Gollnick, D. M., & Chinn, P. C. (1998). *Multicultural education* (5th ed.). Upper Saddle River, NJ: Merrill/Prentice Hall.

Henniger, N. L. (2004). *The teaching experience: An introduction to reflective practice.* Upper Saddle River, New Jersey: Pearson.

Houston, B. (1985). Gender freedom and the subtleties of sexist education. *Educational Theory, 35*(4), 359–370.

Kallen, H. N. (1915, February). Democracy versus the melting pot: A study in American nationality. *The Nation,* 218–220.

Kallen, H. N. (1949). *The education of free men.* New York: Farrar and Straus.

Manno, B. V., Finn, C. E., Bierlien, L. A., & Vanourek, G. (1998, March). How charter schools are different: Lessons and implications from a national study. *Phi Delta Kappan, 79*(7), 489–498.

Martin, J. R. (1994). *Changing the educational landscape.* New York: Routledge.

Nathan, J. (1998, March). Heat and light in the charter school movement. *Phi Delta Kappan, 79*(7), 499–505.

National Council for the Accreditation of Teacher Education (NCATE). (1977). *Standards for the accreditation of teacher education.* Washington, DC: Author.

Newmann, F. M., & Wehlage, G. G. (1995). *Successful school restructuring: A report to the public and educators by the Center on Organization and Restructuring of Schools.* Madison, WI: Board of Regents of the University of Wisconsin System.

Ravitch, D. (1990). Diversity and democracy: Multicultural education in America. *American Educator, 14,* 16–20, 46–48.

Reagan, T. (1985). The deaf as a linguistic minority: Educational considerations. *Harvard Educational Review, 55*(3), 265–277.

Schlesinger, A. M., Jr. (1992). *The disuniting of America: Reflections on a multicultural society.* New York: W. W. Norton.

Sleeter, C. E., & Grant, C. A. (2003). *Making choices for multicultural education: Five approaches to race, class and gender* (4th ed.). Upper Saddle River, NJ: Merrill/Prentice Hall.

Sorgman, M. I., & Sorensen, M. (1984). Ageism: A course of study. *Theory into Practice, 23*(2), 119–122.

Tyack, D., & Cuban L. (1995). *Tinkering toward utopia: A century of public school reform.* Cambridge: Harvard University Press.

Walsh, M. (2002). Charting the landscape of school choice. *Education Week, 21*(42), 1, 18–21.

Williams, P. W. (2002). *America's religions: From their origins to the twenty-first century.* Urbana: University of Illinois Press.

PART THREE

Culture, Schooling, and Educational Development

5

Culture and the Role of Schooling

An understanding of the school–culture relationship is important in developing a theoretical perspective from which to evaluate and interpret the respective roles of school and society in a situation where educational reforms are needed. The relationship between schooling and culture is visible in five major views about the role of schooling as it relates to social class. The social class dynamics in the lives of teachers, administrators, and students influence the educational outcomes of schooling (Knapp & Woolverton, 1995, pp. 548–549), and further, such outcomes may contribute to social-class-related conflicts and resulting social inequities. Historically, we are inclined to see schools as the great equalizer. However, they are bound to be affected by social class and accompanying cultural dynamics in any society because schools always function in a particular social order. For this reason, a study of the theories about the role of schooling may help us understand how the work of schools and their personnel tends to perpetuate social classes or promote socioeconomic mobility. We may also gain insight about the fundamental educational reforms needed to make schools more effective and democratic.

Preceding chapters have discussed the intimate relationship between schools and the sociocultural conditions of the larger society in which they function. Hence, our inability or unwillingness to examine the relationship between school and society usually leads to the erroneous belief that the school is solely to blame for the socioeconomic lags and moral ills of American society. This exaggerated notion about the educational system's capacity as an agent of social change may in turn result in blaming teachers and schools for practically every adversity in our society. Disappointments in and frustrations about our schools are the usual consequences of taking an oversimplified approach to educational reform. Yet, past attempts at major educational reforms in the United States have been focused primarily on organizational and curricular changes. For example, the United States attempted to overtake the USSR in the aerospace race through educational reforms in the late 1950s. But these measures were largely concerned with placing greater emphasis on such academic subjects as the sciences, mathematics, and foreign languages rather than on the so-called life adjustment process.

No more than a decade later, American education was charged as inhumane because it was allegedly preoccupied with only the intellectual growth of the learners. Again, schools and teachers were accused of killing children's love for learning with oppressive and punitive practices. The remedy for this sorry state of American education was to have come from humanistic, or confluent, education, which claimed to nurture the learner's heart as well as the mind. In practice, this approach emphasized developing skills to deal with one's feelings and interpersonal relations. Similar to those of the post-*Sputnik* era, most of the reform measures proposed since the mid-1980s also have sought to improve American education by having students devote more time to studying the liberal arts. In the 1990s, educational reform programs included restructured schools (e.g., charter schools and site-based management), authentic learning, and performance-based assessment. The long-term effects of these measures are yet to be seen.

There is little evidence to suggest that the educational reforms tried since the late 1950s have had a lasting impact on the quality of American education or on the socioeconomic or moral conditions of this society. Indeed, whatever impact the reform programs had were short-lived and superficial. The reformers simply failed to understand that the school is only one of a multitude of institutions in our society and that no amount of tinkering with any single institution could bring about fundamental social, economic, or moral changes. On the contrary, without major social changes, educational reforms are bound to have minimal impact in our lives because the school as a specialized social institution reflects the culture of the larger society. As an illustration, our production-consumption-oriented worldview inclines us to see education as a type of industrial production. Hence, we speak of packaging and marketing educational programs and holding our schools accountable to the consumers of educational products.

CULTURAL TRANSMISSION AND THE ROLE OF SCHOOLING

Every society makes deliberate attempts to transmit its culture to the young. In this way, young people may become full-fledged and contributing members of the society. Culture includes those beliefs, values, and attitudes that a society considers fundamental to its survival and perpetuation. Hence, education is necessarily a deliberate and value-laden (moral) enterprise (Durkheim, 1961). As pointed out in chapter 2, the educative process can be carried on with or without schools. Schools are specialized social institutions specifically designed to transmit the culture of the larger society to the young. This implies that the cultural norms of a society are the primary sources from which schools derive their goals and that each society has its own particular view of the role of schooling.

In a society such as in the United States, where the schools are governed and supported by local communities, the unique values and needs of those communities have direct bearing on the development of specific school goals. For instance, the educational goals of a school district in a politically and religiously conservative agricultural community must not only be consonant with the broad cultural norms of the larger society but must also conform to local demands. More specifically, the district may include agriculture-related subject matter in the curriculum to meet the community's special needs. In accordance with the community's religious and moral perspectives, the district may require school prayer and the teaching of creationism while restricting other activities viewed as liberal. However, the district's responsiveness to the special needs and expectations of the local community may conflict with the role of the school as envisioned by the larger society. Such conflict becomes much more severe if the larger society expects its schools to work toward perpetuating the established culture and also serve as an agent of social change. *Dare the School Build a New Social Order?* by George S. Counts (1932) and the writings of John Dewey, John Childs, Harold Rugg, and William Heard Kilpatrick represent early arguments for making the American school and its teachers agents of social reform.

Disputes regarding the proper role of schooling often are attributable to the fact that cultural transmission as the school's primary goal is usually stated in very broad terms. Hence, there is no consensus about the relative importance of different cultural norms or the order in which such norms are to be transmitted to the young. But even if different interest groups and individuals agree about a school district's general educational goals, there will likely be many disparate views regarding how such general goals are to be translated into concrete school policies, operational procedures, curricula, and a myriad of other school activities. Such court cases as *Board v. Pico* (1982) over book banning, *Wallace v. Jaffree* (1985) concerning silent prayer in schools, and *Lubbock Civil Liberties Union v. Lubbock Independent School District* (1983) on religious gatherings on school premises are only a few examples of attempts to resolve conflicts between disparate conceptions of the role of schooling through legal means. Further, these cases also demonstrate how conflicting beliefs about school activities stem from the divergent ways in which our educators, communities, and other special interest groups interpret the broadly conceived role of the American school.

THE ROLE OF SCHOOLING

If there are disagreements about how schools should translate transmission of culture into specific instructional objectives, policies, and programs, there are even more disparate views regarding the nature of the role of schooling. The following sections will examine five perspectives: (1) structural/functionalist, (2) conflict, (3) critical, (4) interpretivist, and (5) postmodern.

The Structural/Functionalist Perspective

According to the **structural/functionalist theory** (henceforth called the functionalist theory), society is a living organism with many interrelated parts. The life of a society as an organism depends on how well each part performs its distinctive role in relation to the workings of other parts. As one type of institution responsible for the socialization of the young, the school's object "is to arouse and to develop in the child a number of physical, intellectual and moral states which are demanded of him by both the political society as a whole and the special milieu for which he is specifically destined" (Durkheim, 1985a, p. 22). To borrow Talcott Parsons's (1985) words, socialization is "the development in individuals of the commitments and capacities which are essential prerequisites of their future role-performance" (p. 180). The commitments consist of the implementation of the broad values of society and the performance of a specific type of role within the structure of society. Thus, a society cannot survive unless its members possess and perpetuate a set of common physical skills, intellectual knowledge, and ethical values (Durkheim, 1985a, p. 21). The acquisition of these skills, knowledge, and values by the young is too important to be left to chance. Although there are many agents of socialization, according to Émile Durkheim (1985b), schools are primarily responsible for systematically organizing the welter of divergent beliefs, knowledge, and skills to "set off what is essential and vital; and play down the trivial and the secondary" (p. 29).

For Durkheim and Parsons, members of a society need to have a set of common beliefs, knowledge, and values for social unity and cohesion. But they are equally persuaded that the school should provide different and more highly specialized knowledge and skills to certain people, for every society requires that its members have different roles (Durkheim, 1985a, p. 21; Parsons, 1985, pp. 180–182). For example, not everyone in our society can or should become engineers or historians, because our society has diverse needs and problems that require different competencies at varying levels. Further, although both the family and the school socialize the young through transmission of culture, the school has a set of very distinctive roles. According to Parsons (1985), schooling enables the child to emotionally separate from the family and learn to internalize a set of cultural values and norms that are broader than those learned from the family alone (p. 191). Through schooling, children learn to function in the larger society as adults. They also learn that people can be grouped according to such criteria as age, sex, interest, and level of competencies and be rewarded differently according to actual achievements. In a very real sense, the school is a microcosm of the larger society. As such, the school reproduces and perpetuates the established social, cultural, economic, and political structures and norms. As we will see later, other theories of the role of schooling criticize the functionalist perspective. For this reason, it is useful to examine the functionalist view more closely.

Robert Dreeben (1968), a leading contemporary functionalist, argues that the social experiences available to children in schools are uniquely suited for preparing their transition from life in the family to occupation and life in the larger society. More specifically, children are more likely to learn the fundamental social norms of independence, achievement, universalism, and specificity in school than from their family life (pp. 65–76). "The nature of experiences available in [the family] could not provide conditions appropriate for acquiring those capacities that enable people to participate competently in the public realm" (p. 65). But in school, pupils learn to belong to and interact with different groups wherein their social positions are based on personal accomplishments as judged according to objective criteria.

Independence

In school, children learn to accept the need to do certain tasks on their own and to accept the legitimate right of others to expect such independent behavior at various times. *Independence* means more than "doing things alone"; it includes such notions as self-reliance, accepting responsibility for one's actions, "acting self-sufficiently, and handling tasks with which under different circumstances, one can rightfully expect the help of others" (Dreeben, 1968, p. 66). Classroom characteristics such as the number of other children and teacher expectations of pupil behavior demand that the young become independent. Dreeben points out that whereas parents expect their children to act independently only in certain situations, teachers are much more consistent in requiring their students to behave independently in doing academic work. Various occupations and institutions in the larger society require their members to self-initiate activities to accomplish their assigned tasks and to accept personal responsibility for their own actions. Clearly, schools are much more systematic than families in providing conditions for the development of independent attitudes in the young.

Achievement

Another important societal norm taught in school is achievement. In our society, independently attained achievements of individuals are prized highly. However, Dreeben (1968) warns, independence and achievement should be distinguished from each other, because "achievement criteria can apply to activities performed collectively" (p. 71). In developing achievement motivation, there is little doubt that the family's child-rearing practices are influential. But schools provide even more significant conditions for cultivating the achievement-oriented attitude in children. After all, children's positions in school are determined by their personal accomplishments.

Most of what goes on in school is organized in such a way that achievements in curricular and extracurricular activities play a key role in determining the young people's status both in and out of the school environment. In most instances, achievement alternatives are given so that those who do not perform well in one field can do well in another. One student may excel in academic activities but perform poorly in sports; an outstanding athlete may do less than mediocre work in academic programs. These young people must learn to deal with both achievement and failure. For example, an individual may be an honor student to one group but just an egghead to another. Similarly, a star quarterback may be seen as nothing more than a jock to those who are not football fans. And what of the youngster whose talents do not fit neatly into any of the school-sanctioned achievement areas? In many ways, schools do provide a greater variety of opportunities for young people to experience achievement than does the family. But schools may also be less effective in helping pupils to protect their self-esteem in coping with failure.

Universalism and Specificity

Universalism refers to a way in which a person is placed in a particular group according to a set of standards or common characteristics he or she shares with other members of that group. For example, a student may be considered a member of an honor society because he or she shares such common traits as having an outstanding academic record and recognized leadership qualities. On the other hand, *specificity* stands for treating an individual in a group as a unique case because he or she possesses certain traits that differ from those shared by other group members. However, a person is treated "particularistically" if given exceptional treatment even though he or she does not possess special traits as compared with the rest of the group (Dreeben, 1968, p. 75).

To illustrate, universalism requires that a teacher treat all students in one class equally—for example, by not allowing anyone to make up an examination. But the norm of specificity makes it possible to permit one student to make up a missed examination because of illness on the day of the test. However, if another student is allowed to make up the test because he or she says flattering things about the instructor's teaching, then that student is treated particularistically. In other words, particularistic treatment of the student is unfair to the rest of the class. Universalism involves categorizing individuals according to common characteristics and equal treatment of everyone in the group. Specificity permits certain exceptions to be made, but only on legitimate grounds. By accepting categorization, children can learn to deal with other individuals in terms of their positions rather than according to their personal identity. In the larger society, powers and privileges accompany certain social positions. Young people need to understand that individuals exhibit certain behavior when acting in an official capacity and that this behavior stems from the position they occupy rather than their personal rights or privileges. Through the norms of universalism and specificity, children learn to deal with the criteria of equal treatment, or what is fair and what is unfair.

School and Society

From the functionalist perspective, "the family, as a social setting with its characteristic social arrangements, lacks the resources and the competence to effect the psychological transition" from life in the family to life in the larger and industrial society (Dreeben, 1968, p. 85). The school is especially well suited for transmitting the four norms of the society because its organizational structure and the behavioral patterns of the school personnel enable the young to have the kinds of experiences not available in other institutions. More specifically, because classrooms are organized according to age or ability, students are able to compare their own successes and failures in learning the norms of independence, achievement, universalism, and specificity with those of their peers. Schooling is effective in socializing the young because its structural organization, the school personnel's behavioral patterns, and its values reflect those of the mainstream society.

As Parsons (1985) points out, the school serves not only as an agent of socialization but also as a principal instrument of allocating roles in the society. Hence, those who can come close to the society's shared norms in their work and behavior are likely to be rewarded with higher socioeconomic status than those unable or unwilling to do so (p. 191). He goes on to suggest that there is a general and tacit consensus in our society that individuals should be rewarded differentially for different levels of achievement as long as there has been fair and equal access to opportunity. As might be expected, the school incorporates the ways in which the society rewards its successful members into its operational policies and procedures by placing "value *both* on initial equality and on differential achievement" (p. 191).

In industrial societies, the positions requiring complex knowledge and skills lead to greater rewards than those roles that demand simpler and more routine competencies. Because the primary functions of the school are to transmit knowledge, develop special skills, and cultivate attitudes that are consonant with societal norms, the amount of reward (monetary reward and/or status) a person receives depends on the individual's ability in these areas and on his or her level of schooling. Given the nature of the school–society relationship, there are bound to be significant differences among individuals of different socioeconomic classes. For example, more doctors and lawyers occupy the upper classes than the lower classes. The functionalist does not see class differences as due to an inherent superiority of any particular group; rather, they are rooted in the merits of the individual. An individual's success at the highly complex skills of law and medicine is rewarded amply by society, and, thus, he or she earns a high socioeconomic status. This means that the issues concerning equal access to educational, economic, and political opportunities for all people become key concerns in an allegedly meritocratic society such as in the United States.

Functionalists would approach educational reform in at least two major ways. The first approach would be to understand the conditions under which young people can acquire the competencies and attitudes necessary to do better in school so that appropriate conditions could be provided for the poor to succeed in school. This strategy is consistent with the functionalist view that higher academic accomplishments in school lead to higher-paying positions. The compensatory education programs that began in the early 1970s are good examples of such an approach. The second way to accomplish educational reform would be to improve our schools by making instruction more effective. Two assumptions underlie this approach. One is the belief that improved teaching leads to academic success, which in turn will result in socioeconomic success. The other is the premise that the school's primary function is to expand students' knowledge and improve their cognitive skills. In the United States, outcomes of the compensatory education programs begun in the 1970s and other school reform measures during the past four decades suggest that these efforts did help certain individuals to move out of lower socioeconomic classes. But no sufficient evidence indicates that educational and economic equality has been assured for all or that significant changes have occurred in the class structure. Further, the validity of the view that success in school is causally related to socioeconomic success remains to be demonstrated.

The Hidden Curriculum

The school as an agent of socialization and role allocation has an "official" curriculum with a set of explicitly stated goals and objectives. These goals and objectives relate to what knowledge and skills ought to be imparted and attitudes developed. The school promotes the learners' motivation for academic success and their desire to practice the norms and values of the larger society for the established systems of rewards. In addition to the formal curriculum, the school also has an informal set of practices with which the learners are socialized. The expression *hidden curriculum* refers to the school's indirect means of helping young people learn the norms and values of their society. For example, our schools reinforce punctuality, assertiveness, self-involvement, and competitiveness by rewarding such acts as turning in assignments on time, expressing one's own opinions, participating in a classroom project, and asking for extra homework for a higher grade. The hidden curriculum has also been referred to as the **lived curriculum**, emphasizing that these informal sets of practices define the day-to-day experiences of students and often assume a greater importance than the formal, subject matter curriculum.

The hidden curriculum occupies a key position in the functionalist view of schooling, for it is through this informal curriculum that young people learn to adapt themselves to the existing societal values and norms. The ability of the young to work and behave accordingly plays a pivotal role in determining their future social status and economic rewards. But this also means that similar rewards will not be given to individuals whose values and behavioral patterns deviate from the norms sanctioned by the larger society. For this reason, success in school is often correlated with socioeconomic success, and school failure is frequently viewed as causally responsible for poverty.

The use of the hidden curriculum is not exclusively connected with the functionalist perspective. Regardless of our theoretical perspectives, what children learn is affected by the overall school climate, the administrative styles of the school staff, the nature of the teacher–pupil relationship, and the teaching approaches being used to reinforce or discourage. However, the functionalists are accused of holding an erroneous belief that schools impart the same set of attitudes, values, and norms to all children through the use of the hidden curriculum. Critics point out that instructors apply the hidden curriculum differently according to students' social class status. For example, upper-class children are more likely to be taught such qualities as self-control, leadership, and creativity; lower-class children tend to be instructed to respect authority, comply with instructions, and conform to the dominant norms.

The Technological View of Schooling

There are those who argue that the functionalist view of schooling also embodies what has been called an instrumentalist or technological perspective, which views schooling as a form of technology that can be treated as essentially similar to the process of industrial production. Industrial production begins with a predetermined set of product specifications, which then are assembled according to a specified sequence so that the desired product can be manufactured with consistent quality. This process requires a system of quality-control mechanisms that evaluates each unit of the production sequence. The degree of cost efficiency with which each unit can perform its assigned functions then becomes a basis for accountability. An industry is held accountable in terms of (1) how closely the products match the initial set of product specifications and (2) whether the value of the products or outcomes is equivalent to or greater than the resources invested in the production.

When schooling is seen as a form of technology, a learning objective is divided into specific instructional components. These components are then organized according to a predetermined sequence. As students master each component, they move up to the next level until they reach the desired learning objectives. This process necessarily involves translating learning objectives in observable and measurable behaviors or competencies. In general, teachers are held accountable on the basis of how well their students have mastered the learning objectives. Hence, frequent and consistent testing is necessary to monitor each learner's progress toward a specific goal. Although the ways in which this process of industrial production is applied to education and schooling vary, the basic principles remain the same. An emphasis on competency-based instruction, quality control, minimum competency testing, accountability, and cost efficiency reflects the influence of the technological perspective in education.

A fundamental shortcoming of the technological view of schooling is that not all worthwhile educational goals can be exhaustively defined in behavioral or performance terms. By putting so much emphasis on what is quantifiable and measurable, we are likely to neglect such important educational goals as creativity, imagination, and appreciation. The technological approach to schooling is not just a matter of doing the same thing more efficiently, because it necessarily demands predetermined goals and tighter and precise control of learning conditions, the learner, and the quantifiable outcomes. If we are serious about making the American school a place where our children can re-create rather than inherit democracy, then it behooves all of us to scrutinize how technology is used and where the concept of technology is to be applied.

Questions About the Functionalist Theory

As we have seen, functionalists view the role of schooling as the process of transmitting the established sociocultural, economic, and political norms so that the young can become productive and contributing members of the society. Hence, the school enables the society to perpetuate itself by reproducing its existing patterns. But should the primary role of schooling be limited to such a reproductive function alone? If we adopt the functionalist perspective, would the school not become a major force in perpetuating the status quo, which makes the rich richer and the poor poorer? How can the school assure equal and fair access to educational and economic opportunities to all citizens if it is seen as a primary agent of reproducing the established social order? What can the school do to eliminate or minimize the socioeconomic inequities among different classes of people? Can the school perform special functions to isolate those who belong to lower socioeconomic classes? How should we determine the proper role of schooling? These are some of the questions that need to be asked about the strengths and weaknesses of the functionalist theory. In many ways, the conflict, critical, interpretivist, and postmodern theories, which we are about to discuss, are responses to these and other fundamental questions about the proper role of schooling.

Conflict Theories

Marxist Conflict Theory

According to the advocates of **Marxist conflict theory**, schools in a capitalistic society do not reproduce the established social system to fulfill the expanding educational needs of increasingly complex positions in modern society. Nor does the school aid individuals to select high-status positions with greater rewards through better education. Quite the contrary, the school functions to serve the interest of the dominant, the powerful, and the wealthy by perpetuating socioeconomic inequities. According to Marxists, who represent a major segment of the conflict theorist group, the private owners of the means of production maintain their domination of the working class by controlling the process of allocating roles, social status, and rewards. Struggles among the classes are bound to ensue as working-class people become aware of their low status and seek to gain a greater share of the available wealth. For Marxists, the socioeconomic inequities in a capitalistic society cannot be eliminated unless the working class wrests private ownership of the means of production from the dominant group.

Seen from this perspective, schools in a capitalistic society play a central role in enabling the dominant class to maintain the class structure by controlling the kinds of knowledge, skills, and attitudes available to people of different classes. Hence, children of the powerful are educated to self-direct and control others, and working-class youth are taught to conform to the norms of the workplace as prescribed by the dominant group. Educational inequalities are then responsible for maintaining social inequities and the class structure. As two contemporary Marxists, Samuel Bowles and Herbert Gintis (1977), explain:

> The social relations of the educational process ordinarily mirror the social relations of the work roles into which most students are likely to move. Differences in rules, expected modes of behavior, and opportunities for choice are most glaring when we compare levels of schooling. Note the wide range of choice over curriculum, life style, and allocation of time afforded to college students, compared with the obedience and respect for authority expected in high school. (p. 142)

Further, the class differences in school are perpetuated through "the capacity of the upper class to control the basic principles of school finance, pupil evaluation and educational objectives" (p. 142).

Bowles and Gintis go on to argue that differences in intellectual abilities and achievements have very little to do with what status a person is to occupy. They insist that empirical evidence simply does not show that differences in individual IQ scores are significant factors in allocating individuals to different roles in the class structure (pp. 215–225). Because values, personality traits, and class-linked roles are the primary determinants of one's social class, the principle of rewarding academic excellence and the use of cognitive abilities in educational promotion are employed as a way to legitimize the role of schooling as a means of making the society more egalitarian. As Apple and Weis (1983) point out, schools "foster the belief that the major institutions of our society are equally responsive to race, class, and sex," but available data show that "in almost every social arena from health care to anti-inflation policy, the top twenty percent of the population benefit much more than the bottom eighty percent" (pp. 5–6). Schools as agencies of legitimation reflect the social relationship of production as well as "the differences [inequities] in the social class composition of the student bodies" (Bowles, 1977, pp. 142, 149). But schools not only legitimize the socioeconomic system of the capitalistic society, they legitimize their own existence as well (Apple & Weis, 1983, p. 6). This being the case, educational equality cannot be achieved by simply changing the school system. Only by exposing "the unequal nature of our school system and destroy[ing] the illusion of unimpeded mobility through education" can we hope to serve the cause of educational equality (Bowles, 1977, p. 149).

Neo-Marxist Conflict Theory

While proponents of **neo-Marxist conflict theory** agree that schools in a capitalistic society reproduce and perpetuate social hierarchical classes, they argue that the socioeconomic class structure is not the result of each individual's sole or even primary desire to maximize their rewards. That is, the privileged upper class controls the lower class through the means of noneconomic domination because the student is taught the **status culture** (e.g., styles of language, manners, values, and so on belonging to a social class or profession) rather than the social relations of production—the roles of owners, managers, and workers of industry.

Drawing from Max Weber's view, Randall Collins (1985) holds that the basic units of society are **status groups**, associations whose members share common status cultures (i.e, styles of language, conversational topics, manners, opinions and values, and preferences of all sorts, as well as a sense of status equality based on participation in a common culture) (p. 71). Collins explains that each status group distinguishes itself from others in terms of such "moral evaluation" as *honor, taste, breeding, cultivation, property,* and so on. Individuals derive their sense of identity from participation in such cultural groups. From this perspective, the primary role of schooling is to teach status cultures rather than to transmit technical skills and knowledge. In the words of Collins (1985), "schools primarily teach vocabulary and inflection, style of dress, aesthetic tastes, values and manners. The emphasis on sociability and athletics found in many schools is not extraneous but may be at the core of the status culture propagated by the schools" (p. 73). Being schooled is an indication of membership in a particular status group rather than a mark for technical knowledge, skills, or achievements. "Educational requirements may thus reflect the interests of whichever groups have power to set them" (p. 70). Hence, schooling is used to identify and help "insiders" to stay in their status culture and discourage "outsiders" from entering a more prestigious status group. This means that the status group system that controls schooling also controls workplaces, and constant struggles for wealth, power, and prestige are carried out through status groups or classes.

There is no disputing the fact that there has been a profound increase in the educational requirements for employment throughout the last century. But there is no consensus regarding the explanation of this fact. For example, the functionalists interpret the increased educational requirements as a consequence of ever-increasing demands for complex knowledge and technological skills for new and better-paying positions. They see a direct connection between more schooling and greater socioeconomic rewards. However, neo-Marxists regard the same increase in educational requirements for employment as the result of three conditions (Collins, 1985, pp. 79–80). The first is that people have viewed education as a means of entering into an elite status culture. Second, political decentralization or separation of church and state has made establishing schools and colleges much easier than in previous eras. Third, technical changes have also been responsible for the expansion of education because the rapid industrialization of society has reduced the need for unskilled workers and increased the demand for highly skilled technicians and professionals. Notwithstanding these three conditions, Collins observes:

> Once higher levels of education become recognized as an objective mark of elite status, and a moderate level of education as a mark of respectable middle-

level status, increases in the supply of educated persons, and previously superior levels become only average. (p. 80)

This means that high-prestige organizations had to raise their educational
requirements to maintain the high status of the upper-level executives and the
relative respectability of the middle-level managers.

According to Collins (1979), high-prestige professions discourage vertical
occupational mobility by **credentialing**—requiring credentials such as diplomas,
licenses, and certificates for entrance into these positions. Thus, educational
requirements and credentialing serve as a major dividing line between high-
status occupations, such as managerial positions, and such lower-status jobs as
those in manual labor (pp. 46–47). Moreover, because educational requirements
and credentialing are the major sources of socioeconomic inequality, "elimination of educational requirements [including credentialing] for jobs would be a
necessary step in any overall restructuring of the occupational world to produce
greater income equality" (p. 202). The abolition of credentialing is possible if
training sequences and rotation of position-related duties are integrated into
professional activities. For example, university students could be asked to do sec-
retarial work as part of their education while secretaries could be allowed to
receive academic training as part of their work (p. 202). In this way, secretaries
can eventually become members of a better-paying occupation. Eliminating credentialing would no doubt change the structure of power in our society, but
Collins does not expect this radical change to occur in the near future. On the
contrary, he anticipates credentialing to expand with a continuing threat of class
struggle. Unless we find a means more rational than the use of the educational
system for controlling our institutions, he warns, our society may "undergo con-
vulsions from forces beyond [our] control, as in the Reformation" (p. 204).

Limitations of Conflict Theory

According to conflict theorists, socioeconomic inequities result from educational
inequities in capitalistic society. They maintain that the domination of the lower
working class by the wealthy upper class is maintained by having the schools
reproduce the hierarchical class structure inherent in capitalist society. Not all
conflict theorists agree about how capitalist society perpetuates its class structure. For example, Marxists argue that the class structure is maintained because
schools teach social relationships of production. On the other hand, neo-Marxists contend that domination of the lower working class by the wealthy upper
class is accomplished through schools teaching status culture to their students.

In spite of the differences already mentioned, both Marxists and neo-Marxists are convinced that the root cause of inequities in capitalist society is the
school's reproduction of the hierarchical class structure. They are also persuaded
that educational as well as socioeconomic inequities will persist as long as capitalism continues to exist. Yet when we examine the range of factors related to both
educational and social inequities in our society, the Marxist and the neo-Marxist

views, even at best, only partially explain the causes of inequities. Social classes of the young alone do not explain how well or poorly children perform in school and work. In addition to social class backgrounds, a myriad of biological, environmental, and psychological factors—and even luck—enter into people's intellectual, social, economic, and political achievements. Moreover, there is no assurance that educational and social inequities would cease to exist if capitalism were abolished, for such inequities persist in societies that no longer allow private ownership of industry.

Whether the responsibility of educating the citizens of a society is left in the hands of schools, community, or workplace, transmitting societal norms and values is inescapable and indispensable. After all, no society can hope to survive without a means of transmitting and perpetuating its fundamental norms. Accordingly, educational institutions, whether formal or informal, are bound to reflect the social structure and norms of the larger society. Moreover, the hidden curriculum serves as an effective indirect means of transmitting the norms and values of capitalist, Marxist, neo-Marxist, socialist, and many other forms of society. For example, assuming that the neo-Marxist explanation of schooling is sound, schools in Marxist or socialist society also will teach status culture. Given such a relationship between education and society, how is genuine educational reform possible? The suggestion by some conflict theorists that we do away with school may be an interesting notion, but it is hardly a plan that can be implemented. Even if we were successful in disestablishing the school, this change would not bring about educational equality, for the children of the poor are simply not as effective as their wealthy counterparts in utilizing educational resources and opportunities.

Critical Theory

Critical theory encompasses a series of theoretical ideas about the course of twentieth-century history that appeared in Germany in the 1920s and 1930s (Held, 1980). Some of the well-known members of this school of thought are Max Horkheimer (1895–1971), Theodore Adorno (1903–1969), Herbert Marcuse (1898–1979), and Jürgen Habermas (b. 1929). Though varied in certain specific aspects, their thoughts, generally categorized as the Frankfurt school, represent an attempt to reevaluate capitalism and the Marxist explanation of class domination and to reformulate the meaning of human emancipation. Because both capitalists and Marxists view schools as agents of socialization, what the critical theorists have to say about how class structure is reproduced and class domination is maintained has significant implications for the role of schooling. In recent years, the thoughts of the Frankfurt School have stimulated Stanley Aronowitz, Paulo Freire, Henry Giroux, and other educational theorists to work toward developing a critical theory of education (Giroux, 1983).

Because critical theorists sided with Max Weber's position (functionalism) rather than the Marxist perspective, a brief discussion of the Weberian notion of rationalization may be helpful in understanding the general thrusts of critical theory. According to Weber (1947), people in preindustrial societies were educated to lead their lives by learning to perform tasks related to their particular positions. As societies became more industrialized, schools increasingly were required to train individuals for new, specialized roles. Accordingly, modern technological societies moved toward rationalization—that is, institutional organization based on specialized knowledge and skills. The individuals for these roles were selected on the basis of credentials and examinations. Thus, modern society became an organization of specialists and modern government a bureaucracy occupied by experts. This meant that schools had to produce "specialists" rather than "cultivated people." Weber further pointed out that modern schools teach values and norms of the high-prestige positions (i.e., status cultures). Members of the specialist bureaucracy control not only people's lives; they also control schools to maintain their domination over the working class as well as the gender, race, ethnicity, and even age-related groups. In this way, Weber's notion of rationalization leads not to rationality but to technological authoritarianism. Hence, class domination goes beyond economic domination of the working class by the capitalist class. Now, let us examine the ideas of the critical theorists in relation to these Weberian concepts.

Unlike Marxists, the critical theorists of the 1920s and 1930s did not believe that domination of the working class by the capitalist class is achieved by perpetuating the economic class structure alone. Nor did they think that there is only one form of human domination (i.e., economic class domination). For example, in spite of their differences, Horkheimer and Adorno both argued that people's individuality, uniqueness, and creativity would become obliterated by what Adorno called the mass culture. Adorno pointed out that the mass culture—movies, TV shows, and even commercials, for example—contains the norms and values of the dominating groups and, as such, distorts reality to perpetuate the ruling group's interests. Consequently, individuals become unable to think critically about themselves or their society.

In a similar vein, Marcuse contended that as modern society becomes a society of technological experts, people with unique individuality are replaced with "one dimensional [people]" who think neither reflectively nor creatively. Horkheimer, Adorno, and Marcuse agreed that the increasing intrusion of the state into people's lives leads to technocratic authoritarianism, which controls citizens' attitudes, behaviors, and thinking. Even critical thinking is defined within the confines of the dominating group's interest. Habermas (1971) maintained that the interests of the dominating class are legitimized and the most vital and indispensable aspects of human life become threatened when the problems of living are defined as issues with which only specialists can deal. Hence, if human beings are to be emancipated from domination by the authoritarianism of experts, we need to reaffirm the need for self-reflection, critical inquiry, and self-understanding. Further, we must "penetrate beyond the level of particular historical class interests to disclose the fundamental interests of mankind as such" (p. 113).

Although Paulo Freire (1985, 1993), a contemporary Brazilian social and educational reformer, is not considered a critical theorist in the strictest sense, he echoes the critical theorist perspective when he argues that there is no single form of class domination. Just as society includes divergent types of social relations, it also harbors many different forms of domination and oppression:

> The dominated are human beings who have been forbidden to be what they are. They have been exploited, violated, and violently denied the right to exist and the right to express themselves. This is true whether these dominated people represent a unique people, a social group (like homosexuals), a social class, or a particular gender (like women). (Freire, 1985, p. 192)

For Freire, education is more than a process in which the student simply accepts bodies of information provided by the teacher. Education, of which schooling is one part, is a struggle to overcome dominations of all sorts so that each person can grasp the meaning of his or her personal existence and future life. It is the process of self-emancipation. The kind of knowledge that will enable our young people to emancipate themselves from domination and oppression is not verifiable scientific knowledge. Rather, it is radical knowledge through which the young and the oppressed can learn about the conditions responsible for their dominated and subordinated positions (Freire, 1993, p. 32). Only this kind of radical, or critical, knowledge can help students analyze how the dominant society legitimates (justifies) its norms and values. At the same time, young people can also see the possibility of alternative cultural practices, ways of thinking, and social orders. Such knowledge "would function to help students and others understand what this society has made of them (in a dialectical sense) and what it is they no longer want to be, as well as what it is they need to appropriate critically in order to become knowledgeable about the world in which they live" (Aronowitz & Giroux, 1981, p. 132). Helping students, teachers, and others to acquire critical knowledge as a tool of analysis means helping them to develop critical literacy, which will enable them to raise questions about the nature of knowledge and its justification, modes of discourse, and school organization that "reduce learning and social practices to narrow technical dimensions" (pp. 132–133).

Giroux (1983) insists that the development of critical literacy is hampered because the values and norms of the dominant social classes are incorporated into school curricula. Hence, the dominant group's cultural practices, modes of thinking and knowing, lifestyles, language patterns, learning and communication styles, and even political principles are transmitted both overtly and insidiously. A fundamental flaw in the traditional approach to schooling is that it stresses knowledge, social practices, and modes of thinking that have been historically handed down to us. What is necessary in schooling is an emphasis on critical literacy skills that will enable students "to recognize what this society has made of them and how it must, in part, be analyzed and reconstituted so that it can generate the conditions for critical reflection and action rather than passivity and indignation" (p. 231).

Schools need to challenge the established practices, institutions, and ways of thinking and conceive new and alternative possibilities. As Giroux (1983) writes, "Teachers and other educators [need] to reject educational theories that reduce schooling either to the domain of learning theory or to forms of technocratic rationality that ignore the central concerns of social change, power relations, and conflicts both within and outside of schools" (p. 62). Only in this way can schools highlight the human potential and struggle and expose the discrepancies between society as it exists and as we envision it (p. 36).

Dilemmas of Critical Theory

As the proponents of critical theory have pointed out, our society contains many different forms of domination. More often than not, the many and varied conditions responsible for human oppression and exploitation are rooted in the social structure and the cultural norms and conditions of the society. Hence, schools as social institutions reflect the conditions that lead to domination. A dilemma of the conflict theorists is that if teachers and other educators are products of schools controlled by the dominating group, how can they help students develop critical literacy to emancipate themselves? One proposal is to do away with schools and place the control of education in the hands of parents and local communities. However, there is no assurance that families and communities will not work toward perpetuating their own class culture, nor is there a guarantee that the powers of the upper class will not nullify the efforts of lower-class families and communities.

Yet another dilemma faces advocates of critical theory. On one hand, Giroux (1984) advocates for the recognition and support of the public service role of schools. He also insists that educators work with community groups to develop pockets of cultural resistance and to help students become reflective about their life, status, and society. This means that our universities should produce teachers who can encourage students to analyze the assumptions underlying the existing social order and cultural practices and envision alternative forms of society. In spite of Giroux's idea about how our schools should develop critical literacy among the young, he also argues that we cannot rely on existing schools for radical educational reform to promote emancipatory change. The power of schools to control what can and cannot be debated, the disrespect they have toward the oppressed, and their willingness to act against their opponents simply make them unreliable agents for social change (Giroux, 1984). Now, if, as the critical theorists contend, schools reproduce the dominant ideology, who would educate teachers to become emancipating agents? Insofar as schools cannot escape from the influence of the values and norms of the larger society, the critical theorists' demand that schools help students to question and reject the existing system is tantamount to asking teachers and students to pick themselves up by their own bootstraps.

The Interpretivist Perspective

As we have seen, the functionalists, the conflict theorists, and the advocates of critical theory arrived at their views by analyzing the relationship between education and the structural elements of the social class system. However, advocates of **interpretivist theory** maintain that an understanding of the relationship between school and society requires an analysis of interactions among students, teachers, administrators, and various peer groups. They urge us to understand the schooling–society relationship by interpreting the meanings of interactive patterns among these groups, curricula, and school achievements. At the same time, we are admonished not to impose our own preconceived philosophical or theoretical framework on our observation of school and society. In their approach to research, the interpretivists attempt to integrate the structural study of society with analytic studies of interactions among students and school personnel, the nature and contents of school curricula, as well as the consequences of direct and hidden approaches to teaching. Consequently, the interpretivists utilize the findings regarding the linguistic basis of cognition (symbolic interactionism), the role of shared meanings in social situations (ethnomethodology), and the experiential or common-sense views of reality (phenomenology).

According to the interpretivists, social structure consists of a system of class inequality that the family perpetuates by transmitting linguistic codes or patterns of communication to the young (Karabel & Halsey, 1977, p. 63). Thus, although the school is a principal instrument of socialization, it is not the basic agency in which socialization begins. Children learn to play the "game" of living by interpreting the meanings of various rules of behavior, sanctions, lifestyles, and other appropriate norms through speech patterns determined by the family's social position. The child's future class status in society is in turn affected by the communication patterns acquired from the family. Not unexpectedly, the school directly and indirectly expects all children to acquire the dominant linguistic and cultural competencies—those originally produced by families belonging to the dominant class. The lower-class children are required to function according to linguistic and cultural patterns that are alien to them. As Bourdieu (1977) writes:

> The educational system demands of everyone alike that they have what it does not give. This consists mainly of linguistic and cultural competencies and that relationship of familiarity with culture which can only be produced by family upbringing when it transmits the dominant culture. (p. 494)

Because the school reproduces the dominant culture, it creates serious discrepancies between what the lower-class children know and the school norm (Bernstein, 1977, p. 483; Bourdieu, 1977, pp. 493–494). It is not surprising that children from lower socioeconomic classes do poorly in school, for they cannot readily develop those dominant linguistic and cultural abilities needed for academic or socioeconomic success.

According to Basil Bernstein (1977), a leading interpretivist, socialization is the process by which the child, a biological being, is made into a specific cultural being. It is a complex process that gives distinctive form and content to the child's cognitive, affective, and moral tendencies (p. 476). Through socialization the child becomes aware of the various orderings of the society and the roles he or she may be expected to play. Bernstein holds that, of many factors, the family's social class has the most formative influence on the child's education and future work. Further, it is the class system that controls the distribution of knowledge in the society so that knowledge and the modes of thinking available to the upper class become inaccessible to lower-class individuals. This control of knowledge "has sealed off communities from each other and has ranked these communities on a scale of invidious worth" (p. 477). For this reason, the communication and behavioral patterns of the lower class are often considered inferior to those of the higher social classes.

Through social control of knowledge, the class system has affected not only the distribution of material wealth but also communication patterns of different social classes. According to Bernstein, communication patterns of working-class children are much more situation-specific, or particularistic, and restricted than those of middle- and upper-middle-class children, who are given more elaborated, or universalistic, communication patterns in which meanings are not imbedded in specific local situations. Bernstein (1977) explains that "where [the speech] codes are elaborated, the socialized has more access to the grounds of his own socialization. . . . [However,] where the codes are restricted, the socialized has less access to the grounds of his socialization" (p. 478). In other words, individuals with universalistic, elaborated communication patterns are able to respond more flexibly to new and different social situations than those who have particularistic and restricted speech patterns.

The particularistic and restricted nature of the lower-class communication patterns becomes a barrier for working-class children in dealing with situations that go beyond their social class experiences. Further, these children are less able to handle abstract thoughts and generalizations. Socioeconomic inequities in society are maintained because families reproduce the communication patterns and speech codes that are specifically connected with their social status. In addition, higher-status positions require those communication patterns that are reproduced by families belonging to the dominant class. These conditions leading to societal inequities are exacerbated by the fact that schools consider only the universalistic, elaborated communication patterns as acceptable norms. Moreover, they view any pattern that deviates from the dominant norms as "devalued, and humiliated within schools or seen, at best, to be irrelevant to the educational endeavor" (p. 484).

Bernstein asserts that the school is primarily interested in transmitting universalistic speech codes. Hence, serious discrepancies are bound to arise between what the school attempts to accomplish and the communication patterns of the lower-class children. Accordingly, if we are to reduce the amount of social inequities in society, the school must purge all built-in class biases from its curriculum and pedagogy and its conception of educability. Moreover, the school should not try to get lower-class families to provide their children with linguistic and cultural knowledge and skills that these families do not possess. Rather, the school should focus on how it can help these children bridge the gap between their own skills and those that the larger society demands within the context of schooling.

Limitations of the Interpretivist Theory

Interpreting the meanings of various interactive relationships among students, school personnel, the curriculum, and pedagogy is essential in understanding the role of schooling, for schooling occurs among people mediated by curriculum and instruction. The use of this approach in studying the school–society relationship requires that we become participant-observers, just as ethnographers study an alien culture by living in it. One of the difficulties with this ethnomethodological approach is that when the investigator becomes involved in the process or event being studied, the degree of involvement may easily affect the outcome of the study. In addition, because the investigator's focus is on interactions among people and various aspects of the school, not enough attention is paid to the influences of the larger social, political, and economic contexts in which individuals function. For these reasons, the interpretivists are often criticized for not having conducted enough rigorous empirical studies to support their claims with hard evidence. This criticism raises further questions about the nature of the criteria interpretivists use to determine the soundness of their claims.

Another limitation of interpretivism is that although this theory offers an insightful description of the class system and its impact on social inequities, it does not provide a viable plan to resolve class conflicts. Nor does it offer realistic plans to eliminate or even substantially reduce social inequities in society.

Postmodern Perspectives

Undergirding the functionalist, conflict, critical, and interpretivist perspectives are modernist assumptions. Key among these is the idea that social phenomena are characterized by fixed structures and systematic underlying relationships. So, for example, we cannot understand a teacher's activity without examining how that fits together with broader aspects of schooling and society, such as the expectations of the curriculum, the social class of the students, and the regulations of the bureaucracy. From the modernist perspective these relationships are regular and predictable. It is possible to uncover these systemic relationships and thereby understand the social world. Modernism in its functionalist form places great emphasis on the rationalization of the social world. That is, through the establishment of clear, objective procedures and through efficient, unbiased management, social institutions can fairly serve all people. In its functionalist and critical forms, the modernist perspective places great faith in the human ability to control humankind's future and to shape a better world.

Postmodernism/poststructuralism calls these assumptions into question. Poststructuralism, in its contemporary forms, is rooted in the writings of Michel Foucault (1972) and Jacques Derrida (1972). Foucault is interested in the ways in which social and political institutions produce and reproduce ideas about truth and knowledge. Derrida challenges the idea that meaning is fixed. Meaning is only fixed through a consensus of readers and will change, or shift, over time. From the postmodern perspective, what has passed for reason and objective knowledge has in fact been the knowledge, norms, and expectations of those in power. What has been seen as objective truth is defined by postmodernists as a master narrative in which those who hold power determine what passes for knowledge. Henry Giroux (1993) describes the postmodern perspective succinctly:

> Postmodernism rejects a notion of reason that is disinterested, transcendent and universal. Rather than separating reason from the terrain of history, place and desire, postmodernism argues that reason and science can only be understood as part of a broader historical, political, and social struggle over relationships between language and power. (p. 53)

Western culture has defined a privileged canon, a body of literature and ideas that is seen as true and good. This canon has ignored or marginalized the voices and ideas of those with little or no power. The writing and thinking of the oppressed and the poor, for example, have not been seen generally as having equal worth with the voices of the dominant culture. Postmodernists argue for the need for multiple narratives. Rather than one way of knowing and understanding, there are many. Subordinated and excluded groups are given voice and opportunity to discover their worlds and histories.

Postmodernists further argue that it is necessary to examine or deconstruct meanings that we tend to take for granted. That is, language is not simply a medium for transmitting ideas and meaning; it is, in fact, a reflection of existing power structures. Rather than being value-neutral and fixed, meanings are constructed and reconstructed as society and social structures change. As Cherryholmes (1988) writes:

> Some people speak with authority, while others listen as consumers, because power infiltrates the language we inherit; the meanings of our words, utterances, and discourses; and the institutions and practices that shape their use. (p. 50)

For postmodernists, the purpose of education is not to perpetuate the social, political, and economic interests of the few. Rather, it should transform society and empower the marginalized and the oppressed to develop their own personal and social identity based on an understanding of the "whys" of their own status and cultural difference. Not surprisingly, postmodernists seek to deal with problems and issues in society in an integrated way rather than following the lines of discrete and established academic disciplines. Regarding the use of textbooks and knowledge, they point out that these books generally introduce key words with their definitions and examples. Rarely do they indicate that there is likely to be more than one definition. The word *identity*, for example, is likely to have several different meanings and particularly different meanings in different cultures. Further, textbooks make authoritative claims about what is or is not knowledge, with little indication that the claim is controversial or contested. Textbooks determine what knowledge is important or not important by what they include and what they leave out.

Critiques of Postmodernism

Postmodernism raises many important questions about what counts as knowledge and whose voice gets heard in the construction of knowledge. It has been criticized for the very questions it raises. Does the postmodern invitation to open up the curriculum to multiple voices and perspectives threaten the cohesion of our society? Even those who agree that there is a need to analyze the power assumptions embedded in the curriculum question the postmodern critique, which sees the struggle for democracy as based on a politics of difference and power rather than on deliberation and reason (Giroux, 1993, p. 48).

Postmodernism is not a single unified theory. Rather, it is more like a mood or frame of mind (Noddings, 1995, p. 72; Ozmon & Craver, 1999, p. 361). Its subscribers reject the possibility of a universal truth and a single fixed way of knowing. While postmodernists emphasize the importance of allowing cultural diversity, transforming society to establish pluralistic democracy, and helping the oppressed to form their own identity, the difficult and esoteric nature of their language makes us wonder about how well the marginalized as well as the general public understand their message. Further, their views about expected educational outcomes are more abstract and global than concrete and specific. As Ozmon and Craver point out, "postmodernists seem to be more conscious of what they oppose than what they promote; this is revealed in the lack of attention to the sometimes overwhelmingly negative tone of their delivery" (Ozmon & Craver, 1999, p. 371).

Today, "postmodernists" usually refers to deconstructionists. However, there are **constructive postmodernists** (Gang, 1988, 1990; Griffin, 1992; Miller, J. P., 1993; Miller, R., 1997; Moffett, 1994) who hold that the deconstructionist perspective leads to "a disjointed culture of spontaneity and local meaning" and a denial of [the wholeness and] the spiritual dimension of human existence (Miller, R., 1997, p. 71). They argue that human life "has a purpose, a direction, [and] a meaning that transcends our personal egos and our physical and cultural conditioning" (p. 79). Moreover, because reality represents a unified whole with a common ground for truth and values, education should help learners become effective members of a global community. To achieve this goal, the schools must provide the kind of structure and cultural ethos that reflect the wholeness of the world and everything in it. From this **holistic** point of view, the primary purpose of education should go beyond empowering the marginalized and the oppressed.

A REVIEW AND CRITICAL ESTIMATE OF THE FIVE PERSPECTIVES

Before we discuss a critical estimate of the five perspectives, it may be useful to briefly review these ideas because, in spite of their differences, they contain several overlapping views (see Table 5.1).

A Review

Advocates of the structural/functionalist theory believe that, as a social system, the school is an integral part of society. A central role of the school is to pass on the cultural norms of the society to the young so that they can function effectively. Through schooling and other means of education the society is able to maintain social order and perpetuate itself. Critics argue that schools transform culture for the purpose of "helping students meet the institutional requirements of their credentialing" (McNeil, 1986, p. 13). McNeil explains that schools transform culture into pieces of school knowledge and units of courses and sequences that conform to the school's bureaucratic processes. She goes on to say that

> after being processed through worksheets, list-filled lectures and short-answer tests, the cultural content . . . comes to serve only the interests of institutional efficiencies. Its forms may have some utility but its substance has been depleted. (p. 13)

Unlike the functionalists, those who assume a critical perspective take a critical stance toward the status quo of schooling. Conflict theorists argue that the school is an instrument of domination used by those in power to preserve and extend the existing social order. This practice results in an inequitable distribution of wealth, power, and educational opportunities. A new social structure emerges from struggles between the poor and the rich to achieve a more egalitarian distribution of wealth and power. According to critical theorists, there is a genuine need to reconsider the meanings of domination and emancipation because people can be dominated through learning the kind of knowledge, culture, and history that legitimize domination and reinforce the roles of the subjugated. We need to "break the grip of all closed systems of thought and to counter an unreflected affirmation of society" (Thompson & Held, 1982, p. 2). Our reflection about domination must "penetrate beyond the level of particular historical class interests to disclose the fundamental interests of mankind as such" (Habermas, 1971, p. 113). Educationally, schools must help their students learn modes of inquiry, knowledge, and skills to enable them to think critically about how their society may have shaped their positions and prevented them from realizing goals that go beyond the prescribed status. Through such schooling the young should be able to "affirm and reject their own histories in order to

TABLE 5.1
Five Perspectives Toward the Role of Schooling

	Functionalist	Conflict Theory	Critical Theory	Interpretivist	Postmodern
Leaders	Durkheim, Parsons & Dreeben	Bowles & Gintis, Collins	Freire, Giroux	Bernstein	Derrida, Foucault
Present Role	Transmit culture and maintain social order	Reproduce the existing economic order	Legitimize oppression and reinforce the roles of the oppressed through uncritical acceptance of social order	Teach various roles through curricula and learning activities with class bias	Transmit knowledge as defined by those in power
Future Vision	Teach the young to function effectively in society	Provide economic equality through participation in class struggle	Develop critical literacy	Analyze interactions among school participants with a view toward eliminating cultural and class bias from school experiences	Deconstruct taken-for-granted meanings and knowledge; enable multiple voices and perspectives to be recognized

begin the process of struggling for the conditions that will give them opportunities to lead a self-managed existence" (Giroux, 1983, p. 38).

The functionalist and critical perspectives seek to understand the role of schooling based on analyses of the relationship between schools as structural aspects of society and society. But is it possible to adequately understand human society without having sound knowledge regarding human behavior? Interpretivists note that to gain such knowledge we need to examine the norms with which people interpret their experiences and other events in life by assigning significance and values to them. If we grant that culture consists of a system of norms for ascribing meanings and worth to the events in individuals' lives, then those who live in the same culture will tend to give generally similar interpretations to various occurrences. Variations in interpretations are still possible because of the differences in personal experiences and socioeconomic class. In educational terms, the interpretivists are interested in analyzing interactions among students and various school personnel. To these theorists, student behaviors cannot be understood unless we know about their goals and the norms that guide school activities. Children learn the rules and standards that determine their roles and status in school. Hence, schools should evaluate the effects of class bias in teaching, curriculum, and other school-related activities.

The deconstructive postmodernists argue against efforts to strive toward objectivity. What has been defined as school knowledge, as universal and true, has in fact been defined by those in power. Hence, these postmodernists find it necessary to deconstruct both the power relationships and the canon of knowledge which have emerged from them. By seeing knowledge and language within historically constructed contexts we can begin to know and by attending to diverse voices we can really begin to understand the world and our lived experiences within it.

Unlike the deconstructionists, constructive postmodernists insist that there is a universal basis of meaning and knowledge because the world itself is a unified whole. From this perspective, education should (1) give learners a vision of the wholeness of the universe, (2) help them discover the interrelatedness of all disciplines, (3) emphasize a global perspective and common human interests, and (4) enable the young to develop a sense of harmony and spirituality to build world peace (Gang, 1988, p. 14). These four goals of education summarize the basic tenets of the holistic view of education (holism).

A Critical Estimate

These perspectives toward the role of schooling represent five interpretations of the same educational and sociocultural processes found in all human societies. Each of the five perspectives attempts to explain the relationship among schooling, culture, and social structure and proposes different educational measures to make human society more egalitarian. As important as these theories are in helping us analyze the relationship between school and society and class structure and social inequities, all of the theories leave certain aspects of social reality unexplained. For example, social inequities continue to exist in socialistic or Marxist societies. At the same time, educational opportunities are accessible to many more groups of people in the United States than in other capitalistic or even noncapitalistic countries. In the area of their proposed programs for social change and educational reforms, they are intellectually compelling but practically not achievable. In fact, hardly any of the measures proposed by those who hold a critical, interpretivist, deconstructive, or constructive postmodern perspective have had significant impact on how schools are run and children are educated.

At least two possible reasons explain why these theories have had little direct influence on how children are educated. One is that the relationship among education, schooling, and social stratification is extremely complex and multidimensional. Any reform programs based on a theory that is rooted in a single concept— for example, class domination or transmission of communication patterns—will inevitably be inadequate. The impact of such measures will be limited if not superficial. What is needed is the development of a multidisciplinary theory of education that utilizes the findings and methods of a wide range of biological, physical, and social sciences as well as our lived experiences. This does not suggest that these five theories should be discarded, for they do provide insight into certain aspects of the relationship among schooling, culture, and society.

Second, the failure of educational theorists to make a genuine difference in the actual business of educating people may be attributable in large part to the fact that the theorists are outside of the world of educational politics. The theorists become "outsiders" because they are preoccupied with developing and reproducing their own unique languages, which are not accessible to those who do not belong to the same intellectual "class." For example, if the object of critical theory is to "change the world," why "should it describe itself in a language inaccessible to all but a few" (Noddings, 1995)? Because educational politicians and practitioners have their own ordering of meanings that are not open to the theorists, the theorists have very little, if any, power to affect educational establishments and their practices. For the theoretical ideas to make any difference at all, the theorists must become more actively involved in political movements of the larger educational community. Perhaps they should take seriously the following admonition by Feinberg (1975):

> If one is concerned to establish a more human society, then he ought to work to establish that society in the very places where people live and work. If one is intent on having man's work and his machines serve real human needs, then he ought to see to it that a man's work serves his human need and not assume this to be an inevitable by-product of letting talent rise to the top. And if it is believed that the requirements of technology and the nature of work are destroying the humanizing and educative functions of the family and the community, then one should reexamine the requirements of technology and the nature of work. (pp. 283–284)

Cases for Reflection

THE HIDDEN CURRICULUM

The City Academy is an urban school serving about fifteen hundred students in grades seven to twelve. The student population is approximately 19 percent Asian, 41 percent white, 33 percent black, and 7 percent Latino. The school is one of the city's three elite, public "examination" high schools for which admissions are based on results from standardized tests administered by the school district during students' sixth grade. Four out of the school's seventy-one teachers are Asian Pacific American. There are no Asian Pacific administrators. The headmaster is a Hispanic female. The curriculum is traditional with an emphasis on "classics," although students have opportunities to participate in education and cultural activities sponsored by various cultural clubs after school. Following is a description of how the school administration handled a racial incident and student reactions to it.

Racial climate became a focus of the school's attention following a fight in the cafeteria started by a white male student who called Jenny, a Chinese American female, "a fucking gook." After Jenny reported the incident, the school's headmaster scheduled a disciplinary hearing for the white male student, as required by district policy.

An ad-hoc group of Asian Pacific American students, including leaders of the school's Chinese and Asian student clubs, quickly formed after the incident to demand that those responsible for racial harassment be severely punished. They also called for a more diverse curriculum and schoolwide training in prejudice awareness and conflict resolution. To press their concerns, many of the school's Asian Pacific American students agreed to walk out of school en masse the next day when the disciplinary hearing was scheduled to take place. A modest multiethnic coalition also formed in solidarity.

The school administration responded immediately by threatening to suspend any student who walked out of school. Not wanting to jeopardize their academic standing, students agreed to cancel the walkout, and, in its place, to meet with the administration as a group. Following the meeting, the school's headmaster expressed surprise at how marginalized the Asian Pacific American students felt from the larger school community. She asserted, "The kids have always worked together. We pride ourselves on having a nurturing atmosphere." . . .

While describing examples of specific [racial] incidents among peers, many students also criticized school officials for denying that racism was a problem. Sunthon, a Lao American senior, stated, "It's totally swept under the rug, it's never discussed. It's a taboo subject and it goes completely unmentioned." Angel agreed, "The teachers did not seem to want to talk about what happened."

Asian Pacific American students were not alone in these views. Bill, a white male sophomore, observed, "The topic of racism is not really ever discussed in classrooms, but Asians get the most mistreatment as far as racism goes." Tonisha, an African American senior, added, "I've been in the school for six years and this is actually the first incident I ever remember being discussed."

The school's elite reputation figured prominently in staff and student discourse about racial conflict. Many were reluctant to report incidents because of not wanting to damage the school's public image. Jenny explained, "They try to create the impression that this kind of stuff doesn't happen at our school because we are an exam school." However, students also expressed disappointment, if not bitterness, with the lack of support they received from the school's faculty and administration. . . .

Through experiences, Asian Pacific American students learned some hard lessons in how dynamics of race, culture, and power affect relationships in a school community. Although they had articulated a thoughtful, comprehensive set of proposals for school improvement that addressed such areas as school climate, the curriculum, faculty/staff hiring, student activities, and disciplinary policies, only one recommendation for a schoolwide diversity awareness orientation was adopted by the administration. Even then, students had to do the legwork of identifying trainers and community resources to make it happen.

Source: Peter Nien-chu Riang (1998), "We Could Shape It." Reprinted by permission from *Struggling to Be Heard: The Unmet Needs of Asian Pacific American Children,* edited by Valerie Ooka Pang and Li-Rong Lilly Cheng, the State University of New York Press © 1998, State University of New York. All rights reserved.

DISCUSSION QUESTIONS

1. What attitudes and behaviors do you think the headmaster and teachers would encourage and/or reinforce in the school? For example, how would the administration's handling of the incident influence the majority students' view of minority students? How might the minority students' image of themselves be affected?

2. How would you account for the disparity between the headmaster's view that "we pride ourselves on having a nurturing atmosphere" and the students' perception that "they try to create the impression that this kind of stuff doesn't happen at our school"? Are there hidden messages the administration is sending to the students? What are they?

3. How would the functionalists, the conflict theorists, the critical theorists, the interpretivists, and the postmodernists assess the impact of what seems to be going on at City Academy?

4. Which of the five theories discussed in this chapter best represents the headmaster's perspective on the role of schooling? Discuss your rationale. Would you suggest that the headmaster change any aspect of her approach? What suggestions would you make and why?

◼   ◼   ◼   ◼

OTHER CASES OF THE HIDDEN CURRICULUM

The teachers were in the lunchroom discussing the introduction of fractions. They were exchanging ideas about how to explain how fractions work and how to demonstrate in several ways how fractions function and appear. One of the teachers said, "Adding and subtracting aren't much of a problem.

Just wait till you have to teach multiplication and division to three Hispanic students you have. Those kids don't know top from bottom, can't memorize their tables, and they'll just bring down your classroom's score." The rest of the teachers proceeded to give examples about how Hispanic children do not understand English, do not speak English, and, as one summarized, "Can't do."

Source: F. I. Ortiz (1988), "Hispanic-American Children's Experiences in Classrooms: A Comparison Between Hispanic and Non-Hispanic Children." Reprinted by permission from *Class, Race, and Gender in American Education,* edited by Lois Weis, the State University of New York Press © 1988, State University of New York. All rights reserved.

DISCUSSION QUESTIONS

1. What stereotypic views of Hispanic children are reflected in the attitudes of the teachers? How might such stereotypic views affect the academic performance of Hispanic children?
2. How might the teachers' stereotypic views influence the self-image of the Hispanic children?
3. If you were the principal of the school described, what could you do to help the teachers change their views of Hispanic and other minority children?
4. According to each of the five theories discussed in this chapter, what role of schooling is reflected in the teachers' attitudes toward the Hispanic children as given in this case?

"When you sing in our school choir, you sing as proud Negro children," boomed the voice of Mrs. Benn, my fifth-grade teacher. "Don't you know that Marian Anderson, a cultured colored woman, is the finest contralto ever? Haven't you ever heard Paul Robeson sing? It can just take your breath away. We are not shiftless and lazy folk. We are hard-working, God-fearing people. You can't sing in this choir unless you want to hold up the good name of our people."

It never occurred to me in those days that African Americans were not a special people. My education both at home and at school reinforced that idea. We were a people who overcame incredible odds. I knew that we were discriminated against but I witnessed too much competence— and excellence—to believe that African Americans didn't have distinctly valuable attributes.

Source: G. Ladson-Billings (1994), *The Dreamkeepers: Successful Teachers of American Children*, pp. 9–12. Copyright 1994. Reprinted with permission of John Wiley & Sons, Inc.

DISCUSSION QUESTIONS

1. In what ways did the implicit or hidden curriculum function for this author to contradict stereotypic views of African American children? What appears to have been Mrs. Benn's ideas about the role of schooling for her students?
2. How might this incident be viewed from the perspective of each of the theories discussed in this chapter?

REFERENCES

Apple, M. W., & Weis, L. (1983). *Ideology and practice in schooling*. Philadelphia: Temple University Press.

Aronowitz, S., & Giroux, H. A. (1981). *Education under siege*. South Hadley, MA: Bergin & Garvey.

Bernstein, B. (1977). Social class, language and socialization. In J. Karabel & A. H. Halsey (Eds.), *Power and ideology in education* (pp. 473–486). New York: Oxford University Press.

Board v. Pico, 457 U.S. 853 (1982).

Bourdieu, P. (1977). Cultural reproduction and social reproduction. In J. Karabel & A. H. Halsey (Eds.), *Power and ideology in education* (pp. 487–510). New York: Oxford University Press.

Bowles, S. (1977). Unequal education and the reproduction of the social division of labor. In J. Karabel & A. H. Halsey (Eds.), *Power and ideology in education*. New York: Oxford University Press.

Bowles, S., & Gintis, H. (1977). IQ in the U.S. class structure. In J. Karabel & A. H. Halsey (Eds.), *Power and ideology in education* (pp. 137–152). New York: Oxford University Press.

Brown v. Board of Education, 347 U.S. 483 (1954).

Cherryholmes, C. H. (1988). *Power and criticism: Poststructural investigations in education*. New York: Teachers College Press.

Collins, R. (1979). *The credentialing society*. New York: Academic Press.

Collins, R. (1985). Functional and conflict theories of educational stratification. In J. H. Ballantine (Ed.), *Schools and society: A reader in education and sociology* (pp. 60–87). Palo Alto, CA: Mayfield.

Counts, G. S. (1932). *Dare the school build a new social order?* New York: John Day. The writings of John Dewey, John Childs, William Heard Kilpatrick, and Harold Rugg in the journal *The Social Frontier,* published in the mid-1930s, represent the early social reconstructionist position.

Derrida, J. (1972). Discussion: Structure, sign and play in the discourse of the human sciences. In R. Macksey and E. Donato (Eds.), *The structuralist controversy* (pp. 247–272). Baltimore: Johns Hopkins Press.

Dreeben, R. (1968). *On what is learned in school*. Reading, MA: Addison-Wesley.

Durkheim, É. (1961). On the learning of discipline. In T. Parsons, E. Shills, K. D. Naegele, & J. R. Pitts (Eds.), *Theories of society* (Vol. 2, pp. 860–865). New York: Free Press of Glencoe.

Durkheim, É. (1985a). Definition of education. In J. H. Ballantine (Ed.), *Schools and society: A reader in education and sociology* (pp. 19–22). Palo Alto, CA: Mayfield.

Durkheim, É. (1985b). Moral education. In J. H. Ballantine (Ed.), *Schools and society: A reader in education and sociology* (pp. 23–29). Palo Alto, CA: Mayfield.

Feinberg, W. (1975). *Reason and rhetoric: The intellectual foundations of 20th century liberal educational policy*. New York: John Wiley.

Foucault, M. (1972). *The archeology of knowledge*. New York: Harper Colophon Books.

Freire, P. (1985). *The politics of education* (D. Macedo, Trans.). South Hadley, MA: Bergin & Garvey.

Freire, P. (1993). *Pedagogy of the oppressed*. London: Penguin Books.

Gang, P. S. (1988). Holistic education for a New Age. *Holistic Education Review 1*(1), 13–17.

Gang, P. S. (1990). Our challenge. *Holistic Education Review 3*(4), 54–56.

Giroux, H. A. (1983). *Theory and resistance in education.* South Hadley, MA: Bergin & Garvey. *Education Under Siege* (1981) by Stanley Aronowitz and Henry A. Giroux and *Critical Pedagogy and Cultural Power* (1987) by David W. Livingstone et al., both published in South Hadley, Massachusetts by Bergin & Garvey, are also useful books in this area.

Giroux, H. A. (1984). Marxism and schooling: The limits of radical discourse. *Educational Theory, 34*(2), 113–136.

Giroux, H. A. (1993). *Border crossings: Cultural workers and the politics of education.* New York: Routledge.

Griffin, D. R. (1992). Introduction to SUNY Series in Constructive Postmodern Thought. In D. W. Orr, *Ecological literacy: Education and the transition to a postmodern world* Albany: SUNY Press.

Habermas, J. (1971). *Towards a rational society: Student protest, science and politics* (J. J. Shapiro, Trans.). London: Heinemann.

Held, D. (1980). *Introduction to critical theory.* London: Hutchinson & Co. This book presents a scholarly discussion of the thoughts of several major figures of the Frankfurt school from Horkheimer to Habermas.

Karabel, J., & Halsey, A. H. (1977). Educational research: A review and an interpretation. In J. Karabel & A. H. Halsey (Eds.), *Power and ideology in education* (pp. 1–85). New York: Oxford University Press.

Katz, M. B. (1971). *Class, bureaucracy, and schools*: *The illusion of educational change in America.* New York: Praeger Publications. For a description and analysis of bureaucracy, see Max Weber's *The Theory of Social and Economic Organization*, edited by Talcott Parsons, published in 1947 by Free Press.

Knapp, M. S., & Woolverton, S. (1995). Social class and schooling. In J. A. Banks & C. A. McGee (Eds.), *Handbook of research on multicultural education.* New York: Simon and Schuster.

Lubbock Civil Liberties Union v. Lubbock Independent School District, 495 U.S. 1155 (1983).

McNeil, L. M. (1986). *Contradictions of control.* New York: Routledge and Kegan Paul.

Miller, J. P. (1993). Worldviews, educational orientations, and holistic education. In R. Miller (Ed.), *The renewal of meaning in education: Responses to the cultural and ecological crisis of our times.* Brandon, VT: Holistic Education Press.

Miller, R. (1997). *What are schools for?* (3rd ed.). Brandon, VT: Holistic Education Press.

Moffett, J. (1994). *The universal school house: Spiritual awakening through education.* San Francisco: Jossey-Bass.

Noddings, N. (1995). *Philosophy of education.* Boulder, CO: Westview Press.

Ortiz, F. I. (1988). Hispanic-American children's experiences in classrooms: A comparison between Hispanic and non-Hispanic children. In L. Weis (Ed.), *Class, race and gender in American education* (pp. 63–86). Albany: State University of New York Press.

Ozmon, H. A., & Craver, S. M. (1999). *Philosophical foundations of education* (6th ed.). Upper Saddle River, NJ: Merrill/Prentice Hall.

Parsons, T. (1985). The school class as a social system: Some of its functions in American society. In J. H. Ballantine (Ed.), *Schools and society: A reader in education and sociology* (pp. 179–197). Palo Alto, CA: Mayfield.

Thompson, J. B., & Held, D. (1982). Editors' introduction. In J. B. Thompson & D. Held (Eds.), *Habermas: Critical debates.* London: The Macmillan Press Ltd.

Wallace v. Jaffre, 472 U.S. 38 (1985).

Weber, M. (1947). *The theory of social and economic organization* (A. M. Henderson & T. Parsons, Trans.; T. Parsons, Ed.). Glencoe, IL: Free Press. See this work for an instructive description and analysis of bureaucracy. For an analysis of bureaucracy in schools, see *Class, Bureaucracy, and Schools: The Illusion of Educational Change in America* by Michael Katz listed earlier in these references.

6

Culture and the Educational Development of the Learner

KEY *Concepts:*

- Age–stage linkage
- Assessment models
- Authentic assessment
- Concepts of childhood
- Culture of childhood

- Educational development
- Ethnicity
- Moral development
- Psychoeducational assessment

Educational development as a process implies changes in the learner's intellectual competencies, social and sensorimotor skills, emotional dispositions, and moral reasoning. Clearly, these changes are influenced by a wide range of biological, social, cultural, and other environmental factors. Current research studies in educational development continue to be predominantly psychological in nature, although the area of cross-cultural psychology has grown since 1980 (Berry, 1997). These research efforts usually lead to psychological theories that give us partial insight into the nature of educational development and, occasionally, useful educational strategies. Educators need to have a broadly based interdisciplinary perspective both in their research and in their practice because education is a value-laden enterprise that always takes place in specific social, cultural, and political contexts. The worth of certain cognitive abilities, social skills, and attitudes is determined within these varied contexts. Not only do developmental processes conform to cultural demands, even the notions of what is developmentally appropriate or optimal are culturally defined (Montemayor, 2000; New, 1993). Accordingly, this chapter is primarily concerned with the centrality of culture in the learner's educational development.

157

EDUCATIONAL DEVELOPMENT
AND PSYCHOLOGICAL ANTHROPOLOGY

Educational Development

From a societal perspective, **educational development** represents the movement of young people toward becoming full-fledged members of society, which implies changes in many different domains of the learner. But as Edwards and Ramsey (1986) point out, "It is not just any type of change; it is change toward greater differentiation, inclusiveness, and powerfulness of ideas. It involves progress toward more advanced or mature forms of reasoning, judgment, and action" (p. 15). Hence, educational development entails growth in cognitive competencies, acquisition of knowledge and social skills, cultivation of certain attitudes, and formation of moral values and attitudes. Also essential is the ability to make sound judgments about moral, social, and intellectual issues and maintain competent interpersonal relationships.

Although there have been numerous empirical findings and theories about educational development, none have attracted more attention from educators than Jean Piaget's theory of cognitive development and Lawrence Kohlberg's moral development theory. Because of their ongoing widespread influence among educators, it is useful to take a look at these theories as a preface to our discussion of the need for psychological anthropology in understanding educational development.

Piaget's Developmental View

Central to Piaget's theory of cognitive development is the premise that learning involves the learner's active participation in relation to objects or to social relationships. Knowledge is not transmitted; rather, it has to be constructed and reconstructed by the individual learner. Hence, learning, the development of intelligence, is a continuous process of assimilating the external facts of experience and integrating them into the individual's internal mental categories, or schemata. Consequently, activity is indispensable to learning. To know something is not merely to be told about it or to see it, but to act upon it.

Now, if learning and knowing involve the structuring and restructuring of what has been acquired, how do they occur? According to Piaget, the processes of biological and cognitive development occur through the organization and adaptation of the organism to the environment. Organization is the tendency of living organisms to integrate experiences and activities into a coherent system. Thus, organization is said to have occurred when a child is able to perform two originally separate acts, such as grasping and looking, at the same time. Adaptation refers to the organism's ability to interact with its surroundings. In human beings, it is this interaction that leads to the development of an increasingly complex mental organization.

For Piaget (1963), cognitive development takes place as children go through four invariant stages, which are innate and fixed for all children in all cultures. While the precise age at which a specific stage emerges varies from child to child according to individual capacities and culture, the order of the stages remains the same. The first of the four stages is the *sensorimotor stage,* in which children learn motor behavior. In general, this first stage develops between birth and two years of age. The *preoperational stage,* wherein children acquire the ability to conceptualize and use language, develops between the ages of about two and seven. Children's ability to apply logical thought to concrete problems manifests itself in the *stage of concrete operations,* which appears between the ages of approximately seven and eleven. The fourth is the *stage of formal operations,* which takes place between the ages of eleven and fifteen. In this stage, children learn to apply logic to problems of all sorts. Each of these stages leads to the emergence of the next one.

Although the order of the developmental stages is fixed and unaffected by culture, the stages are influenced by organic growth, exercise and acquired experience, and social interaction (Piaget & Inhelder, 1969, pp. 154–158). Organic growth refers to maturation of the nervous and endocrine systems. Although this maturation is an essential aspect of cognitive development, the influence of the child's physical and sociocultural environment becomes increasingly more important as the child grows older. Exercise and the experience of acting upon objects is a critically important factor in cognitive development, for neither assimilation nor accommodation can take place unless children interact with their environment.

Social interaction is particularly important in the development of concepts that cannot be developed by the child alone. In other words, children cannot construct abstract concepts such as love, loyalty, and courage by looking at corresponding objects. They must develop them through interaction with other individuals and through an interchange of ideas. For educators, Piaget's view implies that learning requires the child to interact actively with others and with the learning environment. Piaget and his contemporary followers further insist that the most important goal of education is thinking. For this reason, although language in the forms of reading and writing are important, we should not become preoccupied with them at the expense of learning to think. Consequently, children should be helped to grow by constructing their own knowledge and moral standards through their own thinking and judgment.

Kohlberg on Moral Development

Following Piaget's perspective, Lawrence Kohlberg studied how people reason in dealing with their moral conflicts. Like Piaget, he found that moral development occurs in an invariant or unchanging sequence. Moreover, although the rate of development may vary among individuals, stages are universal and unaffected by social or cultural conditions. According to Kohlberg (1971, 1984), **moral development** proceeds in six stages. The first stage, *punishment and obedience,* occurs around the age of seven. In this stage, "right" conduct is viewed as obedience to authority and avoidance of punishment. In the *instrumental-relativist stage,* which develops between ages seven and ten, right action consists of acting to achieve one's own goals while recognizing the interests of others. Children between the ages of ten and thirteen are found in the *good boy–nice girl stage.* This is the third stage, in which right conduct involves having good intentions and acting according to socially defined roles. In the fourth, the *law and order stage,* meeting one's responsibilities and contractual obligations for the good of the whole constitutes the morally right deed. This stage begins between the ages of thirteen and sixteen. In stages five and six, which emerge after the age of sixteen, the individual makes moral choices based on a *social contract* (the legalistic orientation) and a *universal ethical principle,* respectively. In both of these stages, right conduct is thought of as following a set of consciously chosen principles. These principles may be rooted in legalistic or philosophical concepts of virtue and justice.

These six stages of moral development do not tell us which specific moral beliefs people have in various stages. Rather, they represent how individuals in different developmental stages reason to resolve their moral dilemmas. From Kohlberg's perspective, the educator should encourage the learner to think through conflicting moral situations by presenting realistic ethical issues rather than imparting ready-made solutions. However, learners should not be expected to reason at a level beyond their developmental stage. For example, a child who is at the good boy–nice girl stage ought not be asked to deal with moral issues in terms of abstract and universal principles of justice and morality.

Table 6.1 shows the relationship between Piaget's and Kohlberg's theories.

Discontinuity and Culture in the Developmental Process

The theories of Piaget and Kohlberg are based on two fundamental assumptions: (1) the belief that the developmental process occurs through continuous transformation of earlier stages and (2) the notion that these stages are invariant

TABLE 6.1
Relationship Between Cognitive and Moral Development Theories

Stages/Ages	
Piaget's Theory	**Kohlberg's Theory**
Sensorimotor (0–2)	
Preoperational (2–7)	Punishment and obedience (7)
Concrete operational (7–11)	Instrumental-relativist (7–10) Good boy–nice girl (10–13)
Formal operational (11–15)	Law and order (13–16) Social contract (16+) Universal ethical principle

because the process of development is fundamentally biological and genetic in nature. In other words, although the contents of each developmental stage may be culturally bound and unique to each individual, the order of the stages is the same for everyone and is unaffected by culture. Other theorists—such as Jerome Bruner, Jerome Kagan, and Kieran Egan—dispute these assumptions; their observation and empirical evidence indicate that both cognitive and moral development often occur in spurts or sudden appearances of certain skills or orientations and that these phases are not invariant. This would mean that individuals in different cultures may not go through the same set and sequence of developmental stages. Increasingly these theories have faced criticism because they minimize the influence of sociocultural factors (Eckensberger & Zimba, 1997; Schunk, 2004).

Even those who concur with Piaget's perspective often use the terms *skills, skill levels,* and *tiers* in referring to Piaget's stages. For example, William Damon (1983) found that children not only performed certain cognitive tasks at inconsistent levels, but they often regressed in their developmental levels in understanding concepts. To put it differently, children who can think abstractly think in concrete terms only in some areas. Kurt Fischer (1980), another Piagetian psychologist, discovered that cognitive development proceeds unevenly and that children almost never perform at the same skill level in all areas. Abstract thinkers do not always use their abstract thinking skills evenly in all subject areas. In the area of moral reasoning, the findings of Damon and Fischer imply that individuals who can think about ethical issues according to universal principles may deal with some moral dilemmas in terms only of rewards and punishments.

According to Jerome Kagan (1984), a Harvard psychologist, Western views on human development as a continuous process are based on the assumptions that (1) "each child must step on every link . . . as he or she journeys into maturity" and that (2) a particular adult personality is a necessary product of the past (p. 110). These two beliefs suggest that by looking at an infant, we can get a glimpse of what he or she is going to be like in the future. Kagan argues that grounds that challenge these claims are found both in biology and psychology (p. 111). For example, in the growth of the fetal nervous system, the cells surrounding the future spinal cord move around to various locations in the embryo. Certain cells become part of the heart, the eyes, and the intestine; others end up serving still other organs. Once the cells become part of various organs, they are no longer changeable. Whether a particular cell becomes a part of the eye or the heart has to do with what the cell encounters or where it ends up rather than the unfolding of some innate capacity to become this or that organ. Similarly, in the development of an individual, there are many points at which the person can move in one of many possible directions. The effects of each "choice" or event modify the individual's future. These choices and events can range from traumatic events at birth to the choice of academic majors and occupational fields. According to Kagan, "Once a choice is made, the child will resist being detracted from the path" (p. 111).

Though each individual has been genetically programmed in very broad terms, the specific ways in which such programs become manifested are closely related to what the person encounters in various developmental phases and what special demands those phases make of the individual. As Kagan (1984) writes, "Hence, some of the past is inhibited or discarded. The new pattern may contain none of the elements of the earlier," except some functionally similar competencies (p. 91). Kagan is not insisting that there are no elements of continuity in human development; he is suggesting that major changes in people's cognitive skills, social behavior, and emotional dispositions occur in response to certain life situations and cultural conditions that require special competencies. He is further pointing out that every change in human behavior or attitude does not always contain every part of the earlier developmental phases.

In support of his position, Kagan refers to Paul Bates of the Max Planck Institute in West Berlin (Kagan, 1984, pp. 91–92). According to Bates, both early and later aspects of our development are influenced not only by genetically programmed changes in our central nervous systems but also by a host of other environmental conditions. Such conditions include our society's cultural norms, new inventions ranging from computers to video games, major historical events such as wars and economic depressions, and natural catastrophes like major floods and earthquakes, as well as such other unexpected events as divorce, illness, and accidents. Events like the *Challenger* explosion and the September 11th terrorist attacks are profound public examples of the conditions that can influence growth. These circumstances in our journey toward maturity demand special skills and attitudes; as a result, new competencies may appear and some old abilities and attitudes may disappear abruptly. As Kieran Egan (1979) suggests, educational development "goes by fits and starts, by stages which involve quite sudden shifts of focus and kinds of understanding" (p. 103).

The view that the developmental process is characterized by both continuity and "fits and starts" implies that the special demands of each person's unique social relationships and cultural environments play a key role in influencing how and in which direction that individual will grow. Robert Coles has worked with children and written a series of books that give us a glimpse of these intersections of culture, contexts, and growth. In *The Moral Life of Children* (1986) and *The Moral Intelligence of Children* (1997), he describes how powerful social events contribute to children's moral thinking. This perspective is consistent with Bruner and Haste's (1987) position that the child is a social being who "acquires a framework for interpreting experience, and learns how to negotiate meaning in a manner congruent with the requirements of the culture" (p. 1). Studies in social psychology (Moscovici, 1984; Tajfel, 1981; Williams & Giles, 1978) indicate that children grow intellectually, socially, and morally by giving meanings to personal experiences through the use of the language and culture that represent the world in which they live. Even Damon (1981), a Piagetian psychologist, points out that children do not acquire their knowledge in social isolation. Rather, they "co-construct" their knowledge with others through innumerable social exchanges and the social context in which all knowledge is presented and created.

According to Haste (1987), a dynamic relationship exists between the individual's development and the norms reflected in the folkways and mores of their particular culture (p. 188). Hence, concept development depends on the resources available within the culture, because "it is difficult, if not impossible for a child to develop a concept that does not have an expression within her culture of origin" (Bruner & Haste, 1987, p. 6). A child develops by finding appropriate ways of acting and thinking in various situations through negotiations (transactions) with others. "Culture and individual development are mutually embedded" (Bowman & Stott, 1993, p. 125). This means that "it can never be the case that there is a 'self' independent of one's cultural-historical existence" (Bruner, 1987, p. 91). From this perspective, the Piagetian theory is inadequate because, although it describes how children's ability to reason changes, it is silent on the ways in which cultural factors affect the developmental process.

Charles Harrington (1979), a leading psychological anthropologist, suggests that the very method of conducting cross-cultural studies of Piaget's theory precludes the possibility of discovering what differences might exist in the developmental processes of culturally different children (pp. 28–30). According to Harrington, transcultural research on Piaget's theory is done by translating the standard tasks associated with Piaget's fixed developmental stages into a foreign language and administering them to children of various ages. A typical finding of such studies is that although the stages are validated, the unoriginal group is found to be "slower" (p. 29). A 1997 review of cross-cultural research (Mishra, 1997, pp. 150–153) shows that this bias continues to exist and that researchers themselves "argue that cross-cultural testing of their propositions is a major task that requires immediate attention" (p. 153). Because these studies are based on the assumption that the developmental stages are fixed regardless of culture, no amount of research could show whether the stages vary in different cultures. Unfair and distorted judgments about educability, intelligence, and learning achievements result from psychological and educational practices based on the belief that the development of all children, regardless of their social and cultural backgrounds, follows invariant stages.

Carol Gilligan (1982; Gilligan, Lyons, & Hanmer, 1990) at Harvard University has called into question the universality of Kohlberg's stages. She and her colleagues argue that women generally think differently from men about moral issues. In Kohlberg's work, morality is defined as justice, and higher-level reasoning involves the resolution of moral dilemmas through an objective consideration of abstract principles of justice. Contractual rules and individual rights are key concepts in the development of higher levels of moral reasoning. Nel Noddings, an educational philosopher whose work builds on Gilligan's, is strident in her characterization of Kohlberg's work. "Proponents of caring do not regard the lack of universality as a weakness. On the contrary, many of us feel that insistence on universal models is a form of cultural arrogance" (2002, p. 22). Gilligan and Noddings propose another way of viewing moral dilemmas, which they term the *ethic of care*. Gilligan's studies suggest that women are more likely to conceive of moral dilemmas in terms of human relationships and connections. In this model, higher-level moral reasoning involves the responsibility to care for others and for oneself. The resolution of moral dilemmas comes not from stepping back and objectively applying abstract principles but from "stepping into . . . the situation and by acting to restore relationships or to address needs, including those of one-self" (Gilligan, Lyons, & Hanmer, 1990, p. 42).

The ethic of care is characterized by an acknowledgement of the reciprocal relationship between the *cared for* and the *carer*. The context of each is taken into account in deciding on a course of action. Rather than a series of prescribed stages around which character education programs are built, the ethic of care addresses the contexts and process of being human (Noddings, 1992, p. 22). As such, the ethic of care is a process-oriented model characterized by the components of modeling, dialogue, practice, and confirmation (Noddings, 1984, 1992, 2002).

THE NEED FOR PSYCHOLOGICAL ANTHROPOLOGY

Historically, much of the research on teaching, learning, and educational development has been psychological in nature. This is unfortunate, because preoccupation with the psychological aspects of education gives a one-sided view of how people learn, teach, and grow educationally. This approach ignores the fact that teaching and learning occur in intentional environments in which culturally created meanings and resources are seized and shared (Shweder, 1991, p. 74). As has already been suggested in earlier chapters, the psychological processes underlying human behavior and learning may be essentially the same. However, the specific ways in which these processes manifest themselves are culture bound. For example, human beings tend to avoid situations in which they are punished, but they tend to repeat those behaviors for which they are rewarded. However, the meanings of reward and punishment are culture specific. For this reason, "yelling" at the child is likely to have a much more punitive or aversive meaning to white middle-class children than to Asian youngsters, who are relatively more accustomed to being "yelled at" by their parents while growing up. Because education and schooling always occur in a specific sociocultural context, developing effective instruction must take into account the profound influence culture has on how people learn, teach, and develop. As Bruner suggests, the classroom should be seen as a community of mutual learners in which "children find out what the culture is about and how it conceives of the world" through interaction with each other and the teacher (Bruner, 1996, pp. 20–21). For this reason, the field of psychological anthropology is particularly pertinent in education. But what is psychological anthropology?

According to Francis Hsu (1972), an authority in the field, **psychological anthropology** "deals with human behavior primarily in terms of ideas which form the basis of the interrelationship between the individual and his society" (p. 6).[1] This discipline is also concerned with the characteristics of societies and the ways in which they relate to the wishes, fears, and values of a majority of the individuals of these societies. After all, human functioning in a sociocultural setting is shaped by "culturally devised ways of thinking, searching, [and] planning (Bruner, 1996, p. 169). This means that the so-called culture-free notions of pure thought, pure memory, and perception become fictions (p. 168). For this reason, psychological anthropology is interested in understanding how the norms of a society influence the relationships among its members as well as the manner in which the societal norms and structure affect the hopes, fears, and attitudes of its people. Thus, psychological anthropology not only considers human beings as a source of culture; it also views culture as having a cause–effect relationship with personality. The Society for Psychological Anthropology publishes a professional journal, *Ethos*, with research that provides insights into this intersection and the ways in which youth are "active cultural agents within their social milieus" (Csordas, 2003, p. 358). When we consider that education is the process by which individuals become members of a society through learning its culture, the relevance of psychological anthropology in education should be evident.

A key area of study in psychological anthropology is the development of personality in culture, which directly leads to inquiries about how people acquire their attitudes, values, and behavior patterns. Thus, an examination of the learning process itself, which necessarily raises questions about perception and cognition, becomes a central concern. It is nearly impossible to understand how people learn without knowing how they perceive "things" or what meanings they give to their perceptual experiences and how these experiences in turn affect their styles of thinking. Culture plays a crucial role in determining the meanings that people assign to their experiences, the contents of what is learned, and the way learning occurs. Broadly speaking, teaching is nothing more than the facilitation of learning, and learning is at the heart of education. Thus, reliable knowledge about learning, perception, and cognition and the roles of ethnic, language, and value differences in these processes would be very useful in developing strategies to enable children to learn more effectively. Our discussion will focus on some general findings regarding ethnicity and schooling, which may help us avoid certain pitfalls in working with a culturally diverse school population.

There is no disagreement that our schools are attended by a culturally diverse population. Nor is there any dispute regarding the projection that the number of culturally and racially different children in our schools continues to become significantly larger. As Montemayor (2000) writes, "By the year 2050, when most of today's adolescents will be grandparents, the population of the United States is projected to be about 53% white, 25% Hispanic, 14% Black,

---

[1]See Bruner (1996), Harrington (1979), Shweder (1991), Spindler (1978), and Triandis and Heron (1981), for additional discussion of the aims of psychological anthropology.

8% Asian, and 1% American Indian" (p. 1). Yet there is little consensus regarding how the concept of ethnicity should be understood and used. More often than not, a muddled understanding of ethnicity is at the heart of the failure of school personnel to assess and meet the needs of their students. Ethnicity stands for a complex of characteristics that belong to groups of people. Hence, research findings regarding ethnicity are important because the defining characteristics of the concept must relate to those common traits found among various ethnic groups.

Ethnicity is not a single trait or a rigid category. Rather, it is a complex of interrelated factors such as nationality, language, cultural tradition and values, racial characteristics (e.g., skin color), religion, socioeconomic status, and educational level. Individuals usually define their ethnicity on the basis of some combination of these factors that they share with others in the same group. Studies indicate that these factors influence teachers' images, expectations, and evaluations of students from different ethnic groups (Harrington, 1979, pp. 67–86; Levine & Levine, 1996, pp. 296–351). To meet the needs of all learners, we need to understand how each child deals with his or her own ethnicity as well as the ethnicity of others. We should also be aware of possible conflicts among the values of various ethnic groups and the norms of the dominant culture according to which the school operates.

Specific knowledge about ethnic groups and their relationship with each other and with the mainstream society has to be acquired through studying individual groups. Nevertheless, school personnel must exercise some general cautions in dealing with young people's ethnicity. Although individuals identify with a particular ethnic group on the basis of a combination of factors associated with ethnicity, schools usually categorize minority students into four general groups: African Americans, Hispanics, Native Americans, and Asians. The criteria by which students are placed in one of the four categories are neither clear nor consistent. The common belief is that the members of each group share common cultural, linguistic, and racial characteristics and needs. Indeed, not all African Americans come from the same socioeconomic backgrounds, nor do they have the same educational level or a common religion. Hispanics as a group consist of even more diverse groups with divergent legal, economic, and social status. For example, those from Puerto Rico, the Dominican Republic, Mexico, and Cuba may speak Spanish. But all Puerto Ricans are American citizens, whereas Hispanics from the Dominican Republic, Mexico, and Cuba may be recent immigrants or illegal or undocumented aliens. Parents of Puerto Rican children may be more likely to participate in school functions than others, if for no other reason than that of their legal status in this country. The Native American group too consists of individuals from diverse cultural, linguistic, and religious heritages related in part to their tribal affiliation. Asian Americans as a group include those who came from China, India, Japan, Korea, the Philippines, and several Southeast Asian countries. Like the Hispanics, Asian Americans also have greatly varying kinds of legal status, sociocultural history, educational backgrounds, language patterns, and economic achievements.

Although there are wide variations in the backgrounds of individuals even in a single ethnic group, evidence suggests that school personnel make erroneous conclusions about their students—conclusions based on a single or very limited number of factors (Gollnick & Chinn, 1998; Harrington, 1979; Levine & Levine, 1996; Nieto, 2004). For example, teachers tend to assume that youngsters who speak a nonstandard dialect are intellectually inferior, and children with light skin color are treated more favorably than those with darker skin. There is also an indication that children of highly educated parents tend to receive special attention from teachers and other school personnel. In a different vein, one of the authors recalls a case of a U.S.-born Asian American child who received a D on a well-written essay. When the child's father pressed the teacher to explain the grade, the teacher responded, "I thought that someone else had written the paper for her because, being an Asian, I assumed that she would naturally have problems in writing an English essay."

In yet another instance, a teacher who had spent part of her summer taking a Spanish immersion class would walk to the back of her elementary school classroom to repeat directions for a class activity in Spanish to a young student who never spoke up in class. Because of the student's last name, the teacher assumed that the quiet student was Hispanic. During a parent conference, however, she found out that the child was painfully shy, that she was Navajo, and that she spoke English.

There are two primary purposes for citing these examples. One is to stress the view that a person's ethnicity consists of several factors and that the individual's own perception of his or her ethnicity should play a part in placing the person in a particular group. This point is particularly important because how we use the concept of ethnicity, as well as our image of ethnic groups, influences the ways in which we work with and evaluate ethnic children. The second purpose is to point out the need for our school personnel to learn about the cultural values of different ethnic groups and the manners in which these values influence the children's performance in school. Not all cultural or ethnic groups have the same view of education, schooling, or learning. Thus, it is essential for educators to know how or at what point the values held by the various ethnic groups may come into conflict with school goals. With this knowledge, teachers can help students from various ethnic groups to apply these values appropriately according to different cultural contexts. For example, schools reward students for individual competence, achievements, and involvement. On the other hand, Navajos are said to prize group harmony and hence conformity to the group norm. In this situation, a school's staff can help a Navajo child to learn to function differently in school and in the Navajo community while at the same time the school works to broaden its own notions of achievement and participation.

The wide gap between the school's view of extracurricular activity and that of Asian American parents is another example of how two different views of education can conflict with each other. In general, school personnel see schooling as a process of developing the whole person. Hence, nonacademic school activities are considered an important part of the child's education. However, Asian American parents tend to view schooling as the process of training the child's intellect only and, consequently, they regard nonacademic activities as distractions. Teachers may be able to persuade these parents to encourage their children's involvement in school activities by discussing with them the notion of school as a microcosm of the larger society wherein children learn to live and grow socially, intellectually, and emotionally.

To help culturally different young people learn more effectively, we must be aware of the cultural and value differences among various ethnic groups and the school. Further, teachers and administrators need to have specific information about those cultural and linguistic variables that are likely to affect the teaching–learning processes. But such specific data are difficult to obtain without some systematic study of and experience with different cultural groups. This suggests that teacher education and in-service programs should include how divergent value systems, child-rearing practices, thinking styles, and patterns of communication influence children's learning patterns. In addition, schools need to (1) increase the diversity of educational environments so that children can find an environment in which they function more effectively, (2) nurture the legitimacy of multiple educational outcomes that foster cultural diversity without reinforcing discrimination based on social class, and (3) develop the kinds of curricula that incorporate the examination of what goes on in school as part of a larger context, such as children's lives, the larger society, and so on (Harrington, 1979, p. 100). For Charles Harrington, these "programs" reflect some of the pressing concerns of psychological anthropology in education.

Finally, much of this discussion about ethnicity has been centered on non-white ethnic groups. However, ethnicity is no less important in the lives of such cultural groups as the Irish, the Poles, the Italians, and the Jews. Divergent patterns in social norms, linguistic forms, and cognitive and communication styles, as well as approaches to learning, are found among members of both the dominant and ethnic minority groups. As educators, we should not categorize individuals into certain ethnic or cultural groups on the basis of one or two characteristics they possess. Rigid and stereotypic labeling of the learner is likely to result in an unfair assessment of his or her educability, which in turn may limit the child's social and intellectual growth.

Rather than becoming preoccupied with categorizing children into various cultural, ethnic, age, or gender groups, we should be concerned with how each learner's unique social, linguistic, and attitudinal patterns influence educational development. For example, we need to determine the extent to which the child's use of a nonstandard English dialect or bilingualism may influence academic performance. We must also examine how the learner's docility and conformist attitude based on respect for authority may affect the teacher–pupil relationship. Whether these abilities and attitudes become assets or liabilities for the child depends on the nature of his or her goals and the contexts in which they are to be achieved. One's unwillingness to express personal opinions and feelings or to assert one's rights may even be a virtue in certain ethnic or cultural environments, but these same attitudes can become liabilities in many academic and social situations in the larger society. A central responsibility of educators is to help learners achieve their goals by utilizing appropriate knowledge, skills, and attitudes in divergent social and cultural environments.

How we use our knowledge of the learner's needs, aspirations, and sociocultural background in facilitating the child's educational development depends on our conception of the nature of childhood. That is, if we regard children as little adults with immature judgments, we may view their needs and aspirations as childish or foolish desires to be suppressed. On the other hand, if children are considered individuals traveling through a natural and necessary phase of their life process, their wishes and future goals may be thought of as legitimate and important aspects of their development. In this sense, childhood is no more an abnormal state than adulthood. In a very real sense, all educational models, theories, and practices are based on either implicit or explicit beliefs about the child (Cleverley & Phillips, 1986). The following sections will examine today's conceptions of the nature of childhood and the educational implications of those conceptions. For this discussion, the terms *childhood* and *youth* will be used interchangeably to refer to the phase of life from birth to late adolescence.

CONCEPTS OF CHILDHOOD AND EDUCATIONAL DEVELOPMENT

Early Concepts of Childhood

Concepts of childhood are formulated by societies at various times and in different contexts. Hence, the meanings of the nature of childhood vary from one historical period to another and from culture to culture (Super & Harkness, 1997). Historically, the idea of childhood as a state distinct from adulthood did not always exist in most parts of the world. In the medieval Western world, children participated in the work and play of adults as soon as they were able to live without the help of an adult. Hence, children were viewed as miniature adults who, by the age of seven, became participating members of adult society (Packard, 1983, p. xv; Suransky, 1982, p. 6). The recognition that infancy was an early stage of life was implicit in this perspective. However, no clear distinctions were made between childhood and adulthood, for children and adults shared common types of work, games, and even clothes.

An interesting contrast to the Western images of children is the conception of children found in many Eastern cultures, which have been heavily influenced by the Confucian ideal of filial piety. In these cultures, children are not only taken for granted, but their importance is minimized (Hsu, 1981, pp. 80–84). In the parent–child relationship, parents are more concerned about what children can do for them than what they can do for their children. Consequently, although parents may be amused by childlike behaviors and attitudes, their children's worth is based on the extent to which they conform to adult norms.

The concept of childhood as a distinct state did not appear until the seventeenth century. Even then the idea of childhood as a period requiring prolonged training and preparation for adult life was associated only with the children of the nobility (Suransky, 1982, p. 7). Childhood as a separate state did not apply to working-class children. In this way, the concept of childhood became a phenomenon linked with a social class. In the late seventeenth century, games and play for adults and nobility were delineated from those of children and the poor. This is how "the lower classes were infantilized, and the concept of childhood became linked to subservience and dependency" (Suransky, 1982, p. 7). Unlike in the preceding eras, childhood was seen as something separate from adulthood in nineteenth-century America. During this period, children were viewed as having economic value not only because they represented an important source of the labor force but also because they were useful in the household division of labor. But with the recognition of childhood as a distinct state and the rise of schooling came a growing trend toward the separation of children from adults (Packard, 1983, p. xviii).

Contemporary Concepts of Childhood

Children as Victims

In the United States, child labor laws and compulsory education introduced in the early twentieth century to protect children from economic exploitation gradually led to the transformation of the conception of American children from economically useful to economically useless but emotionally priceless (Zelizer, 1985). Children are to be kept off the labor market and the streets. Frequent reports in today's mass media of physical, sexual, and emotional abuse of children and public policies protecting children from abuse seem to support the image that children are indeed victimized by their elders. In *Pricing the Priceless Child,* Viviana A. Zelizer (1985) argues that American children became objects of sentimentalization regardless of social class. And "the new sacred child occupied a special and separate world, regulated by affection and education, not work or profit" (p. 216). In this way, the United States is considered a uniquely child-centered society. Yet, as Suransky (1982) insists, we separated childhood from adulthood so completely that we have failed to recognize the significance of our children's contribution to the "cultural forms of everyday life" (p. 8). Children are seen neither as meaningful participants in their society nor as possible contributors to certain human problems. We do not see children as thinkers and doers. Rather, we consider them sheltered and victimized members of society who are immature, incompetent, and manipulable for their own good (Boulding, 1979).

Children as Adults

According to Postman (1981), in the United States we have returned to the pre-seventeenth-century notion of the child as a miniature adult by "adultifying" children (p. 174). Children have been prematurely pushed into adulthood by merging their taste and style with those of adults in almost every aspect of their life. Postman insists that children's interests, language, dress, and sexuality as portrayed in television shows, TV commercials, and movies do not differ significantly from those of adults (pp. 120–125). Even in the areas of alcoholism, substance abuse, sexual activity, and crime, distinctions between childhood and adulthood become less and less clear.

The fading differentiation between childhood and adulthood is aggravated by the fact that adulthood is often represented by "childified" or childlike adults. For example, consider the childlike traits of the main characters in such popular television shows as *The Simpsons, Malcolm in the Middle,* and *Will and Grace.* For Postman, the rapidly fading distinction between childhood and adulthood—the disappearance of childhood—made the compulsory nature of schooling seem arbitrary by the early 1980s (p. 140). Because they were already adults, there was nothing left for the children in school to become. For this reason, educators became uncertain about what to do with schoolchildren, and they were willing to accept "education for the entry into the marketplace" (p. 140). This meant that learning history, literature, and art became less and less worthwhile.

Notwithstanding Postman's (1981) discouraging view, he does think that two social institutions—the school and the family—can stem the tide of disappearing childhood. He points out that the school can help maintain the distinction between childhood and adulthood by teaching children to be literate and allowing them to grow as children. But this task is difficult for the school to accomplish because it tends to reflect the social trends rather than direct them.

The family, like the school, exists and functions in a particular cultural context. Hence, it is doubtful that the family as one institution can resist "the spirit of the age" any more than the school can, for it too reflects the social trends more than directs them. But Postman is correct in observing that children are being rushed into adulthood, and the nature of childhood as we understood it in previous eras has declined, if not disappeared. If Postman is correct, or at least on the right track, the current trend in adultification of children will lead to a distorted view of childhood and unfair judgment of our children's capabilities and contributions to the larger society. There is little doubt that this view of childhood will impede children's educational development. Even if Postman's view is not sound in any definitive sense, his perspective gives educators important caveats in helping children grow as children on their way to becoming adults.

Children as Undeveloped Adults

The conceptions of childhood discussed thus far have all been descriptions of the nature of childhood derived from the experiences and observations of adults. As Montagu (1981) insists, these images of childhood are preconceptions of what adults believe the nature of childhood ought to be (p. 121). From such a biased point of view, adults are bound to fail in what the child is trying to become, "to develop not as an adult, but as a child—in other words, to realize the promise of the child" (p. 121). Thus, if we are to understand the meaning of childhood and its significance for educational development, we need to gain insight into the child's experiences as he or she views them. Although we cannot see the world as a child might interpret it, we could infer the child's-eye view of the world from children's own reports of their experiences and studies of child-rearing practices and socialization of the young. The *culture of childhood* is an expression used by Mary Ellen Goodman (1970), an anthropologist and the author of *The Culture of Childhood*, to get at the child's-eye view of children's experiences (p. 2; Suransky, 1982, pp. 27–28).

According to Goodman, the image of childhood held by American adults differs radically from children's view of themselves in that the former is based on two mistaken assumptions. She finds that these assumptions underlie American pedagogy and child-rearing practices (pp. 2–3). One is the fallacy of universal **age–stage linkage** and the other is the underestimation fallacy. The first is reflected in the belief that adolescence anywhere at any time is necessarily a period of storm, stress, and confusion. Hence, adults characterize adolescent behavior as confused whenever it deviates from the adult norm. The second assumption suggests that children and adolescents are incapable of appreciating interpersonal relations and unable to cope with their frustrations, tensions, and problems. Hence, when the child does not behave according to the demands of adults, he or she is thought to have symptoms of behavioral or emotional problems. Consequently, children and adolescents are thought of primarily in terms of incapacities and inabilities. Patricia Hersch calls adolescents "a tribe apart" (1998), because in her three years of work with young adolescents she found that adults' "piecemeal attempts to mend, motivate, or rescue them obscure the larger reality: we don't *know* them" (p. 14).

Because the notion of age–stage linkage and the underestimation fallacy are so widely held by adults, the behavior and value patterns of the young are often described as senseless, irrational, confused, irresponsible, and insensitive. For this reason, "children and adolescents are usually treated with a kind of amiable tolerance; little is expected of them in the way of learning, control or responsibility" (Goodman, 1970, p. 11). In other words, the behavior and belief systems of children and adolescents are not seen as a functionally viable means of coping with their problems. Adults in our society have rejected the notion of the culture of childhood and adolescence just as the mainstream culture has rejected minority and ethnic patterns as different but legitimate means of dealing with problems of living.

In a similar vein, Ashley Montagu (1981) points out that the belief in "stages" is educationally damaging because stages are generally correlated with chronological age, which is then considered an indicator of a specific developmental stage in which the child is expected to function in a particular way (p. 125). The fact that every child has his or her own rate of development is likely to be ignored because the age–stage linkage leads us to believe that children of the same age are at the same stage of development in all respects. Montagu warns that it is unreasonable and destructive to expect a child to do equally well in all areas of growth because the rates of developing aptitudes and learning different subjects and skills vary significantly.

What is implicit in the views of Goodman and Montagu is that what the young can accomplish in the areas of cognitive, social, and even motor skills is determined not only by maturation and training but also by the level of culturally patterned expectations. The lower the expectation, the less the achievement. For example, in our society we have minimal expectations with respect to the kinds of social responsibilities and cognitive skills the young are to achieve. Consequently, if children or adolescents lack "social grace" in relating to older people, they are usually excused because adults believe that "kids are kids and they can't be expected to behave and talk properly."

The fact that children and adolescents in other societies work and behave at a much more sophisticated level is due largely to the high level of culturally patterned expectations. For example, in a three-year study of 564 Korean American early adolescents and adolescents (in grades five through twelve), the youth attributed their high aspiration and achievement in academic performance to the high level of their parents' expectations (Pai & Pemberton, 1987). The study participants also viewed their parents' expectations as unreasonably high. In the area of "what I want in life," more than 79 percent of those studied reported that "doing well in school" is "very important" to "at the top of the list" (p. 63). In comparing these Korean American youth with their counterparts in a similar study of 7,000 early adolescents conducted by the Search Institute, more than 70 percent of the Korean American youth and 56 percent of the Search group indicated that they worry "quite a bit" to "very much" about school performance (Search Institute, 1984). Although we cannot discern a clear cause–effect relationship between the levels of parental expectations and young people's academic performances, they do give us useful clues regarding the cultural conditions that are closely related to culturally established expectations and young people's performance levels.

In "Cultural Influences Shaping the Role of the Child," Solon Kimball (1974) argues that American adults place their children in a difficult and confusing world. On the one hand, they expect little from their children. But on the other hand, they evaluate them according to the adult norm. More specifically, the grown-ups in the United States expect their children to have a strong commitment to change and to desire constant progress and improvement (pp. 91–92). They are expected to seek to achieve goals higher than what they have already accomplished. In addition to committing themselves to constant improvement and self-fulfillment, they are also required to assume a posture of perpetual optimism (pp. 92–93). Our culture demands that they maintain this euphoric façade. These three criteria of evaluation coupled with our underestimation of children's ability to deal with their problems present young Americans with an unresolvable dilemma, because although they are not expected to act like adults, they are judged according to adult standards.

Valerie Polakow (1992) argues that childhood has been eroded by the imposition of adult agendas and rigid planning on the lives of children. In the absence of national social policies for working mothers, families find themselves increasingly relying on institutional childcare. In a study of childcare centers all over the country, Polakow found that children in general experienced a dulling of curiosity and the regulation of imagination and exploration:

> In short I saw the fostering of a leveled landscape of compliance and the bureaucratization of young children's experiences. Stripped of the power to play and invent, children were denied the opportunity to become meaning makers in their own small worlds. (p. 203)

Blurred Childhood: A Postmodern Dilemma

Postmodern thinkers point out that in the late twentieth century the traditional notion of childhood as a time of innocence and adult dependency has been broken down by children's access to the adult world through electronic media (Steinberg & Kincheloe, 1997, pp. 16–17). Thus, while the contemporary adults may continue to believe that they can protect and guide the lives of their children, reality of the postmodern times makes them encounter a bewildering dilemma. With an incredibly rapid development of technology and equally fast growth of electronic media and related products, children learn about the world not only from what schools present but also from such sources as video and computer games, e-mail, chat rooms, websites, television, and movies. According to Kincheloe (1997), parents and teachers find that they are no longer able to control or regulate the kinds of information their children obtain from electronic media and popular culture:

> As postmodern children gain unrestricted knowledge about things once kept secret from non adults, the mystique of adults as revered keepers of secrets about the world begins to disintegrate. No longer do the elders know more than children about the experience of youth, given social/technological changes (video games, computer, TV programs, etc.). They often know less. (p. 46)

The postmodern condition blurs clear distinctions between information and entertainment and does away with boundaries between adulthood and childhood so that a clearly defined notion of childhood becomes "an object of nostalgia—a sure sign that it no longer exists in any unproblematic form" (Lipsky & Abrams, 1994). Children are no longer seen as dependent or incapable, for they now know what only grown-ups used to know. Many of them are often experienced in sex, drugs, and alcohol. In short, as seen in the movies *Home Alone I* and *Home Alone II*, they are "kids-with-adult-knowledge" (Steinberg & Kincheloe, 1997, p. 16) with power who may become a threat to adults. This phenomenon makes the relationship between adults and children ambivalent because it impairs the adults' ability to influence the values and worldviews of their children. Children become "adultified" and adults become "childified" (Best & Kellner, 1991).

In postmodern times, a great deal of children's knowledge of the world comes from artificially created electronic media and products of popular culture. This means that children's view of reality is heavily influenced not by knowledge and real-life experiences but rather by what corporate America produces for profit, including today's glut of reality television shows, which purport to put reality on a public stage. Given the nature of and the ways in which information and entertainment are passed on to the young, we can no longer assume that what children learn can be presented in a sequentially ordered manner. Nor should schools be viewed as institutions for delivering information only. Rather, schools should be places "where meaning is made, where understanding and interpretation are engendered" (Steinberg & Kincheloe, 1997, p. 18). Further, the curriculum should not be viewed only in terms of what is developmentally appropriate but should take into account the children's experiences in their lived world (Lipsky & Abrams, 1994).

Few of us would disagree that Americans are preoccupied with and anxious about their children and uncertain about how to deal with them. Thus, on the one hand, we claim to respect the rights and dignity of the young as intrinsically worthwhile, but on the other hand, we evaluate them according to the criteria used for adult members of the society. Despite the postmodern phenomenon of the blurred distinctions between adulthood and childhood, it would appear that adults continue to assume that children's behavior and belief patterns are deficit forms of adult norms (Burman, 1994; Morss, 1990; Rogers & Rogers, 1992). Children are regarded "as either deficient (and hence in need of education); delinquent (and hence in need of control); or dysfunctional (and hence in need of therapy) (Griffin, 1993). From this kind of deficit view, children are treated as inadequate adults who must depend on "real adults" for a prolonged period of time. Hence, grown-ups are unable to recognize children's problem-solving capabilities and their potential contribution to the family, the school, or the larger society. In today's world, children and adults should be seen as interdependent members of a community in which they contribute to their own development by participating in various social and cultural events (New, 1998, pp. 265–267). As Spaggiari (1994) points out, children should not be treated as mere recipients of a "prepackaged culture." Rather, they should be seen as capable co-constructors of their understandings of "the meanings and rules of serious life" (Rogoff, 1990, p. 186).

The postmodern message (Lesnik-Oberstein, 1998) is that the nature of childhood (i.e., how children ought to be viewed) is not a hidden entity waiting to be discovered either by speculation or scientific studies of the child development processes. Rather, the notion of childhood is created by society and its meaning changes when there are significant social and cultural changes. According to the postmodernists, children should not be treated as property, inadequate adults, victims, or "adultified" children who represent a threat to grown-ups. Rather, we should view them as individuals with their own possibilities and limitations as well as the right to participate in co-constructing their own identity with their peers, teachers, parents, and others (Montemayer, Adams & Gullotta, 2000).

The "Culture of Childhood" and Education

The conceptions of childhood represent three very different perspectives regarding the nature of childhood. All three images—children as victims, as miniature adults, or as undeveloped grown-ups—underestimate the potential of young people. If, as Montagu argues, children know a lot more about growing than adults do, they are also well aware of their own abilities. Studies of the culture of childhood or the child's-eye view of his or her own culture (Boulding, 1979; Goodman, 1970; Kimball, 1974; Kozol, 2000; Kurth-Schai, 1985; Montagu, 1981) indicate that young people are conscious of the ways in which the contradictory expectations of the adult world make their social participation and contribution difficult.

For the present, as well as the future of our society, we need to revise our conception of childhood, for, as Margaret Mead (1970) once pointed out, grown-ups can learn to cope with a rapidly changing world more effectively by observing the young. We need to have the young "ask the questions that we would never think to ask, but enough trust must be reestablished so that the elders will be permitted to work with them on the answers" (p. 95). Our youth are less fettered by excess historical baggage to imagine and explore a much wider range of social alternatives than their elders. For the future, it is essential that we reconceptualize the nature of childhood in terms of children's own views of their world or the culture of childhood rather than by the degree to which they conform to or deviate from the adult norm. We need to redefine children as thinkers, doers, creators, and sharers of knowledge and arts, as well as participants in promoting human welfare. Once the nature of childhood is defined in this way, education should be the art and science of helping the child to realize his or her potentialities. Accordingly, education should (1) emphasize the personal meaning and social significance of children's learning experiences, (2) promote critical evaluation of knowledge claims and integration of knowledge and experience, (3) encourage reflective inquiry into the moral implications of what is learned, and (4) stimulate the exploration of new and different ways of knowing and valuing.

CULTURAL INFLUENCE IN THE PSYCHOEDUCATIONAL ASSESSMENT OF THE LEARNER

If we conceive education as the art and science of aiding the child to fulfill his or her promises, an accurate and unbiased assessment of the child's needs, abilities, and aspirations becomes critically necessary. From this perspective, psychoeducational assessment is much more than administering standardized intelligence, achievement, or aptitude tests to obtain such global indicators as IQ or percentile scores on children.

What Is Psychoeducational Assessment?

Broadly speaking, **psychoeducational assessment** is a process of obtaining information about the learner and communicating it to the intended users for making the best possible decisions about the learner's education (Shellenberger, 1982). For most young people who do not have apparent behavioral, emotional, or learning difficulties, the assessment process usually does not go beyond the use of a limited number of standardized intelligence and achievement tests and pupil evaluations done by classroom teachers. In general, student performance on teacher-made achievement tests and more or less systematic observations of the pupil's behaviors by other school personnel constitute the classroom teacher's assessment of the child. The teacher shares information obtained through this process with the parent in making decisions about the child's educational program.

Ideally, a systematic and comprehensive psychoeducational assessment includes, but is not limited to, the use of standardized intelligence and achievement tests, evaluation of the child's social or adaptive behaviors, and tests of sensorimotor and cognitive skills. Observations of classroom teachers, counselors, principals, school psychologists, social workers, physicians, and other psychological and educational specialists are an integral part of the process. The learner's parents are also viewed as active participants in assessing the child's needs, abilities, and goals. We can safely say that all of the elements in this assessment process may be affected by a wide variety of cultural factors. Consequently, if the assessment is to be both comprehensive and nondiscriminatory, we must guard against possible biases of the assessor, the instrument, and the assessment process as well as the environment or context in which the assessment is to take place (Hillard, 1977; Lutey & Copeland, 1982; Suzuki, Ponterotto & Meller, 2001; Torrance, 1982). Following a brief discussion of assessment models, we will examine how the cultural aspects of these key assessment process components may influence the outcomes and their uses.

Assessment Models and Culture

Approaches to psychoeducational assessment can be grouped into five conceptual **assessment models**: (1) the medical model, (2) the social system model, (3) the ability training model, (4) the task analysis model, and (5) the pluralistic model, or system of multicultural pluralistic assessment (SOMPA) (Mercer & Ysseldyke, 1977; Torrance, 1982, pp. 489–491).

The Medical Model

The medical model is based on the belief that learning difficulties are caused by some biological conditions. Hence, the sociocultural characteristics of the person with behavioral or learning difficulties are thought to be irrelevant in the assessment process. Treatment programs for the learner are based on assessing physical factors. Although this model is not believed to be culturally bound, it may become culturally discriminatory if those who administer the model view certain behaviors caused by physical conditions as resulting from cultural conditions. For example, educators may prescribe inappropriate and even harmful educational programs for a minority child, if he or she judges reading difficulties caused by neurological conditions as stemming from the child's cultural background.

The Social System Model

According to the social system model, the learner is evaluated in terms of the extent to which the child meets the expectations of the group in which he or she functions at the time of assessment. In the context of schooling, deviant or undesirable behaviors are those that do not conform to the expectations of the school and its rules and policies. The child's failure to learn the necessary role behaviors as defined by the school is considered primarily responsible for the child's poor academic performance. Although many conditions contribute to the child's failure to master the necessary social norms, educators need to carefully examine conflicts between values of the learner's culture and those of the school and the lack of opportunity to learn the necessary role expectations.

From the social system's perspective, educational "treatment" involves helping the child learn the norms of behavior for various roles in the school. Such an educational strategy is useful insofar as the role expectations to be learned fit a particular social setting—for example, school. However, the social system approach becomes culturally biased if the norms of one group are taught as universal norms to be adopted by all groups and at all times. To many culturally different children, this attitude may lead them to believe that only the mainstream or the school norms are legitimate. But after all, role expectations vary from group to group, and no one acts according to only one set of norms at all times.

The Ability Training Model

The ability training model is based on the premise that children learn differently and that academic failures occur because a child has certain disabilities or deficits. The primary objectives of this model are to identify the underlying causes of failure through testing and to help children improve their school performance by teaching them the necessary skills. Within the ability training model, deviations from average or model performance levels are considered deficits or disabilities according to which children are labeled.

The ability training approach to assessment relies heavily on children's performance on norm-referenced tests, which are given to a large and representative group of individuals who presumably have comparable academic and cultural backgrounds. Hence, a child's score on a norm-referenced test tells us about where he or she stands in relation to others who took the same test. The score does not indicate how much the child has learned in relation to a specific educational objective. Most standardized intelligence and achievement tests are norm-referenced instruments. This means that minority children's scores on these tests will not give us unbiased information about their abilities and achievements as individuals, only their abilities as members of a representative group. Because minority children are compared with mainstream children with whom they do not share comparable intellectual or sociocultural backgrounds, a heavy use of norm-referenced tests frequently results in discriminatory assessment and placement of minority children. Many suggest that this practice is partly responsible for the overrepresentation of black and Hispanic children in educable mentally handicapped (EMH) classes and their underrepresentation in gifted programs.

The Task Analysis Model

For advocates of the task analysis model of assessment, the main concern is analyzing specific skills that make up certain target behaviors or educational objectives. Because the primary focus of this assessment model is integrating identified individual skills into desired objectives, there is minimal concern for disabilities or deficits based on a group norm. In the 1990s, a resurgence of interest in this approach appeared in the form of *mastery learning*. Based on the earlier work of Benjamin Bloom (1976), mastery learning is based on the assumption that all children can learn, given sufficient time on task. Some students may require more time than others, and instruction must be modified to meet individual differences. Mastery learning advocates stress the importance of assuring that students experience success at each level of instruction. Another approach that gained popularity in the 1990s, outcomes-based education (OBE), also places emphasis on the clear identification of outcomes and the construction of individual knowledge through mastery.

This assessment model stresses the use of criterion-referenced instruments to evaluate children's progress. Unlike norm-referenced tests, criterion-referenced instruments measure how much a child has learned in relation to a particular educational objective. Once a child's strengths and weaknesses are assessed in relation to a specific goal, instructional objectives are written to enable the child to reach his or her goal by developing necessary skills. This test-teach-retest process can be repeated until the individually planned educational programs are successfully achieved. Because each child is treated as an individual rather than being judged in relation to others, the assessment process is less likely to be biased or discriminatory. However, educators need to capitalize on the different ways children think and learn so that each child can be helped to reach his or her goals effectively.

The Pluralistic Model

The pluralistic model, pioneered by Jane Mercer and also known as the system of multicultural pluralistic assessment (SOMPA), represents an attempt to estimate "learning potential in a manner which is not racially or culturally discriminatory" (Mercer & Ysseldyke, 1977, p. 85). It was originally developed to help school psychologists and others in their work in the educational placement of elementary school children. In the 1980s Mercer's approach included a "group-adjusted scoring procedure" that was banned with the passage of the Civil Rights Act of 1991 (Padilla, 2001, p. 12). Even though more than thirty years have elapsed since its initial development in 1973, Mercer's model is still a part of discussions about culturally sensitive assessments (Austin, 1999; Padilla, 2001). This model takes into account the possible impact of sociocultural and health factors on the measurement of learning potentials (Torrance, 1982, p. 490). SOMPA is based on two basic premises. One is the belief that learning potential is similarly distributed in all racial and cultural groups. The other is the view that all tests used for estimating learning potential are culturally biased. Hence, individuals whose cultural backgrounds are similar to those of the persons who belong to the group used for test standardization (the norm group) tend to perform better on such tests than those who have different cultural heritages.

In addition to the use of standardized intelligence tests, the child's role performance in the family, the neighborhood, and the school and his or her perceptual-motor development and health conditions are assessed. The assessment is accomplished through an interview with the child's parents or guardian and direct examination of the child. Once the specific skills the child needs to learn have been identified, he or she is taught those skills and then tested to estimate the amount of growth gained as a result of the teaching. In this context of test-train-retest, intelligence is viewed as the child's ability to profit from experience (Mercer & Ysseldyke, 1977, p. 83). Similarly, educability of the minority child should be seen as his or her ability to learn new cultural patterns.

In reviewing the five assessment models, we find that each model can yield information about some specific aspect of the child (see Table 6.2). For example, the medical model can tell us about the physical factors related to the child's performance in school. The task analysis model can yield information about what specific skills the child needs to develop in order to master a particular subject matter. On the other hand, the pluralistic model can give us a measure of the child's learning potential in terms of the cultural heritages within which he or she has been reared. It would appear that nondiscriminatory assessment for educational development requires an approach that can utilize the unique techniques and methods of a wide variety of disciplines such as counseling psychology, anthropology, social psychology, psychometry, ethnography, social work, certain health sciences, and even subject matter specialization. Parents' observations of the child and the child's self-perception, as well as his or her optional performance of untested skills, can also provide valuable information for fair assessment and sound educational planning.

In general, a multidisciplinary staff conference is held for evaluating and placing special education students. This conference usually involves the parents, psychologist, school personnel, social worker, and, at times, the child. Similar meetings involving a smaller number of individuals could be held to assess both the mainstream and minority students who experience minor difficulties or desire special educational guidance.

TABLE 6.2
Summary of Assessment Models

		Models			
	Medical	**Social System**	**Ability Training**	**Task Analysis**	**Pluralistic**
Learning Difficulties	Biological or physical deficits	Not behaving according to the school norm	Lack of abilities to do schoolwork	Lack of specific skills to achieve terminal behaviors	Not having certain culture-specific skills to do schoolwork
Assessment	Physical and/or neurological conditions	Degree to which the child meets the school's expectations at the time of assessment	Norm-referenced measures used to compare with the norm group	Criterion-referenced measures used to determine how much the child has moved toward a target behavior	Standardized IQ tests, sociocultural and health factors, and personal interviews
Treatment	Remedy physical or neurological conditions	Teach the behavioral norms for various roles in school	Teach skills to reach the group norm	Develop specific skills to master a subject matter; test-teach-test	Develop culture-specific skills necessary to do well in school; test-train-retest
Discriminatory Effects	Behaviors resulting from physical conditions may be viewed as stemming from cultural backgrounds	Deviation from dominant norms viewed as deficits or pathological conditions	Only the dominant group norm is used to define educability	Less discriminatory because learned skills are specifically related to a learning objective	Least discriminatory because sociocultural factors are considered in defining educability

Cultural Factors in Psychoeducational Assessment

All approaches to psychoeducational assessment share at least three common components: (1) the person who is doing the assessing, (2) the instrument used for assessment, and (3) the person who is being assessed. These components contain certain cultural elements that may contribute to biased assessment and discriminatory decisions leading to harmful influence on the educational development of the child.

The Assessor

The beliefs, values, and biases of the person responsible for carrying out the assessment can make a significant difference in the outcome, the interpretation, and the use of the data. One of the major issues regarding the interactions between the assessor and the child being evaluated is the concern that the assessor's attitudes toward minority cultures, the opposite sex, and the aged may negatively affect the outcomes of testing. The assessor's ethnocentrism as well as his or her failure to understand the child's culture, values, cognitive styles, language usage, and unique approach to interpersonal relationships may influence the assessment results adversely. The child may have similar difficulties in understanding the assessor's attitudes and behavior patterns. When we consider that most minority children are evaluated by white assessors, it is not difficult to see how poor performance on standardized tests can result from poor communication and misunderstanding between the assessor and the assessed. The negative influence of these factors on how tests are administered, scored, interpreted, and used can lead to biased assessment, which in turn can result in unfair and inappropriate placement. Most school personnel, including school psychologists and counselors, are monocultural in both experience and education. Unless they have had special training in cross-cultural studies they are most likely to interpret the attitudes and behaviors of minority children in terms of the mainstream culture. Hillard (1977) insists that "when the [assessor's] frame of reference is imposed on the experience of people alien to him [or her], confusion and invalid interpretation are almost certain to result" (p. 108).

Evidence regarding the relationship between the assessor's attitudes and evaluation outcomes appears to be inconclusive (Lutey & Copeland, 1982, pp. 131–133). However, it would be prudent for psychoeducational assessors to know as much about their own attitudes and values, other cultural norms, and the cultural biases built into all forms of testing instruments and processes as possible. After all, assessment is a form of social interaction among individuals whose values and worldviews are bound to affect how they think and what they do.

The Assessment Instrument

One of the most frequent criticisms against the use of standardized intelligence and achievement tests is that the tests' contents are biased in favor of white middle-class Americans. For example, neither African American nor Hispanic cultures give minority students opportunities to be exposed to many commonly used test items. Moreover, because the norms are established by testing predominantly white students, the culturally different tend to do poorly on these tests. The use of minority children's test scores for placement purposes is said to be unfair and unsound, because these norm-referenced measures of intelligence and academic achievements do not indicate how much minority children have learned in an alien culture, the school. Even for white middle-class children, the use of IQ scores and percentile scores on standardized tests for educational placement may be inappropriate because the scores on these tests only indicate where the youngsters are in relation to others who took the same test.

Another area of concern in the use of standardized tests for minority children has to do with their cognitive styles and language usage. For example, studies indicate that many African American and Hispanic children are not concerned with the details of a concept or a situation or with "hurrying" to do a job (Carter & Segura, 1979, pp. 83–89, 97; Grossman, 1984, pp. 175–186; Hillard, 1977, pp. 114–115). However, timed-standardized tests require that analytic and detail-specific responses be given within a fairly short period of time. It is generally known that even among white children, urban children do much better on timed tests than rural children because rural residents tend to place less emphasis on a time-oriented lifestyle than urban city dwellers. In addition, the fact that minority cultures may consider certain test items as simply unimportant may also contribute to poor test performance by minority children.

A most serious barrier to nondiscriminatory assessment is the lack of appropriate instruments for assessing minority children's learning potential, personality characteristics, and social behavior. This problem is believed to be rooted in the differences in concepts, behaviors, values, and measurement techniques that exist between mainstream American and minority cultures (Koh, 1988, p. 7). Tong-He Koh, the Research Director of the Bureau of Child Study of the Chicago Board of Education, reports that when the Minnesota Multiphasic Personality Inventory (MMPI) was administered to Koreans who had recently immigrated to the United States, they were found to have a highly elevated level of depression and other psychological disturbances (Koh, Sakauye, Koh, & Liu, 1986). However, such a level of depression and other psychological disturbances were considered common or "normal" among Japanese in Japan and Chinese in China (Clark, 1985; Song, 1984). On the other hand, when another well-established psychiatric interview schedule was given to Koreans in Seoul and to Chinese in Taiwan and Shanghai, the subjects were found to have significantly lower levels of psychological disturbances than Americans in the United States (Koh, 1988, p. 8). Koh concludes that diametrically opposing findings can come from established and well-translated assessment instruments because of their cultural contents and the contexts in which the instruments were administered. It is quite likely that Asians prefer not to disclose their own problems to others or tend to give socially acceptable responses in face-to-face interview situations. These research findings suggest that a person's performance on an assessment instrument varies with the cultural contents of the instrument and culturally induced ways in which the individual responds to written or oral questions. This has important implications for assessor–subject, teacher–pupil, and counselor–client relationships. Some of these ramifications will be discussed in the following chapter.

Finally, all of this is not to suggest that standardized, norm-referenced instruments are useless, for they can give us information about where a particular person or a group stands in relation to a larger norm group. But a central point of our discussion is that each child's unique learning potential or attitudinal characteristics cannot be determined on the basis of the child's scores on norm-referenced instruments alone. The emergence of efforts toward authentic or performance assessment is, in part, a reaction to the criticisms of standardized, norm-referenced testing. **Authentic assessment** (Chittenden, 1991) seeks to engage students in assessment tasks that are more clearly reflective of articulated goals and emphasize process as well as products. Rather than choosing from predetermined options, the emphasis is on having students create or construct responses (Fredricksen & White, 2004, pp. 76–77). For example, if the expectation of students is that they be able to analyze and think critically about a work of literature, the assessment should give students the opportunity to demonstrate that ability rather than respond to a multiple-choice test. Expectations and standards for success are to be made clear to learners at the outset, and instruction is focused around the attainment of those goals; however, different learners may be able to demonstrate their attainment of particular goals in somewhat different ways. Students are not assessed against one another but rather against the attainment of clear goals. Both mainstream and minority children's learning potential can be estimated without comparing their learning rates with those of others.

The Assessed

When we consider the complex nature of the psychoeducational assessment process, it is not surprising that anyone about to undergo an evaluative experience might be apprehensive. As compared with mainstream youth, most minority students face much more severe psychological stresses at the prospect of having to be evaluated because, for them, the evaluation represents an alien cultural setting. However, studies indicate that not all forms of anxiety have a negative effect. Of the two types of anxiety, trait and state anxieties, only the latter tends to adversely influence test performance (Lutey & Copeland, 1982, p. 130). According to Lutey and Copeland, *trait anxiety* is a pervasive condition that affects the person's daily life. On the other hand, *state anxiety* is brought on by the person's emotional reaction to immediate conditions. It is state anxiety that tends to disrupt test performance. Although it is not unusual to be apprehensive in a testing situation, the assessor needs to be aware of the potential adverse influence of state anxiety. Anything that the assessor can do to establish a positive rapport with the assessed may help reduce negative effects of state anxiety.

Findings regarding the effect of bilingualism on test performance seem mixed (Lutey & Copeland, 1982, pp. 129–130). For example, Spanish-English-speaking children tend to do significantly better on the verbal section of the Spanish version of the Wechsler Intelligence Scale for Children (WISC) than on the English version. However, when another intelligence test was given to African American children in black dialect, their performance did not vary significantly from the scores of African American children who were given the Standard English version of test. Other studies dispute these findings. However, there appears to be enough data to suggest that children seem to do significantly better when they are assessed by those whom they see as most like themselves. In any event, this is an area that requires much more intensive and extensive study.

Finally, children's own worldviews, values, attitudes, and perceptions of their roles are likely to have direct and/or subtle effects on the assessment outcomes because evaluation processes invariably involve interactions among many different people. For example, African American and Hispanic children's preference for dealing with people rather than things (Carter & Segura, 1979; Grossman, 1984; Hillard, 1977) may influence how these children respond to test items. The deferential attitude toward adults and authority figures held by Asian, black, and Hispanic children could have a significant impact on how these young people relate to the assessor (Carter & Segura, 1979; Hillard, 1977; Hsu, 1981). Changes in the assessor's perception of minority cultures may in turn affect the evaluation results and their interpretations as well as how they are used to make educational decisions.

Educators need to keep in mind that the primary purpose of psychoeducational assessment is to gather information that can be used to make the most appropriate decisions for the child's educational development. This process goes beyond obtaining quantitative scores on a variety of standardized devices that are incapable of providing insights into the child's problems, needs, aspirations, and other constraints in his or her life. The test data give us limited information about certain aspects of the child. Interpretation of test scores should be enriched with an understanding of the complex sociocultural milieu in which the child has been reared and now lives. On the basis of one of the authors' own involvement in the psychoeducational assessment of minority children, the experience of having lived in both the mainstream and the child's own culture adds immensely to understanding him or her. Yet the insights one derives from such experiences are neither quantifiable nor describable in precise empirical language.

Literary depictions of other cultures can give educators a sense of what it feels like to live in two or more cultures at the same time. We all have stories to tell about our own childhoods, and we can learn from the stories others tell as well. As Minami (2000) writes, "to tell and interpret stories should be regarded as a culturally deep-rooted activity." (p. 76). Some writers listen carefully to children and write about what they hear (Coles, Testa & Coles, 2001; Kozol, 2000; Paley, 1999). In other instances, writers depict their own recollections. Polingaysi Qoyawayma recalls the disorienting experience of leaving her home on the Hopi reservation in order to go to school in California in the early 1900s. Her book, *No Turning Back: A Hopi Indian Woman's Struggle to Live in Two Worlds* (1977), chronicles her confusing experiences as a young student and her resolve to return to the Navajo and then Hopi reservations eventually as a teacher. Many writers have penned portraits of growing up that are rooted in their own experiences. A series of books with such descriptions give readers insights into a range of childhood experiences: *Growing Up Asian American* (Hong, 1993); *Growing Up Chicana/o* (Lopez, 1993); *Growing Up Native American* (Riley, 1993); and *Growing Up Poor* (Coles, Testa & Coles, 2001). In these books the perspectives provide us with insights into the many textures of childhood.

The importance of learning about the more technical aspects of the assessment process should not be minimized. Indeed, school psychologists, counselors, administrators, social workers, school nurses, classroom-teachers, and other subject matter specialists must be competent in their own fields of specialization and appropriate professional "crafts." But they should also be required to do ethnographic, observer–participant studies of other cultural groups found in their communities. Psychoeducational assessment without the experiential ingredient can become a mechanical means of classifying students according to predetermined categories from which children, particularly the culturally different, may never escape.

Torrance (1982) provides two categories of "solutions" related to psychoeducational assessment of children (pp. 485–486). First-order solutions, also called the "more and better of the same" solutions, involve such changes as reducing the teacher–pupil ratio and providing smaller classes, more teaching aides, and paraprofessionals. Second-order solutions involve working collaboratively with principals, teachers, other school personnel, children, parents, community agencies, and special consultants to bring about genuine alterations in the system. Torrance points out that second-order solutions, rather than the "more and better of the same," are more effective in dealing with the special needs and problems of the culturally different. The creative use of ethnic, cultural, and other special resources in the community is essential in making second-order changes truly effective.

Assessment and Cultural Diversity

As has been pointed out in the preceding sections, a major criticism of the established traditional assessment process is related to the pervasive use of standardized intelligence and achievement tests. This objection stems from the use of these test scores to compare the performances of children without considering the differences in their sociocultural experiences, racial ethnic backgrounds, and the disparities in educational opportunities. The critics claim that these comparisons are often used to place poor and culturally different students in inappropriate programs that have deleterious effects. Thus, some even argue that standardized tests be eliminated from educational assessment (Wiggins, 1993).

A variety of measurement instruments and more than one model of assessment procedure are necessary if our schools are to provide effective learning environments for their culturally diverse population. For this reason, the use of the new forms of alternative (authentic) assessment (i.e., performance and portfolio assessments) can play an important role. Performance assessment measures the student's mastery of specific tasks in different contexts, while portfolio assessment focuses on collecting what the student has achieved during a specific period of time. An enriching aspect of the latter is that it involves the learner's self-assessment of learning (Walters, Seidel, & Gardner, 1994) because the student is required to choose his or her own best work. Unlike the traditional norm-referenced approach, the alternative assessment is learner centered and the student can participate through self-evaluation and reflection.

The new forms of alternative assessment give us potent tools in making educational assessment nondiscriminatory and effective in facilitating learning. But unless we take into account the various ways in which social and cultural factors affect how children learn, the new alternative assessment procedures too can discriminate against poor and culturally different children by sorting and tracking. Further, even with all the criticisms directed against the use of standardized tests, schools will continue to use them as long as the test scores are considered to be indicators of how well schools have achieved their educational mission. Clearly, assessment is crucial in helping individual students meet their instructional needs and goals. Our choice of assessment procedures then must be consistent with our educational objectives for helping diverse children achieve their aspirations. In principle, what needs to be done to make the assessment process nondiscriminatory and educationally enriching is no different from what we have to do to make our culturally diverse classroom and schools more effective and humane.

 Cases For Reflection

THE CONVENTION ON THE RIGHTS OF THE CHILD

The Convention on the Rights of the Child (CRC), a human rights treaty adopted by the United Nations more than a decade ago, has been used by countries around the world to help promote the rights of children, strengthen government efforts to serve families and build upon the efforts of non-governmental organizations (NGOs) on behalf of children. The Convention sets forth basic norms and standards that individual nations agree to pursue on behalf of their children.

Emphasizing the primacy and importance of the role and authority of parents, the treaty calls for governments to respect the responsibilities, rights, and duties of parents to provide direction for the development of their children. It also calls on governments to develop policies conducive to families and communities that will allow children to grow up in an atmosphere of happiness, love, and understanding. The CRC's internationally recognized norms include:

- Protection from violence, abuse, and abduction.
- Protection from hazardous employment and exploitation.
- Adequate nutrition.
- Free compulsory primary education.
- Adequate health care.
- Equal treatment regardless of gender, race, or cultural background.

Recognizing the special vulnerability of children and their need for guidance, all of these goals are expressed with respect to the child's age and maturity; the child's best interests are always the paramount concern.

Source: UNICEF: http://capwiz.com/unicefusa/issues/alert/?alertid=32697

DISCUSSION QUESTIONS

1. The Convention on the Rights of the Child has been approved by 192 member nations of the United Nations. What adult behaviors and activities do you think have made this Convention necessary?
2. The United States is among the very few nations not to have ratified the Convention. Do you think such a statement of children's rights is necessary in a developed country like the United States? Explain your rationale.
3. Does the Convention represent a particular concept of childhood? If not, does it provide some hints for formulating a concept of childhood that may be sound and appropriate for democratic education?
4. What rights do you think that children in a democratic nation should be assured of? Why?

ABOUT JOHN

The report that follows was given by an actual school psychologist. Comments regarding the outcome of this situation are given after the discussion questions.

I met [John's] parents by invitation of the principal at a teacher conference requested by [his] parents. [His] parents were upset at [John's] teacher. She was doing a world history month in her (fifth-grade) class and asked the five "Oriental" students, including [John], to work together and prepare to tell the class about Oriental customs in their homes (e.g., food, dress, dance). [John] was a third-generation (sansei) Japanese American whose parents were born and raised in California; [his] grandparents were from Hawaii.

When the "Oriental" group met together to discuss and plan their presentation, [John] felt embarrassed and out of place. [He] was embarrassed because as the only American-born student in the group, [he] had never considered [himself] an Oriental, and [he] didn't want to be "one of the Orientals." [He] had not interacted with these Asian students and [his] friends were mostly white students. Furthermore, [he] didn't know much about Japanese customs, let alone Oriental customs!

[He] went home and told [his] parents about the assignment and [his] uneasiness with the group and [his] parents concurred. They were upset that the teacher had failed to recognize the differences in Asian groups and had simply lumped everyone together. They also did not want to be called "Orientals."

Source: Brian P. Leung (1998), "Who Are Chinese American, Japanese American, and Korean American Children?" Reprinted by permission from *Struggling to Be Heard: The Unmet Needs of Asian Pacific American Children,* edited by Valerie Ooka Pang and Li-Rong Lilly Cheng, the State University of New York Press ©1998, State University of New York. All rights reserved.

DISCUSSION QUESTIONS

1. What do you think are some possible historical, social, cultural, and emotional reasons why John felt embarrassed and out of place in the "Oriental" group?
2. Do you think that John's parents had legitimate or reasonable grounds to be upset at the teacher? Why or why not?
3. In what sense is "Oriental" more pejorative than "Asian"?
4. What would you have said or done at the teacher–parent conference? If you were the principal, what would you have done to prevent a similar situation in the future?

OUTCOME

I began this joint conference by restating the (good) intention of the assignment and the fact that it had upset [John] and [his] parents. I then proceeded to discuss the differences among various "Asian" groups and the need to treat each separately. . . . The use of the term "Asian" was also introduced to the teacher. . . .

This conference presented an opportunity for the teacher to learn first hand about the multicultural nature of her students, especially the differences within large categories like Asians. The principal also saw the opportunity, and, as a direct result of this parent conference, scheduled a staff development discussion about the differences within the rapidly changing student population in his schools.

Source: Brian P. Leung (1998), "Who Are Chinese American, Japanese American, and Korean American Children?" Reprinted by permission from *Struggling to Be Heard: The Unmet Needs of Asian Pacific American Children,* edited by Valerie Ooka Pang and Li-Rong Lilly Cheng, the State University of New York Press ©1998, State University of New York. All rights reserved.

JENNIFER IN LA VICTORIA

[La Victoria] consists of no more than 17,000 people with an average family income of less than $17,000, and a lower net household income for Chicanos than for non-Chicanos. Over 40 percent of La Victoria residents were Chicanos who had resided in the Southwest for over five generations. . . . The majority spoke only English in their family. Isolated Spanish words accented family conversations but no detection of an accent was heard which indicated that Spanish was not a frequent medium among family members. . . .

A major concern within the Chicano community in La Victoria was the lack of quality education for Chicano youth evidenced by the consistently high dropout rates. Of Chicanos between the ages of sixteen and twenty-five, at least 33 percent had not completed high school. . . .

In La Victoria, no single motive could be cited for leaving school, nor is there a single model of a student dropout. Parents who both worked in the school as nurses, secretaries, and teachers' assistants and who lived in the community concluded that tracking of students was one of the worst problems and one that began in the elementary school. The tracking system ostensibly followed the students throughout their schooling years. [According to one teacher, everything is geared towards the mainstream culture.] . . .

[Jennifer consciously decided to] leave La Victoria High School when she could not keep up with her classes in the tenth grade. She tells, "As I got to be a sophomore they [classes] got to be boring. The classes were harder, and like in Geometry, I kept telling the teacher that I didn't understand, but he didn't try to slow down, so then I just gave up. He kept telling me to keep up but I needed more help. I didn't want to put up with anything like pressure in classes. I was flunking the classes because I didn't go. I would go to school, but I wouldn't go to class. I would just ditch."

Jennifer . . . experienced a vague disturbing boredom in the classroom. Jennifer, like her brother, Bob, had always been placed in accelerated or advanced classes. In Jennifer's transition from junior high school she became interested in her social life. Her boredom in school and new interest in boys led Jennifer to become pregnant.

Jennifer felt self-conscious about continuing in the high school program although the school did have a program for pregnant girls and teenage mothers. Jennifer's mother did not pressure her to stay in school but she told her . . . that if she did not attend school, she had to get a job especially now that she had a child to support.

Source: C. Delgado-Galtan, "The Value of Conformity: Learning to Stay in School." *Anthropology & Education Quarterly*, Vol. 19, No. 4: 354–381. © 1988, American Anthropological Association. All rights reserved. Used by permission.

DISCUSSION QUESTIONS

1. How would you go about identifying Jennifer's problems and needs? How helpful do you think some of the standardized instruments (tests) would be in making educational plans for Jennifer?
2. What do you think are some key conditions that led to Jennifer's decision to leave school?
3. What recommendation(s) would you make to Jennifer's mother? Discuss your rationale. Should Jennifer be allowed to leave school and find a job? How about having Jennifer enroll in the program for pregnant girls and

teenage parents? Would the school district's alternative school be more appropriate for Jennifer? One student in the alternative school made the following comment about the school: "The teachers tell you what you have to do there . . . and they help you. The teachers in the regular school talk to the whole class. The classes are also smaller in the alternative school and I guess that's how the teachers can help you a lot" (Delgado-Galtan, 1988, p. 369).

4. Can you think of some programs the La Victoria High School can introduce to make the school experiences more culturally relevant to its students?

◼ ◼ ◼ ◼

OUTCOME

Jennifer decided to go to the alternative school, where the barriers to her learning were reduced. The following is a brief description of the alternative high school (AHS) in La Victoria:

The classroom usually provided a casual and relaxed environment for the student in the AHS. The halls were lined with bulletin boards announcing employment, dances, and concerts in the neighboring cities. The language arts classroom, for example, had seven round tables, newspapers, and student compositions scattered all over; a couple of soda cans sat on top of the teachers' desk and a can of hair spray on top of a girl's desk. An Aztec Calendar, with 20 days drawn up, hung on a large board. On the blackboard a few written statements appeared as story starters using local vernacular—for example, "Yesterday was a real drag . . .,"—which the teacher used as a way to open up dialogue during the first part of class as she walked around the room. Although this was a language arts class, the teacher explained the need for using the reading and writing tools to learn about science, history, and other subjects. Thus, students brought their books from other classes which lay open on various desks. . . .

In La Victoria, the AHS existed to accommodate students who could not succeed socially or academically in the [La Victoria High School]. . . . Students were able to work the necessary hours to help their family while completing their requirements to graduate. They could work at their own pace without the fear of failure, and they could work faster with the appropriate teacher support. . . . Social and academic competition became manageable because it was not the force governing the school. Rather, the school was based on caring, individualized instruction and alternative academic and skill training programs.

Source: C. Delgado-Galtan, "The Value of Conformity: Learning to Stay in School." Reproduced by permission of the American Anthropological Association from *Anthropology & Education Quarterly* 19:4, 1988. Not for further reproduction.

REFERENCES

Austin, J. T. (1999). Culturally sensitive career assessment: A quandry. Eric Digest no. 210 [On-line]. Available: http://www.cete.org/acve/docgen.asp?tbl=digests&ID=94

Berry, J. W. (1997). Preface. In J. W. Berry, P. R. Dasen, & T. S. Saraswathi, (Eds.) *Handbook of cross-cultural psychology: Basic processes and human development* (2nd ed., pp. xi–xvi). Boston: Allyn &Bacon.

Berry, J. W., Dasen, P. R., & Saraswathi, T. S. (Eds.) *Handbook of cross-cultural psychology: Basic processes and human development* (2nd ed.). Boston: Allyn & Bacon.

Best, S., & Kellner, D. (1991). *Postmodern theory: Critical interrogations.* New York: Guilford Press.

Bloom, B. S. (1976). *Human characteristics and school learning.* New York: McGraw-Hill.

Boulding, E. (1979). *Children's rights and the wheel of life.* New Brunswick, NJ: Transaction Books.

Bowman, B. T., & Stott, F. M. (1993). Understanding development in a cultural context: The challenge for teachers. In B. L. Mallory & R. S. New, (Eds.), *Diversity and developmentally appropriate practices.* New York: Teachers College Press.

Bruner, J. (1987). The transactional self. In J. Bruner & H. Haste (Eds.), *Making sense* (pp. 81–96). New York: Methuen.

Bruner, J. (1996). *The culture of education.* Cambridge: Harvard University Press.

Bruner, J., & Haste, H. (1987). Introduction. In J. Bruner & H. Haste (Eds.), *Making sense* (pp. 1–25). New York: Methuen.

Burman, E. (1994). *Deconstructing developmental psychology.* London: Routledge.

Carter, T. P., & Segura, R. D. (1979). *Mexican Americans in school: A decade of change.* New York: College Entrance Board.

Chittenden, E. (1991). Authentic assessment, evaluation, and documentation of student performance. In V. Perrone (Ed.), *Expanding student assessment* (pp. 22–31). Washington, DC: Association for Supervision and Curriculum Development.

Clark, L. A. (1985). A consolidated version of the MMPI in Japan. In J. N. Butcher & C. P. Spielberger (Eds.), *Issues in personality assessment.* Hillsdale, NJ: Lawrence Erlbaum Associates.

Cleverley, J., & Phillips, D. C. (1986). *Visions of childhood: Influential models from Locke to Spock.* New York: Teachers College Press. This book deals with how various conceptions or paradigms of childhood have influenced "the way humans have understood, cared for, and educated their young" (p. 141).

Coles, R. (1997). *The moral intelligence of children.* New York: Random House.

Coles, R. (1986). *The moral life of children.* Boston: Atlantic Monthly Press.

Coles, R., Testa, R., & Coles, M. (Eds.). (2001). *Growing up poor: A literary anthology.* New York: The New Press.

Csordas, T. J. (2003). Trials of Navajo youth: Identity, healing, and the struggle for maturity. *Ethos, 31*(3), 357–384.

Damon, W. (1981). Exploring children's social cognition on two fronts. In J. H. Flavell & L. Ross (Eds.), *Social cognitive development* (pp. 162–163). Cambridge: Cambridge University Press.

Damon, W. (1983). *Social and personality development: Infancy through adolescence.* New York: Norton.

Delgado-Galtan, C. (1988). The value of conformity: Learning to stay in school. *Anthropology & Education Quarterly, 19*(4), 354–381.

Eckensberger, L. H., & Zimba, R. F. (1997). Development of moral judgment. In J. W. Berry, P. R. Dasen, & T. S. Saraswathi (Eds.), *Handbook of cross-cultural psychology: Basic processes and human development* (2nd ed., pp. 299–338). Boston: Allyn & Bacon.

Edwards, C. P., & Ramsey, P. G. (1986). *Promoting social and moral development in young children.* New York: Teachers College Press.

Egan, K. (1979). *Educational development.* New York: Oxford University Press.

Fischer, K. W. (1980). A theory of cognitive development: The control and construction of hierarchies of skills. *Psychological Review, 87,* 473–531.

Frederiksen, J. R., & White, B. Y. (2004). Designing assessments for instruction and accountability: An application of validity theory to assessing scientific inquiry. In M. Wilson (Ed.), *Towards coherence between classroom assessment and accountability.* 103rd Yearbook of the National Society for the Study of Education, Part II (pp. 74–104). Chicago: National Society for the Study of Education.

Gilligan, C. (1982). *In a different voice: Psychological theory and women's development.* Cambridge: Harvard University Press.

Gilligan, C., Lyons, N. P., & Hanmer, T. J. (1990). *Making connections: The relational worlds of adolescent girls at Emma Willard School.* Cambridge: Harvard University Press.

Gollnick, D. M., & Chinn, P. (1998). *Multicultural education in a pluralistic society* (5th ed., pp. 100–109). Upper Saddle River, NJ: Merrill/Prentice Hall.

Goodman, M. E. (1970). *The culture of childhood: Child's-eye views of society and culture.* New York: Teachers College Press.

Griffin, C. (1993). *Representations of youth.* Cambridge: Polity.

Grossman, H. (1984). *Educating Hispanic students: Cultural implications for instruction, classroom management, counseling and assessment.* Springfield, IL: Charles Thomas.

Harrington, C. (1979). *Psychological anthropology and education.* New York: AMS Press.

Haste, H. (1987). Growing into rules. In J. Bruner & H. Haste (Eds.), *Making sense* (pp. 163–195). New York: Methuen.

Hersch, P. (1998). *A tribe apart: A journey into the heart of American adolescence.* New York: Ballantine.

Hillard, A. G. (1977). Intellectual strengths of minority children. In D. E. Cross, G. C. Baker, & L. J. Stiles (Eds.), *Teaching in a multicultural society: Perspectives and professional strategies* (pp. 97–120). New York: Free Press. This chapter discusses ways in which cultural factors influence several key aspects of the process of assessing minority children's intellectual abilities. It also examines how biases against minority cultures can lead to unfair and erroneous placement of children.

Hong, M. (Ed.). (1993). *Growing up Asian American.* New York: Avon Books.

Hsu, F. L. (Ed.). (1972). *Psychological anthropology.* Cambridge: Schenkman.

Hsu, F. L. (1981). *Americans and Chinese* (3rd ed.). Honolulu: University of Hawaii Press.

Kagan, J. (1984). *The nature of the child.* New York: Basic Books.

Kimball, S. T. (1974). Cultural influences shaping the role of the child. In S. T. Kimball (Ed.), *Culture and the educative process* (pp. 85–98). New York: Teachers College Press.

Kincheloe, J. L. (1997). The advent of postmodern childhood. In Shirley R. Steinberg & Joe L. Kincheloe (Eds.), *Kinderculture: The corporate construction of childhood.* Boulder, CO: Westview Press.

Koh, S., Sakauye, K., Koh, T. H., & Liu, W. T. (1986). *Mental health and stress in Asian-American elderly.* Chicago: University of Illinois, Pacific and Asian American Mental Health Research Center.

Koh, T. (1988, June). *Cognitive and affective adaptation of Korean-American school children: Service and research priorities.* Paper presented at the invitational conference on Asian-American research priorities funded by the Pacific and Asian American Mental Research Center and held at the University of Illinois–Chicago.

Kohlberg, L. (1971). Stages of moral development as a basis for moral education. In C. M. Beck, B. S. Crittenden, & E. V. Sullivan (Eds.), *Moral education: Interdisciplinary approaches.* Toronto: University of Toronto Press.

Kohlberg, L. (1984). *Essays on moral development: The psychology of moral development* (Vol. 2). New York: Harper & Row.

Kozol, J. (2000). *Ordinary resurrections.* New York: Crown Publishers.

Kurth-Schai, R. (1985). *Reflections from the hearts and minds of children: A Delphi study of children's personal, global, and spiritual images of the future.* Unpublished doctoral dissertation, University of Minnesota, Minneapolis.

Lesnik-Oberstein, K. (Ed.). (1998). *Children in culture: Approaches to childhood.* New York: St. Martins Press.

Levine, D. U., & Levine, R. F. (1996). *Society and education.* Boston: Allyn & Bacon.

Lipsky, D., & Abrams, A. (1994). *Late bloomers.* New York: Times Books.

Lopez, T. A. (Ed.). (1993). *Growing up Chicana/o.* New York: Avon Books.

Lutey, C., & Copeland, E. P. (1982). Cognitive assessment of the school-age child. In C. R. Reynolds & T. B. Gutkin (Eds.), *The handbook of school psychology* (pp. 121–155). New York: John Wiley. This is a helpful discussion of the goals of assessment, evaluations of tests, aspects of the testing process, and interpretation of test results in schoolchildren's cognitive assessment.

Mead, M. (1970). *Culture and commitment.* New York: Doubleday.

Mercer, J. R., & Ysseldyke, J. (1977). Designing diagnostic-intervention programs. In T. Oakland (Ed.), *Psychological and educational assessment of minority children* (pp. 70–90). New York: Bruner/Mazel.

Minami, M. (2000). The relationship between narrative, identity, and culture. *Narrative Inquiry, 10*(1), 75–80.

Mishra, R. C. (1997). Cognition and cognitive development. In J. W. Berry, P. R. Dasen, & T. S. Saraswathi (Eds.), *Handbook of cross-cultural psychology: Basic processes and human development* (2nd ed.; pp. 143–175). Boston: Allyn & Bacon.

Montagu, A. (1981). *Growing young.* New York: McGraw-Hill.

Montemayor, R. (2000). Paths to adulthood: Adolescent diversity in contemporary America. In R. Montemayer, G. R. Adams, & T. P. Gullotta (Eds.), *Adolescent diversity in ethnic, economic, and cultural contexts* (pp. 1–8). Thousand Oaks, CA: Sage Publications.

Montemayor, R., Adams, G. R., & Gullotta, T. P. (Eds.). (2000). *Adolescent diversity in ethnic, economic, and cultural contexts.* Thousand Oaks, CA: Sage Publications.

Morss, J. (1990). *The biologising of childhood.* Hove, England: Lawrence Erlbaum.

Moscovici, S. (1984). The phenomenon of social representations. In R. Farr & S. Moscovici (Eds.), *Social representations.* Cambridge: Cambridge University Press.

New, R. S. (1993). Culture, child development, and developmentally appropriate practices: Teachers as collaborative researchers. In B. L. Mallory & R. S. New (Eds.), *Diversity and developmentally appropriate practices* (pp. 70–72). New York: Teachers College Press.

New, R. S. (1998). Theory and praxis in Reggio Emilia: They know what they are doing, and Why. In C. Edwards, L. Gandini, & G. Forman (Eds.), *The hundred languages of children* (2nd ed.). Greenwich, CT: Ablex Publishing.

Nieto, S. (2004). *Affirming diversity: The sociopolitical context* (4th ed.). Boston: Pearson Education.

Noddings, N. (1984). *Caring: A feminine approach to ethics and moral education.* Berkeley: University of California Press.

Noddings, N. (1992). *The challenge to care in schools: An alternative approach to education.* New York: Teachers College Press.

Noddings, N. (2002). *Educating moral people: A caring alternative to character education.* New York: Teachers College Press.

Packard, V. (1983). *Our endangered children.* Boston: Little, Brown.

Padilla, A. M. (2001). Issues in culturally appropriate assessment. In L. A. Suzuki, J. G. Ponterotto, & P. J. Meller (Eds.), *Handbook of multicultural assessment: Clinical, psychological, and educational applications* (2nd ed., pp. 5–27). San Francisco: Jossey-Bass.

Pai, Y., & Pemberton, D. (1987). *Findings on Korean-American early adolescents and adolescents.* Kansas City, MO: School of Education, University of Missouri–Kansas City.

Paley, V. (1999). *The kindness of children.* Cambridge, MA: Harvard University Press.

Piaget, J. (1963). *The psychology of intelligence.* Paterson, NJ: Littlefield, Adams.

Piaget, J., & Inhelder, B. (1969). *The psychology of the child* (H. Weaver, Trans.). New York: Basic Books. (Original work published 1966)

Polakow, V. (1992). *The erosion of childhood.* Chicago: University of Chicago Press.

Postman, N. (1981). *The disappearance of childhood.* New York: Delacorte Press.

Qoyawayma, P., with V. Carlson. (1977). *No turning back: A Hopi Indian woman's struggle to live in two worlds.* Albuquerque: University of New Mexico Press. (Original work published 1964)

Riley, P. (Ed.). (1993). *Growing up Native American.* New York: Avon Books.

Rogers, R. S., & Rogers, W. S. (1992). *Stories of childhood: Shifting agendas of child concern.* Helmel Hempstead, England: Harvester-Wheatsheaf.

Rogoff, B. (1990). *Apprenticeship in thinking: Cognitive development in social context.* New York: Oxford University Press.

Schunk, D. H. (2004). *Learning theories: An educational perspective* (4th ed.). Upper Saddle River, NJ: Pearson Education.

Search Institute. (1984). *Young adolescents and their parents: Project report.* Minneapolis, MN: Author. More than 80 percent of this study population consists of white middle- and upper-middle-class children.

Shellenberger, S. (1982). Presentation and interpretation of psychological data in educational setting. In C. P. Reynolds & T. B. Gutkin (Eds.), *The handbook of school psychology* (pp. 51–81). New York: John Wiley. This is a technical discussion of a wide variety of issues related to gathering, interpreting, and reporting psychological evaluation data for the purpose of making educational recommendations.

Shweder, R. A. (1991). *Thinking through cultures: Expeditions in cultural psychology.* Cambridge: Harvard University Press.

Song, W. Z. (1984). A preliminary study of the character traits of the Chinese. In W. S. Tseng & D. Y. H. Wu (Eds.), *Chinese culture and mental health.* New York: Academic Press.

Spaggiari, S. (1994, September). *History and philosophy of Reggio Emilia.* Paper presented at Reaching Potentials: The Challenge of Reggio Emilia Conference, University of Melbourne, Melbourne, Australia.

Spindler, G. D. (Ed.). (1978). *The making of psychological anthropology.* Berkeley: University of California Press.

Steinberg, S. R., & Kincheloe, J. L. (1997). Kinderculture, information saturation, and postmodern childhood. In S. R. Steinberg and J. L. Kincheloe (Eds.), *Kinderculture: The corporate construction of childhood.* Boulder, CO: Westview Press.

Steinberg, S. R., & Kincheloe, J. L. (Eds). (1997). *Kinderculture: The corporate construction of childhood.* Boulder, CO: Westview Press.

Super, C. M., & Harkness, S. (1997). The cultural structuring of child development. In J. W. Berry, P. R. Dasen, & T. S. Saraswathi (Eds.), *Handbook of cross-cultural psychology: Basic processes and human development* (2nd ed., pp. 1–39). Boston: Allyn & Bacon.

Suransky, V. P. (1982). *The erosion of childhood*. Chicago: University of Chicago Press.

Suzuki, L. A., Ponterotto, J. G., & Meller, P. J. (Eds.). (2001). *Handbook of multicultural assessment: Clinical, psychological, and educational applications* (2nd ed.). San Francisco: Jossey-Bass.

Tajfel, H. (1981). *Human groups and social categories*. Cambridge: Cambridge University Press.

Torrance, E. P. (1982). Identifying and capitalizing on the strengths of culturally different children. In C. R. Reynolds & T. B. Gutkin (Eds.), *The handbook of school psychology* (pp. 481–500). New York: John Wiley. Implications of the cultural characteristics of the assessor, the assessed, and the assessment instrument and process, and the context of assessment are discussed.

Triandis, H. C., & Heron, A. (Eds.). (1981). *Handbook of cross cultural psychology* (Vols. 1–6). Boston: Allyn & Bacon.

Walters, J., Seidel, S., & Gardner, H. (1994). Children as reflective practitioners: Bringing metacognition to the classroom. In C. Collins & J. Mangieri (Eds.), *Mindfulness: Creating powerful thinkers*. Fort Worth, TX: Harcourt Brace Jovanovich.

Wiggins, G. P. (1993). *Assessing student performance: Exploring the purpose and limits of testing*. San Francisco: Jossey-Bass.

Williams, J., & Giles, H. (1978). The changing status of women in society: An intergroup perspective. In H. Tajfel (Ed.), *Differentiation between social groups*. New York: Academic Press.

Zelizer, V. A. (1985). *Pricing the priceless child*. New York: Basic Books.

7

Culture and the Learning Process

KEY *Concepts:*

- Cognitive styles
- Discovery learning
- Genres of language
- Guided learning
- Intercultural competence
- Learning as information processing

- Learning styles
- Shared-function groups
- Social structure
- Styles of communication
- Styles of language

Today, numerous psychological theories explain how human beings and other animals such as monkeys, mice, and even flatworms learn. Educationally and in the context of schooling, these theories may be classified into three broad types or models: (1) guided learning, (2) discovery learning, and (3) learning as information processing (Spindler & Spindler, 1987, pp. 64–66).

Guided learning begins by breaking down a learning objective into a set of specific skills or bodies of information. By mastering each of the components according to a carefully prearranged sequence, the learner is able to achieve the objective. The guided learning model is frequently called behavioristic because the component skills and knowledge must be stated in behavioral terms. This view of learning has been advanced by B. F. Skinner, Robert Gagné, and David Ausubel in somewhat varied ways.

Although not new in concept, the modern version of **discovery learning** was formulated by Jerome Bruner. According to Bruner (1966), learning is the process of discovering regularity and relatedness by ordering and organizing one's experiences for solving problems. In other words, the more one tries to work out solutions to problems and independently figure things out, the more one gains new insights. Hence, greater emphasis is placed on the process of discovering than on mastering knowledge and skills.

197

As a model, **learning as information processing** is based on the view that a goal-oriented, problem-solving process helps the learner cope with simplified models of real problems, as with a computer (Schunk, 2004; Simon, 1979). The ways in which children organize and structure newly acquired knowledge and skills are viewed as similar to the way a computer works. The data that the child has interpreted and organized by using such skills as attention, encoding, and comparing with other information are either immediately used to solve problems or stored in long-term memory. From this perspective, the process of learning a subject cannot be analyzed into individual components, because the learner has to understand the interrelationships among different parts and may have to revise what has been learned earlier. Hence, proponents of the learning as information processing model do not focus on the outcomes of instruction. Rather, they are more concerned with cultivating skills that will enable them to (1) represent their problems schematically and (2) identify relations among the problem elements and recombine them into new patterns (Kneller, 1984).

Today, behavioral objectives are no longer in vogue except in certain areas of special education. However, concepts such as "competencies" and "performances" are used to assess observable learning outcomes. Though these are not behaviorist terms, the use of these notions reflects the concern that we should attempt to evaluate how learners apply their knowledge rather than how they store what they have learned. As for discovery learning and the information processing model, the subscribers of these approaches to learning have contributed much to the development of constructivism by emphasizing the importance of discovery, critical and reflective thinking, and the ability to generalize (Bruner, 1996; Eggen & Kauchak, 1996). Constructivists hold that learners construct their knowledge and meanings in collaboration with their teachers through active participation in the learning process.

CULTURAL CONDITIONS FOR LEARNING

The preceding discussion may give the impression that these types of learning represent three distinct and perhaps incompatible processes; on the contrary, these models do have certain overlapping aspects. Thus, some guided learning may be necessary in helping children raise appropriate questions for discovery learning, and learning as information processing may require that the learner discover new relationships among things he or she already knows. However, learning is not purely a psychological phenomenon, because it almost always takes place in some social and cultural setting. Many complex physical as well as cultural factors affect how people learn. Accordingly, regardless of one's own conception of learning, any attempt to understand the learning process must deal with questions about the relationships among the learner, the teacher, the context, and the purposes for learning certain knowledge or skills. These queries inevitably lead to questions regarding the role of social relationships among a wide range of individuals related to the learning environment.

In their article on primate learning and educational thought and policy, Marion Lundy Dobbert and Betty Cooke (1987) suggest that four kinds of factors affect the learning process: (1) observation and modeling, (2) social experience, (3) social conflict, and (4) play (pp. 106–113). In observation and modeling, the individual learns by watching others do things and attempting to repeat them. This process usually occurs within a group that provides a supportive climate, allowing the learner to try out things. Learning through observation and modeling is not an act the learner does alone. On the contrary, a supportive social relationship between the individual and others is an important condition.

Learning in a formal or informal educational setting involves other people. Hence, the learner's ability to maintain complex relationships with others influences how he or she learns. Such an ability, as well as the learner's own sense of personal identity and roles, is developed through social experiences of associating with others. As social experience is an essential aspect of learning, so is social conflict. Through encounters with interpersonal conflicts, an individual may learn to work cooperatively with others to resolve various problems stemming from aggression, competition, and struggle for power.

For young children, play is neither a trivial nor a useless activity because it contains most of the physical, cognitive, and behavioral elements of adult life. In their play, children learn to solve problems, work cooperatively with others, cope with conflict and competition, and maintain complex social relationships. Beresin (2002), for example, observed that children responded to the terrorist attacks of September 11, 2001, by incorporating references to the events in their play. These responses showed the children coping with their own physical and emotional saftey. Through play, children also learn their own culture. Not surprisingly, we can often find out about the norms of another culture by observing the rules according to which children communicate, behave, and learn in their play. For example, "playing house" involves trying out different roles, reversing roles, punishing bad behaviors, rewarding good deeds, and dealing with conflicting interests. For this reason, "the more children play freely, the more experience they build up and the more likely they are to be able to solve complex problems in later life" (Dobbert & Cooke, 1987, p. 108).

Dobbert and Cooke's discussion of observation and modeling, social experience, social conflict, and play gives us useful insight into the roles these factors play in learning. But whether or not one agrees with Dobbert and Cooke's classification of learning mechanisms, their view does point out a fundamental aspect of the learning process. Although there are psychological conditions for learning, their significance cannot be known unless we understand what meanings they carry in different cultural contexts. Christine Bennett (1997) points out that in her work in schools, it is evident that "we must be able to cue into the characteristics that affect the way a person learns. Some of these references are accurately labeled individual differences, others are cultural differences, or, preferably, cultural alternatives" (pp. 130–131). For example, psychology tells us that rewards are reinforcing and punishments lead to avoidance behavior. But it cannot tell us whether giving a hug to a person is equally rewarding in all cultures. Nor can it inform us about how punitive the act of yelling at a person is in one culture as opposed to another, because specific acts or events have no inherent meaning unless seen from a particular cultural perspective.

Like all human behavior, learning must be viewed in the context of the total sociocultural setting in which it takes place. The specific values, attitudes, norms of behavior, ways of thinking, styles of communication, and modes of interpersonal relationships the larger society expects from its young become the bases of formulating the school's policies, procedures, curriculum, and pedagogy. These norms of the dominant society and the changing conceptions of childhood are the cultural factors that influence how and what people learn.

In a society as diverse as in the United States, students come to school with many distinct cultural backgrounds. The ways in which these young people think, interact, and communicate with others, as well as their value priorities, often clash with those of the school and its personnel. These cultural differences or discontinuities often become a source of misunderstanding and conflict. Gutmann (2003) calls this "asymmetry of cultural belongingness" and says it presents a challenge to institutions like schools if the democratic ideal of equal participation is to be achieved (p. 196). These consequences of cultural differences may lead to inappropriate educational evaluation of, and planning for, culturally different young people. For this reason, the remainder of this chapter will (1) discuss the relationship among social structure, communication styles, and the teaching–learning processes and (2) examine cross-cultural implications for practitioners.

SOCIAL STRUCTURE, COMMUNICATION STYLES, AND THE TEACHING–LEARNING PROCESS

Social Structure

The concept of **social structure** can be defined in many different ways. For the purpose of our discussion, the school's social structure is that complex of formal and informal role relationships that exists among students, teachers, counselors, administrators, and other school personnel. Integral to this structure are the school's academic, social, and behavioral expectations. The social structure of the school functions as an official agent of the dominant society. It defines and rewards culturally approved values, skills, and attitudes; punishes deviance; and provides opportunities for the young to learn various adult roles (Gay, 2000; Sieber & Gordon, 1981). However, the learner must function not only within the social structure of the school but also within that of his or her own family and community.

For most white middle-class children, the social structures of the school and their families share essentially the same characteristics. However, many minority children will find the school's social structure radically different from that of their family or ethnic community. Consequently, to these minority children, going to school means having to function according to two divergent social structures with fundamentally different sets of rules (Thomas, 2000). Hence, the effectiveness with which the child can function and learn in school is related to the degree of continuity between the school and the family environment. The greater the differences between the norms of the school and the culture of the child's family, the more difficulties he or she is likely to encounter in learning. For example, in general, white middle-class children are more likely to interact with adult members of their family in a way very similar to the manner in which they relate to teachers and other adults in school. However, minority children who have been reared to be docile and conforming to grown-ups' demands may find it difficult to meet the school's expectation that good students be more assertive in exchanging their views with other students and the teacher.

According to a study of Native American and non-Native American young-sters' classroom participation patterns (Philips, 1972), Native American children tended to become involved more effectively in classroom activities that did not require a great deal of teacher control. On the other hand, non-Native American middle-class children participated more effectively in typical classroom activities. The Native American children's participation patterns appear to be a result of growing up in a cultural environment in which peer relationships were more important than the hierarchical relationship between adults and children. However, the non-Native American children's patterns of classroom participation seem to be attributable to growing up with role-differentiated relationships between children and their elders. Other studies of minority youth not only support these findings but also suggest that the learning failures of Native Americans (Erickson & Mohatt, 1988; Smith & Shade, 1997), African Americans (Kochman, 1972), and Hawaiian Americans (Au, 1980) are attributable to differences in the participation structures of these ethnic communities and their schools. These studies amply illustrate the kinds of difficulties minority students may encounter when they move from the social structure of their own ethnic communities to that of the school.

Frequently, a child unable to perform according to school norms receives poor evaluations and is unfairly labeled, a result not only of academic performance but also of his or her interactional patterns (Rist, 1985; Shade, 1997). Unfair labeling often contributes to the teacher's minimal academic expectations from minority students. These lower expectations become self-fulfilling prophecies when the labeling is accepted by students. White middle-class children, too, may be affected adversely by unfair labeling practices and self-fulfilling prophecies. One of the crucial problems of cultural discontinuities between the school and minority students is that these differences "trigger implicit evaluations which in intricate ways reinforce larger institutional patterns of unequal treatment" (Collins, 1988, p. 309).

To minimize, if not eliminate, unequal treatment of schoolchildren and help them learn optimally, the school needs to take into account the negative impact of cultural discontinuities between the social structures of the school and ethnic communities in assessing the educability of the culturally different. In addition, the school can initially provide the kinds of learning environments to which minority children have been accustomed so that they can learn successfully. Then, the "ethnicity of a child's learning style undergoes modification of the child to his or her broader culture" (Pepper & Henry, 1997, p. 168). Following their successes in such supportive school conditions, the culturally different children can be guided to function equally well in a social structure that operates according to the norms of the mainstream culture.

Styles of Communication

Forging and maintaining appropriate relationships within a social structure are achieved through effective communication. In this sense, communication is neither a simple matter of transmitting a body of information to another person nor receiving messages from others. Rather, it is a process by which people try to influence one another by "interpreting one's own and others' actions, and . . . performing actions that will be interpreted" (Pearce & Kang, 1988, p. 25). Here, the term *actions* refers to both verbal and nonverbal behaviors. Certain principles or norms of interpreting other people's actions emerge when individuals act by adjusting themselves to the behavioral patterns of others (Carroll, 1981). Individuals who share these norms have certain expectations of behavior for each other. For example, in the United States, waving one's hand to another person in a particular manner is understood as "Good-bye," because most of us share a common set of criteria for interpreting this behavior. However, to persons from a different culture or social structure, such a behavior may carry an opposite meaning, such as "Please come here."

All individuals and groups have distinct **styles of communication** that include style of speech, varied forms of language, and such nonverbal behaviors as postures and gestures. As one of the keys to understanding students, the significance of knowing about styles of communication cannot be overlooked. As Gay (2000) points out, when "teachers know about the discourse styles of ethnically diverse students, the better they [teachers] will be able to improve academic achievement" (p. 109). In the material that follows, different pairs of styles illustrate the continuum of communication patterns. This range of preferences provides a glimpse of the richness of communicative relationships. However, which mode of communication one uses in a given situation depends on the nature of the social relationships that characterize a particular social structure or culture.

Direct and Indirect Styles

Direct, or low-context, communication refers to the style in which the speaker expresses his or her thoughts and intentions directly in explicit verbal messages. This style, often known as "straight talk," is sender-oriented in that the speaker is responsible for delivering clear, accurate, and convincing messages. On the other hand, in indirect, or high-context, communication the speaker uses indirect verbal and nonverbal expressions to convey his or her messages. Here, the receiver is responsible for accurately inferring or interpreting the hidden meanings and intent of the verbal messages. "Reading between the lines" is often required in this process (Ting-Toomey, 1999, p. 101). For example, the Korean expression *nunchi* (pronounced "noon-chi") refers to a person's ability to "size up the situation correctly" without talking or asking questions. This notion is so important in communication that having good *nunchi* is tantamount to having high intelligence.

In the United States, mainstream culture places primary emphasis on the individual. For this reason, communication tends to be explicit and direct. However, in cultures that focus on the relationship between individuals (e.g., Asian, Native American, and Hispanic cultures), communication is likely to be indirect, and the meanings of the messages will vary according to the context of interaction (Ibarra, 1999, 2001). In other words, U.S. culture is person-centered rather than human-relationship centered. It is not difficult to see why those who use the direct communication style may view the indirect communicators as "beating around the bush" and the latter may see the former as being "pushy" or rude. This kind of misunderstanding between teachers and students may become a serious barrier in teaching and learning.

Informal and Formal Styles

These styles are also known as person-oriented and status-oriented styles (Ting-Toomey, 1999, pp. 106–107). Informal, or person-oriented, communication reflects an egalitarian worldview that de-emphasizes the differences in individuals' status and prescribed roles. In this mode, informal verbal expressions are used without complex codes of behavior or ritualized language. Further, each individual's uniqueness, rather than social or professional status, is recognized. For this reason, communication often occurs on a first-name basis. The informality characterizes the communication styles of both African American and Anglo-American groups (Grossman, 1995).

Unlike the informal style, the formal, or status-oriented, style uses verbal and nonverbal expressions that are prescribed as appropriate for honoring individuals' status and roles. For example, Koreans and Japanese use expressions that distinguish others according to their status, prescribed roles, age, and gender. Their languages have several different terms for the English word *you* that are used in addressing others according to their status, gender, and age. Even after many years of close personal relationships, Koreans and Korean Americans tend to address each other with expressions that reflect their professional positions and social status (e.g., President Kim, Professor Lee, Dean Park, Elder Yoon). The predominant communication style for Hispanic Americans and Asian Americans tends to be formal and status-oriented (Grossman, 1995). This kind of communication style is also found in the cultures of Iran, Egypt, and Turkey (Samovar & Porter, 1997, p. 105). It should not be surprising to find that teachers in U.S. schools may interpret the formality of children from the already mentioned cultural groups as being shy, timid, or unmotivated (Ruan, 2003).

Self-Enhancement and Self-Effacement Styles

Self-enhancement, or expressive, communication style focuses on the importance of clearly communicating one's accomplishments and abilities (Ting-Toomey, 1999, pp. 107–109). This means the speaker has the responsibility of presenting his or her own accomplishments to persuade others regarding one's own ability. Self-enhancement style becomes extremely important in any self-evaluation process. In the Western cultures where this style is valued, a person who is convinced that his or her work has been good believes that good performances should be documented so that the person could "sell" oneself. In this context, self-assertiveness becomes an important trait. On the other hand, self-effacement, or understated, style emphasizes the value of being humble and modest about one's own success (pp. 107–109). It stresses the importance of exercising verbal restraint in talking about personal successes and capabilities. The self-effacement style in Asian cultures is reflected in such common remarks as "Well, what I did was really nothing," or "I really haven't done anything," or "My work is OK but there are others who can do this much better than I can." Such self-effacing and self-deprecating statements are based on the belief that the person's success would be recognized by others in his or her behavior. This attitude contributes to the tendency of Asian Americans to self-evaluate themselves more modestly than their white counterparts. It is not difficult to see why Asians often misunderstand Westerners as boastful while the latter perceive the former as lacking in self-confidence.

Self-enhancement and *self-effacement* are relative terms. That is, one group is more or less self-enhancing or self-effacing when compared with another group. What is important is not identifying which cultural group always self-enhances or self-effaces but rather determining which communication style is most appropriate in a given cultural context. For example, as self-enhancement is self-defeating in Japan, so is self-effacement self-defeating in the United States.

Topic-Centered Communication and Topic-Associating Communication Styles

In approaching a particular topic, some communicate in a topic-centered manner and others use the topic-associating style (Stefani, 1997, p. 353). Topic-centered speakers tend to focus on the matter in question and other closely related topics. On the other hand, topic-associating persons are likely to relate the topic to episodes involving certain events, persons, or themes. One of the authors recalls that when a group of white middle-class college students were asked about the meaning of freedom, they enumerated several definitions of the term and then pointed out the one they considered most appropriate and sound. However, when the same question was raised with a number of African and Hispanic Americans, they recounted the personal experiences of oppression, which reflected their conviction that more freedom is necessary for minority groups.

While these students were convinced that they had successfully communicated the meaning of freedom through their personal experiences, others did not see the relevance of the stories to the question at hand. Because U.S. schools emphasize topic-centered communication, children who have a topic-associating communication style may be misunderstood as not properly responding to their teachers or as intellectually deficient.

Nonverbal Communication

All cultures have varied forms of nonverbal communication, including such non-linguistic behaviors as the use of personal space, gestures, facial expressions, eye contact, and silence. The uses of nonverbal behaviors in conveying explicit and implicit messages vary according to culture, ethnicity, and nationality as well as gender, age, and even the circumstances under which interactions occur. More specifically, the use of personal space or how far or closely people stand next to each other and how much touching and gesturing go on between them indicate the nature of relationships and attitudes toward each other. Some cultures encourage their members to use facial expressions to show personal emotions of approval or disapproval. Other societies discourage such expressions. Similarly, maintaining direct eye contact is considered as showing attentiveness, respect, and self-confidence to others in certain cultural groups. In other cultures, avoiding direct eye contact is thought of as reflecting respect and deference. In such a society, looking directly at an older person or someone who occupies a higher position is viewed as showing disrespect and insolence.

Like other nonverbal behaviors, silence also conveys different meanings. For example, in East Asian and Far Eastern societies, being quiet is usually seen as a sign of respect for authority, wisdom, and knowledge. Silence is also a means of dealing with either an awkward or ambiguous social situation in which one is not clear about what to do. Personal disapproval is often expressed by not speaking. In Western cultures, silence is frequently viewed as implying ignorance, indifference, disrespect, or even hostility. In general, these societies tend to be less tolerant of silence, for it is thought to reflect a nonparticipatory attitude.

The frequency with which nonverbal behaviors are used for communication varies according to cultural norms and the contexts of interaction as well as age and gender. This suggests that there is likely to be as much variation in the uses of different kinds of nonverbal communication modes across cultural groups as there is within one culture. Clearly, teachers' misunderstanding of their students' nonverbal communication could impair the teaching–learning processes. As Stella Ting-Toomey (1999) so aptly points out,

> Intercultural clashes arise when we unintentionally use our own culture-bound evaluations in judging dissimilar [nonverbal behaviors]. Our mindless versus mindful orientations in interpreting these different . . . communication styles can ultimately influence the quality of our intergroup relationship development with dissimilar others. (p. 101)

Intercultural Competence

As citizens and educators in a multicultural society, how can we become competent and effective intercultural communicators? Assuming that we are interested in communicating with those who have different cultural backgrounds than our own, there are two major components of **intercultural competence**, including cognitive and affective components. The cognitive component consists of knowledge about other cultures as well as our own. It is essential to have specific knowledge about the norms and communication styles of other cultures. This knowledge is a significant component of what Gay (2000) calls "culturally competent instructional action." In order to act on the commitment to teach all students effectively, Gay stresses that educators must "have knowledge of the cultural characteristics of different ethnic groups and of how culture affects teaching and learning" (p. 209). We also need to have skills of interacting with those who are different from us. While much effort is necessary to gain knowledge about other societies and develop the skills of managing our interactions with them, having a clear and critical understanding of our own culture may require even more work. Like air, our own culture is all around us and we tend to think of it as being "naturally right." If we are to avoid being ethnocentric, we must understand both the strengths and weaknesses of our own culture.

The affective component of intercultural competence includes such attitudes as "empathy," "tolerance for ambiguity," "nonjudgmentalness" (Martin & Nakayama, 1997, pp. 268–271), and "caring" (Gay, 2000, pp. 45–76). Empathy refers to the ability to see things from another person's perspective. This involves asking "If I were in those shoes, how would I feel?" Clearly, we are not able to see the world as another person would because we cannot become that person. Yet, we may find some aspects of our own experiences that are close to the other person's experience. For example, in attempting to empathize with a newly arrived minority child who feels awkward and uncomfortable in school, we could try to think back to our own experiences of being new in a group of strangers whose experiences and backgrounds were significantly different from our own. This requires self-reflection as well as knowledge about and experiences in other cultures and worldviews.

Tolerance for ambiguity is related to the willingness and ability to deal with a situation, which requires that we act according to unfamiliar norms and rules. Recognition of and openness to other cultural practices as different but legitimate ways of achieving the same purpose are essential in effective intercultural communication. When we judge the behaviors of culturally different people according to our own cultural norms, we are being judgmental. This approach frequently leads us to misunderstand the intentions and meanings of others, which often contributes to unintended cultural conflicts. We may avoid such conflicts by first describing, rather than interpreting or evaluating, the person's behavior. For example, saying that a person talked loudly and rapidly is giving a descriptive account. However, reporting that the person spoke angrily is making a judgment about the person's behavior. In other words, reporting to the teacher that "Nancy was silent in the class" describes her behavior. But saying "Nancy was indifferent in the class" is being judgmental. Effective intercultural communication is made possible by first describing other people's behaviors, then asking about their meanings in a given cultural context. Martin and Nakayama (1997) suggest that when we show such culture-general behaviors as being respectful, showing interest, and being friendly as well as polite, we may contribute to effective intercultural communication (p. 271). For Gay (2000), the interpersonal classroom relationships characterized as "caring" include the teacher's demonstration of "patience, persistence, facilitation, validation, and empowerment" for the students (p. 47). She further points out that while most teachers have good intentions, when students of color do not act according to the mainstream culture's norms, those same well-intentioned teachers can see the students as "unlovable, problematic, and difficult to honor or embrace without equivocation" (p. 46).

Much research has been done in the area of intercultural communication. Given the scope of this book, our explanations of the various communication styles have been very broad and general. However, the following discussion of the communication styles of Asian Americans, African Americans, Hispanic Americans, and Native Americans may help us see how these different modes of communication may help or hinder the educational development of culturally different students in our schools.

There is danger of overgeneralizing, and thus stereotyping, when we describe the characteristics of any one group of people. As Pickering (2001) points out, "stereotyping attempts to deny any flexible thinking within categories" (p. 3). In the strict sense, findings of an ethnographic study of a group should apply only to that group. Yet, as Heath (1986) aptly points out, "The public at large uses inclusive labels for groups of people: Chicanos, Native Americans, Indo-Chinese, Asians, Blacks, Hispanics, etc." (p. 153). Little attention is paid to variations of characteristics based on people's age, gender, length of stay in the country, educational levels, socioeconomic status, and regional locations, as well as their religious affiliations. For the sake of an accurate understanding of another ethnic group, subdivisions of the group ought to be studied separately. Notwithstanding the wide variations found within a racial or ethnic group, some broad characteristics are more or less ascribable to groups as a whole. For example, the deferential attitude young people have toward their elders may be common to all Asian Americans as well as to Hispanic and Native American groups. What is important in this discussion is that educators recognize the legitimacy of divergent styles of communicating, thinking, and learning so that children who exhibit nonmainstream patterns are not judged as possessing pathological conditions (Fitzberg, 2001). As stressed in early chapters, this is not to suggest that every communication style is as functional as every other style, for some modes may be more effective than others for certain purposes. Thus, rather than attempting to have all learners use only the mainstream style of communication, educators ought to help each child use the mode most appropriate for achieving his or her educational goals.

Asian Americans

Cultural values and worldviews have significant influence on behaviors and communication styles. Thus, the fact that Asian Americans come from a strongly family-centered tradition with a rigidly hierarchical interpersonal relationship has a strong impact on their communication style (Dao, 1997; Hsu, 1982; Pang, 1997; Ruan, 2003; Sue, 1981; Suzuki, 1980). Within the hierarchical social structure of Asian American communities, the roles of individuals are defined according to age, sex, and status. Further, individuals are expected to deal with problems indirectly so as not to offend others. Docility, respect for authority, and restraint of strong feelings are encouraged, while direct expression of feelings and thoughts is strongly discouraged. Because communication flows from higher to lower positions in the hierarchy, it is considered inappropriate for children to participate in adult conversation or decision making. Accordingly, elders frown upon children asking "why" questions.

Clearly, radical differences exist between these traits of Asian Americans and the school's emphasis on assertiveness, informal social relationships, spontaneity, direct communication, and active involvement in various activities. Because of these differences, Asian Americans are frequently judged as less autonomous, less assertive, more conforming, less expressive, and hence "inscrutable." Although these are general descriptions of Asian Americans, these characteristics manifest themselves in the behaviors of Asian American young people. For example, in general, Asian American students are not likely to participate actively in classroom discussions, seek explanations or other forms of help from teachers, or become involved in open discussions about academic matters or personal problems. On the other hand, their deferential attitude toward teachers and willingness to conform to the rules of the school and the classroom may lead teachers to see them as either shy or "model students." This image often hides other underlying emotional, social, or even academic problems, which are usually disclosed to family members or intimate friends only (Leong, Chao, & Hardin, 2000).

African Americans

Although African Americans have a very strong oral/aural tradition of storytelling with an emphasis on stylish delivery, nonverbal behaviors are also considered important elements in their mode of communication. Elsie Smith (1981) points out that African Americans are prone to spend much time unobtrusively observing people to see "where they are coming from." Moreover, they do not have to maintain direct eye contact while talking to each other. School personnel often interpret this behavior as an indication of disinterest, fear, or lack of self-confidence.

Similar interpretations are given to this nonverbal behavior of Asian American, Hispanic American, and Native American children. Shade (1997), who conducted a comprehensive review of the research on the cognitive patterns of African Americans, asks, "How do African Americans come to know the world?" From this review she concludes that "their knowledge is gained most effectively through kinetic and tactile senses, through keen observations of the human scene, and through verbal descriptions" (p. 86). In a cross-national comparison of African American cultural forms in schools, Solomon (1988) found that African Americans in U.S. schools use both Black English and Standard English as a means of communication as well as a symbol of their identity (p. 256). Many African American students respond to their teachers in Standard English but communicate with their peers in Black English. Claudia Mitchell-Kernan (1985) is probably correct in reminding us that the use of Black English does "symbolize a spirit of liberation in the black community, and the separatist function of Black English has become more explicit" (p. 209). However, in the area of nonverbal behavior, teachers and counselors often interpret African American youngsters' stylized sulking gestures and body movements as an expression of resistance and a challenge to the school authority. Not surprisingly, African American students who display such a "bad attitude" are frequently denied opportunities for participating in special enrichment or honors programs (Solomon, 1988, p. 257). This is only one illustration of how differences in communication styles can result in unequal education because "attitude" is considered more important than academic achievement.

Hispanic Americans

The Hispanic American category includes several different ethnic groups with many varied historical, linguistic, cultural, and even legal backgrounds. However, studies suggest that the following general communication characteristics would apply to all of the groups in varying degrees (Carter & Segura, 1979; Castro, Boyer & Balcazar, 2000; Heath, 1986; Levine & Levine, 1996; Ramirez & Castaneda, 1974).

In general, Hispanic children are socialized to observe and emulate adults, who do not usually give them specific instructions. Nor do children orally report what they are doing. As is the case with Asian Americans, communication flows from adults to children generally in the form of commands and demands. Children are expected to follow or conform to these commands or demands without questioning. The young rarely initiate social conversations with adults, who neither consider children as conversational partners nor accept them as active participants in decision making. In the area of thinking, Hispanic children are much more sensitive to the global or overall view of a situation or a concept than to its component parts. Moreover, because these young people are more concerned with social or interpersonal relationships and opinions of others than with impersonal facts, they tend to mix the cognitive with the affective aspects of their experience. Of course, whites also are interested in social and interpersonal relationships; however, in school, children are encouraged to separate expressions of personal feelings from reports of factual information.

Not surprisingly, the school requires that students think objectively and analytically and express their ideas in a logical and detail-specific way. In addition,
the young are expected to respond promptly to their teachers' questioning and
to frequently express their thoughts and feelings in public. When Hispanic children are judged solely in terms of these school norms, they are likely to be seen
as having little interest in education and as intellectually inferior to white middle-class children. A key point of this discussion is not to argue that either the
way of the school or of Hispanic children should be discarded, because each has
its own strengths and weaknesses. Much more important is the responsibility of
educators to help these children learn to communicate effectively by using the
most appropriate means of relating to others. This requires that the teacher be
able to appreciate the "lived" culture of the child because "the inability of
schools to accomodate these differences may be one of the major factors which
exacerbates academic and social failure" (Shade, 1997, p. 39).

Native Americans

The Native American group includes many different nations, each with a unique
historical and cultural heritage. An increasing number of research studies have
reported the communication styles of these groups in relation to education
(Pewewardy, 2002; Swisher & Deyhle, 1992), but many of the characteristics of
Native American communication style have to be gleaned from information
about other aspects of Native American cultures and described in rather general
terms. Although general work like this provides some broad-brush information, it
overlooks the significance of local contexts and needs to be viewed with caution.
According to Edwin H. Richardson's (1981) comparative study of Native American and mainstream norms, several Native American values have significant bearing on their communication style. The Native American emphasis on personal
humility, respect for elders, learning through storytelling or legends, intuitiveness, preference for a low-key profile, concern for group harmony, having few
and flexible rules, and simplifying problems would directly influence communication style. This tendency toward intuitiveness, learning through storytelling,
simplification of problems, and preference for few and flexible rules may contribute to the global rather than analytic character of the Native American cognitive style. When Cornel Pewewardy (2002) reviewed the studies of American
Indian/Alaskan Native students' learning styles, he found that such generally
shared cultural values are "deeply rooted in the teachings of elders" (p. 23).

A study of Sioux and Cherokee children (Dumont, 1985) revealed that Sioux
children have an extremely complex system of communication, combining both
verbal and nonverbal behaviors. They seem to communicate with each other
excitedly and more frequently in the absence of an adult Sioux or white supervisor. Moreover, they tend to hesitate and restrain themselves when they are speaking to persons outside of their family or when they are singled out to read or
answer questions. Not surprisingly, when these children perform a task at the
teacher's request, they seem to be neither interested nor excited about their

involvement. According to Dumont, the Cherokee believe that the ways in which people relate to each other verbally or nonverbally are a form of moral transaction (p. 364). Hence, how something is said is as important as what is said.

Like others, Native American children communicate with verbal and non-verbal behaviors, but their attention is also focused on actions and visual elements related to words. This implies that exercises that analyze meanings and sentence structure are likely to have very little meaning to Native American children. John (1985) reports that Navajo children may be attentive to the teacher's voice, but they are just as likely to watch his or her actions (p. 334). On the basis of what the mainstream society and the school consider the "normal" and proper mode of communication, we may considerably underestimate the Native American children's educability, intellectual ability, motivation, and interest in formal education. Such misjudgment is bound to hinder these children's educational development.

Styles and Genres of Language Use

All people use both verbal and nonverbal behaviors to communicate. However, not all groups rely on written, spoken, and body language with equal emphasis. Even in the use of language, some use certain styles and forms more often than others. The frequency with which one style or form is used may be related to the purpose of the person's communicative act. On the other hand, the individual may simply be more accustomed to using one particular style or form because of his or her cultural background. Like individuals, groups, including schools, vary in their uses of language. Thus, major discrepancies between the linguistic styles of the school and those of culturally different students may contribute to the latter's serious academic as well as interpersonal difficulties (Korn & Bursztyn, 2002).

Styles of Language Use

In *The Five Clocks,* Martin Joos (1967) names five major **styles of language**: (1) the intimate style, (2) the casual style, (3) the consultative style, (4) the formal style, and (5) the frozen style. The *intimate style* is used by those who have especially close personal relationships—husbands and wives, boyfriends and girlfriends, and lovers. Thus, the intimate style contains jargons and private "codes" understandable only to the communicants. The *casual style* is used by individuals who share a close but not intimate personal relationship. These individuals use certain expressions understood only by "insiders." Telling "inside jokes" is a good example of the use of the casual style. The style often used by peers or acquaintances to convey specific information and instructions to accomplish a particular task is called the *consultative style*. In this style, the listener often becomes involved in the communication process by injecting such expressions of acknowledgment as "I see," "I understand," or "OK." Unlike the styles already mentioned, the *formal style* does not allow for listener participation, for it is the style most frequently used in prepared lectures and speeches. The *frozen style,* which is used solely for print, does not involve active interaction between the writer ("speaker") and the reader ("listener").

The styles commonly used in school tend to be more formal and frozen than intimate, casual, or even consultative. Many African American, Hispanic, and Native American students are likely to find learning through the exclusive use of formal and frozen language styles to be difficult because these styles do not permit meaningful interactions between students and their teachers. On the other hand, teachers who prefer to relate to their students through the intimate or casual styles might find that Asian American young people appear to be reticent or uncomfortable. Each of the five styles serves unique and special functions, but not all groups use them with equal emphasis. Thus, schools may be able to help their students learn more effectively by using a wider variety of styles, which are at once familiar to students and appropriate for certain instructional purposes. Indeed, there is no good reason to believe that only the formal and frozen styles are educationally sound and desirable.

Genres of Language Use

In addition to the different styles of language use, there are also divergent forms of language related to varied linguistic functions. According to Shirley Brice Heath (1986), **genres of language** are synonymous with forms, schemas, or molds of language use that stand for "maps or plans for stretches of discourse" (pp. 166–167). Heath describes (1) label quests, (2) meaning quests, (3) recounts, (4) accounts, (5) eventcasts, and (6) stories as basic genres of uses of language (pp. 168–171). Each genre has its own set of rules, which are organized so that initial clues enable listeners to predict the nature of the coming discourse. For example, "When I was your age . . ." would clearly suggest that a lecture about one's behavior might be coming.

As cultural groups differ in their uses of language styles, so do the range of genres and the extent to which certain genres are used by these groups and families vary. Similarly, schools use some oral and written genres more frequently than others. This suggests that the proficiency with which children can effectively use the genres valued highly by the school can profoundly influence their school success.

According to Heath, label quests and meaning quests are the two genres most frequently used in school learning activities. The remaining four genres are used by children as they integrate and expand the first two genres in their acquisition of language.

The language activities related to *label quests* include asking questions about the names and properties of objects, places, persons, and body parts. These questions generally begin with such words as *what, where,* and *who.* In school, students, particularly those in early primary grades, are asked to give names and properties of things found in their learning environment. When *meaning quests* are used, children are asked to give meanings or interpretations of words, events, behaviors, pictures, and combinations thereof. Moreover, adults often explain their interpretations of children's own behaviors. Uses of meaning quests are illustrated in the teacher's requests that students explain an author's intended meaning of his or her work or interpret the meanings of certain written passages. In school, teachers of reading, literature, and other humanities courses frequently rely on this genre.

In the use of the genre called *recounts,* a person retells certain events or repeats information already known to the teller and listener. A child may be asked to repeat a story read in a book or recount something that happened while playing with others. In a school setting, students may be asked to summarize a class discussion, a lecture, or a chapter they have just read. Proficient use of this genre is particularly important in doing well on tests that require accurate recounting of materials read, heard, or discussed. Studies of Chinese and Mexican American families by Heath (1986) reveal that recounts occur rarely in these groups (pp. 172, 173). Given the hierarchical nature of the parent–child relationship and the predominant communication styles of African American, Native American, and Asian American families, we might reasonably suspect that adults in these groups infrequently request recounts from their children.

Children telling their parents about what happened at school or at a party, or a spouse explaining the details of an automobile accident, are examples of the *accounts* genre. The use of this genre is initiated by the teller for the purpose of conveying new information or reinterpretations of known events (e.g., an insurance adjuster's description of how the accident "really occurred") to the listener. Characteristic uses of the accounts genre in school occur in creative writing classes, show-and-tell sessions, and advanced classes that require students to interpret what they have learned on the basis of their personal experiences.

In *eventcasts,* the speaker gives a running description of an event in progress, as a media correspondent might explain what is going on at a Senate hearing or a sportscaster might cover a Super Bowl game. The eventcasts genre consists of giving an account of future events. For example, statements such as "After dinner, we'll go bowling" or "After I finish my homework, I'll go to the movies" are good illustrations of the use of this genre. Children as well as adults often use the eventcasts genre by talking aloud to themselves while they are engaged in play or other activities. These speech acts either describe what the speakers are doing or refer to something they will do after completing their current activity. Teachers provide eventcasts by explaining their semester plan in a particular course to students or by giving step-by-step instructions to those who are about to engage in a physical exercise activity in the gym.

The genre of *stories* involves telling stories about certain facts, which are elaborated or exaggerated to make them interesting to the listener. Uses of the stories genre frequently involve the listener's imagination, as children often imagine when they listen to bedtime stories. In school, historical studies or science lessons are sometimes supplemented with historical fictions, docudramas, and science fiction tales to clarify and illustrate key points and infer certain ethical implications from them.

These six genres of language use by no means exhaust all possible uses of language. However, they appear to be the patterns most frequently employed by middle-class families and the school in teaching children the uses of language (Heath, 1984). Heath explains that when a mainstream child is asked to "read" a book with only pictures, the child is asked to label, give *meanings* of events portrayed by the pictures, *recount* the story, and compare it with personal *accounts*. In art classes, children are asked to give an *eventcast* by explaining what they are doing or may do in the future. They are further asked to illustrate and clarify the important points of their work by providing *stories*.

Patterns of Language Use and the School

The school, as well as other institutions in the larger society, requires all six or more genres of language use. Hence, much of our children's success in school and in their future workplaces depends largely upon the degree of proficiency with which they can use a wide range of these genres. However, not all cultural groups use the same range or kinds of genres with equal emphasis. Although the school as a whole values and utilizes a much larger repertoire of linguistic genres than individual families, the number of different patterns used in individual classrooms tends to be quite limited. For this reason, it is important for teachers to help children practice as many different patterns of language use as possible, both within and outside their classroom setting. In their review of the history of American Indian education, Reyhner & Eder (2004) voice the view that "Native people, on the whole, have favored schools that teach their children non-Indian ways without forcing them to forget their Indian ways" (p. 330). By cooperating closely with families and ethnic communities, schools may be able to help children learn genres not commonly used in their own cultural groups. This can be accomplished through youth group activities, community service projects, and church programs, in conjunction with formal and informal school offerings. Heath (1986) is correct in pointing out that "it is the responsibility of the school to facilitate expanded language uses in English and other languages for students from all sociocultural and class backgrounds" (p. 179).

LEARNING STYLES AND EDUCATION

Much of the current literature on the relationship between culture and learning indicates that ethnicity and culture have greater influence on how people learn than social class (Banks, 1988; Hollins, King, & Hayman, 1994; Nieto, 2004). Yet, there are some who point out that, because of insufficient research in this area, we do not know enough about the role of social class in learning in different cultural groups (Shapiro, Sewell, & DuCette, 1995, p. 66). Despite such disagreement, there is sufficient evidence to say that learners do follow distinct and consistent patterns of processing information—that is, **learning styles**—that are preferred by their own cultures (Shade, 1997; Thomas, 2000). For example, in some cultural groups, learners rely more heavily on auditory input and others tend to depend on visual experiences. Further, while individuals in some cultures learn with others in a cooperative climate, there are those who choose to work independently in a competitive environment. A main premise underlying today's discussions about learning styles is the claim that instruction becomes more effective and enriching when a person's learning style is matched with the key elements of teaching strategies and environment.

Cognitive Styles

In recent times, the terms *cognitive style* and *learning style* have been used interchangeably. But more accurately, **cognitive style** is the broader and more basic term (p. 54) because it refers to "a person's way of responding and performing in diverse situations" (Saracho, 1997, p. 9). It influences the latter, but not vice versa. For this reason, a brief discussion of two major cognitive styles—field-independent and field-dependent—is useful.

Field-Independent Style

The individual who is field-independent tends to think analytically and in detail-specific ways. This style focuses on organizing the various elements of a situation into a cause–effect, or sequential, framework. In doing so, factual and rational aspects of the problem are separated from personal feelings or emotion. "Let's just consider the facts!" illustrates this approach. Field-independent learners are also task-oriented, and they usually prefer to work independently. For example, in planning for a picnic, field-independent people decide on a precise time and place of the picnic and identify all necessary items and responsibilities for the occasion. The items and responsibilities are then assigned to specific individuals. Prior to the actual picnic, all the elements for the event are likely to be sequentially organized. The success of the picnic depends on how the event is carried out according to the predetermined plan and time line. In the United States, members of the mainstream culture tend to be field-independent, and the schools emphasize this cognitive style as well.

Field-Dependent Style

Unlike the field-independent style, this approach focuses on the global aspect of a problem. Field-dependent individuals approach a problem holistically, thus often combining the factual elements with the emotional aspects of the situation. Field-dependent learners usually prefer to work with others in a collaborative way. Returning to the example of picnic planning, the field-dependent individuals are likely to select a suitable place for the event and agree on an approximate time to get together. The participants will be asked to bring food, drinks, and other necessary supplies. Participants are likely to be given some broad responsibilities. As a result of this rather global planning, unanticipated last-minute activities often occur. In this society, the cognitive style of shared-function groups may be characterized as field-dependent.

It is not unusual to have field-independent people view field-dependent individuals as unorganized and unsystematic, while field-dependent persons see those who are field-independent as being too mechanical and lacking in warmth. The cognitive styles we have just discussed represent two distinctive ways of responding to a variety of situations, but they are not mutually exclusive, nor is one style inherently superior to the other. In reality, a field-independent person may have certain elements of field-dependency, and vice versa. For example, a person who approaches a problem in an analytic way may often combine objective information and personal feelings. On the other hand, a field-dependent learner may deal with a situation only in terms of cognitive elements of the situation. It appears that field-independent learners tend to do better academically than field-dependent students (Cushner, 1994, p. 122). This phenomenon is consistent with the tendency for our schools to emphasize learning facts, cognitive activities rather than affects, and individual achievements.

Learning Styles

The term *learning styles* refer to distinctive patterns of behaviors, attitudes, and dispositions that reflect different cognitive and social characteristics of individuals in processing information. Although cultures prefer their own distinctive patterns, learning styles are not right or wrong. However, some styles may be more appropriate for certain kinds of learning objectives than others. Additionally, the style that works well for one person may not be effective for others. While there are numerous learning style variables, a discussion of the following major groupings is appropriate for our purpose.

Reflective and Impulsive Learning Styles

These styles are defined in terms of the amount of time learners spend on solving a problem. Certain cultures encourage individuals to think about a problem and come to a solution as quickly as possible. In such an environment, impulsive learners tend to respond to questions promptly and complete their assigned tasks rapidly. On the other hand, reflective style emphasizes taking sufficient time to think thoroughly about all possible aspects of a problem to reach the most correct answer. Here, not only are quick responses unrewarded, but the mistaken or partially correct solutions are usually considered as a consequence of hasty deliberation.

Active and Passive Learning Styles

Students in some cultures are encouraged to be personally involved in learning by actively asking questions and participating in class discussions. Not infrequently, active learners in U.S. classrooms are rewarded for contributing to the class by speaking up promptly and often. Learner initiative and leadership are also considered as desirable qualities. In contrast, passive learners in other societies are encouraged to function as passive recipients of information from teachers. They are expected to be mentally alert and attentive, but their active participation in learning is not emphasized. In this type of cultural environment, learners rely heavily on the guidance and authority of those who teach. Listening, watching, and emulating are usually considered positive characteristics of a good passive learner. Native Americans, Hispanic Americans, and Asian Americans tend to be passive learners (Grossman, 1995, p. 265). In the United States, wherein active learning is highly prized, we need to be cautious so that passive learners from other cultures are not judged as shy, unmotivated, or deficient in academic ability.

Cooperative and Independent Learning Styles

Whether individuals prefer to learn on their own or with others is influenced by culture. Cooperative learning style emphasizes high rates of peer interaction, in which learners ask for and give help as well as support each other. This cooperative learning style is encouraged by such cultural groups as African Americans, Asian Pacific Americans, Hispanic Americans, Hawaiian Americans (Hollins, King, & Hayman, 1994, p. 19) and Native Americans (Pewewardy, 2002). The independent learning style is emphasized in the mainstream culture of this country. In this context, self-initiated learning, critical thinking, and creativity, as well as individual accomplishments are prized. As compared with cooperative learners, independent learners are likely to function more effectively in a competitive learning environment.

Modalities of Learning

Cultures rely on different types of sensory channels, or modalities, that influence how individuals learn. Some learners prefer aural input more than visual, while others favor either visual or oral experiences. For example, Native Americans tend to be visual learners in that they rely on imagery to understand concepts. On the other hand, African Americans, Hispanic Americans, and some Southeast Asian Americans are more aural in their approach to learning (Grossman, 1995, p. 269). This learning by listening is usually connected to a preference for oral activity. As Saracho (1997) points out, "People learn by listening and demonstrate understanding by speaking. African American persons are more effective when they present their work orally" (p. 16).

Different cultures emphasize different learning styles, but we should not assume that all members of a particular cultural group use the same style, because individuals are capable of modifying their styles. Although learning styles have numerous components, individual learners exhibit certain consistent and habitual patterns, however knowledge of these generalized patterns must not stand in the way of gaining information about individual students. When

Bergstrom, Cleary, and Peacock (2003) interviewed 120 Native American youths, they found general preferences, but a range of uses. One of the students, Gina, explained that when her teacher used a learning style test with the class, "'it kind of made me feel like this teacher's going to think he knows how to teach this to me'" (p. 103). It is important to keep in mind that a person's learning style tells us about how an individual generally learns but not about the most appropriate way of learning for that person. In other words, a person's style is not necessarily the most effective means of learning just because the learner prefers a particular style. For example, a heavy reliance on imagery may not be the best way of learning abstract concepts to a visual learner. Nor is the verbal approach the most effective means of learning to appreciate music. Educationally, our task should be more than simply matching teaching strategies to the students' learning styles. Rather, it should be one of providing the kinds of learning environments and teaching styles that will enable learners of all types to achieve their purposes. As important as learning styles are in understanding their influence on learning in a multicultural society, we should be careful not to exaggerate their role in developing instructional strategies and curricular programs. "What is clear, however, is that people learn differently and that some learners have strengths in areas that are unique to them and that make them different from other learners" (Shapiro, Sewell, & DuCette, 1995, p. 66). Our knowledge of culturally preferred learning styles may help us utilize the strengths of individual learners to make learning more effective. Moreover, an understanding of the learning style preferences of those who come from different cultural backgrounds could prevent us from making hasty and stereotypic judgements, which may be unfair and harmful to the educational development of the culturally different learners.

CONNECTING CULTURALLY WITH STUDENTS

Come for a moment to the playground of the Franklin Elementary School in Oakland, where black girls like to chant their jump-roping numbers in Chinese. "See you mañana," one student shouts with a Vietnamese accent. "Ciao!" cries another, who has never been anywhere near Italy. And let it be noted that the boy who won the National Spelling Bee . . . was born in India . . . and speaks Tamil at home. . . . Graffiti sprayed in a nearby park send their obscure signals in Farsi. . . . The Los Angeles County court system now provides interpreters for eighty different languages from Albanian and Amharic to Turkish and Tongan. (Friedrich, 1985, p. 36)

This excerpt from Otto Friedrich's portrait of an elementary school clearly reflects the range of cultural diversity found in our schools today. It also reinforces the need for the contemporary U.S. school to find effective means of working with myriad special needs and problems of children from divergent sociocultural and ethnic groups. Teachers and other school personnel need to know about and appreciate minority cultural patterns represented in school, but they should also be aware of the assumptions underlying their own worldviews, values, and attitudes.

Cultural Differences Between Mainstream Society and Shared-Function Groups

To work effectively with culturally different children, we must know about their cultural backgrounds and their historical heritages. Current discussions of inclusive models of schooling address the importance of recognizing cultural features shared by different cultural groups (Gay, 2000; Ibarra, 2001; Korn & Bursztyn, 2002; Oaks & Lipton, 2003; Pewewardy, 2002; Shade, 1997). We have been, as Markus, Steele, and Steele (2002) point out, "reluctant to see that these group differences in lived experience and perspective might be relevant to the goal of inclusion" (pp. 453–454). In addition, we must be sensitive to the degree of conflict these children may be experiencing in relating to the cultures of the mainstream society and their own community. Some young people live in families that have been almost completely assimilated to the norms of the dominant culture; others come from traditional families in which their own ethnic ways are strictly practiced. Many from the latter environment often must deal with contradictory expectations, what Pewewardy (2002) calls "lack of 'cultural synchronization' between students and teachers" (p. 37); they literally have to live in two distinct worlds. To help culturally different students cope with disparate cultural forces in school and society, teachers and counselors must be cognizant of the cultures of the mainstream society and several ethnic groups in the United States. As a helpful guide, some of the basic characteristics of the mainstream and shared-function groups—Asian Americans, African Americans, Hispanic Americans, and Native Americans—are listed in Table 7.1 and Table 7.2 in very broad terms. **Shared-function groups** tend to be collectivistic in that the group members tend to emphasize the importance of the group's identity and interests over the individual identity and interests. Collectivistic groups promote interdependence, harmony, and collation among in-group members (Triandis, 1995). In contrast, the mainstream culture as an individualistic culture stresses the value of individual identity over the group's rights and needs. It promotes personal autonomy, self-efficiency, and individual responsibility (Hofstede, 1991).

The characteristics listed in Table 7.1 are very broad generalizations that do not give us a picture of how such general traits are manifested in disparate cultural groups. Hence, intragroup distinctions are provided in Table 7.2 so that a clearer understanding of individual groups can be had. The reader should be warned that these distinctions are very general descriptions of complex beliefs, attitudes, values, and cognitive styles of various cultures. These generalizations are useful in coming to understand the general range of preferences, but they are counterproductive if they are viewed as rigid categories that individual students must disprove. Such stereotyping demeans both students and educators.

TABLE 7.1

Cultural Differences Between Mainstream Society and Shared-Function Groups

	Mainstream Culture (Norms of the American School)	Shared-Function Groups
Worldview	Person-centered world See others as equals Informal human relationship	Human-relationship-centered world Hierarchical and formal human relationships
Values	Emphasis on individual rights Stress assertiveness and competitiveness	Emphasis on personal duties Respect for authority Group harmony and conformity
Learning	Through personal involvement Emphasis on active communication	Through docility Emphasis on observation and emulation
Identity	Based on personal competence Emphasis of self-motivation	Based on group membership Motivation derived from group
Cognitive Style	Objective, analytic, and detail-specific thinking Separating facts from feelings	Global approach to conceptual thinking Combining facts with feelings
Communication Style	Reciprocal (give-and-take) mode Direct expression and exchanges Serial exchanges (taking turns in speaking and listening)	Hierarchical (commands and demands) Indirect expression Spontaneous expression

In the same way that judging all students against the norms of the dominant society limits their participation, using general cultural knowledge as stereotypes treats students as "types" rather than as individuals.

One of the approaches some educators take is to ignore all cultural generalizations in favor of what Markus, Steele, and Steele (2002) and others call "color blindness." This choice to do so "rests on the faith that not seeing differences is the surest route to reducing the inequalities and improving inclusion" (p. 454). Because the institution of school itself reflects both the history and norms of the dominant culture, such an approach—no matter how well intentioned—creates a barrier to that inclusion. Being knowledgable about the dimensions of cultural diversity can enable teachers to approach classroom instruction in a way that draws on the contexts of learners rather than ignores it (Thomas, 2000, p. 115). With this in mind, we will now examine some of the major differences among Asian American, African American, Hispanic American, and Native American groups.

As can be seen in Tables 7.1 and 7.2, the mainstream society as well as the school view the individual person as central to the world. Consequently, rights of the individual and assertion of these rights occupy a crucial place in the mainstream culture. Because individuals see one another as equals in the person-centered world, relationships among individuals tend to be less formal. The codes of behavior and uses of language are not inclined to be complex. When each person is seen as having a central place in the society, people are encouraged to demand their rights and compete with each other for just rewards for their accomplishments. The same qualities are fostered among schoolchildren. They are encouraged to learn their social roles as well as academic subjects by becoming actively involved in classroom activities and schoolwide programs. For both children and adults, their identity is rooted in individual competence and actual achievements. Consequently, the qualities of autonomy and self-reliance are valued by the larger society and its schools. It is not surprising that a lack of self-motivation is frequently seen as a main cause of the person's failure to achieve in his or her own field of endeavor.

In the area of cognitive styles, the young are taught to think objectively by separating facts from their personal feelings and experiences. Perhaps because the Western world places such importance on science and technology, a child's ability to solve a problem by breaking it down into minute component parts, or atoms, is given a very high premium in the school and society. The ways in which our schoolchildren are taught to plan a family trip in their social studies class is a good illustration of this approach to thinking and problem solving. In a project of this sort, students are required to plan their trip by calculating how many miles or hours they must drive each day to reach their destination within a specified period of time. They are also asked to figure out where to find lodging and how much money to spend on gasoline, food, entertainment, and other unexpected contingencies. Finally, in an egalitarian society, communication flows in both directions, so the young and the grown-ups can freely exchange ideas and opinions. Issues are usually clearly and directly addressed and their resolutions are to be given in an unambiguous manner.

Implications for Teachers

In the context of schooling in the United States, students are judged in terms of their willingness and ability to participate and compete in academic and nonacademic activities as well as their competence in thinking objectively and analytically. They are required to give detail-specific answers without mixing personal feelings with facts. Students are also expected to raise questions to and share their thoughts and feelings with teachers and counselors. The ability to communicate clearly and directly is another essential requisite to being judged a good student. Although the foregoing description of the school's expectations is general, children growing up in white middle-class families are less likely to experience conflicts between their family norms and those of the school.

As we have come to see, "culture produces meanings, guides actions, assigns identities, makes particular events possible, and structures social relationships and power relations among people" (Foster, Lewis, & Onafowora, 2003, p. 262). So,

TABLE 7.2
Intragroup Distinctions Among Asian, African, Hispanic, and Native American Groups

	Asian Americans	African Americans	Hispanic Americans	Native Americans
Worldview	Hierarchical and formal human relationships with complex rules of behavior and language use	Focus on people and their activities rather than on things	Subjugation to nature Present-time orientation Time is to be enjoyed Obedience to will of God Sensitive to the opinions of authority figures	Mother Earth belongs to all Everything belongs to all people Life is to be enjoyed Few rules are best; be simple
Values	Emphasis on personal duties Respect for authority Value formal education Conformity to established role expectations	Concern for others Attach importance to creativity, freedom, and justice	Preference for conformity to status quo Humility Achievement defined in terms of interpersonal relationships Work for present needs Sharing	Group harmony Respect for nature Respect the elderly for their wisdom Sharing; all belong to the Great Spirit Accept others Be carefree
Learning	Docility: follow instructions Listen, observe, and emulate	Words and actions Responds to social rather than nonsocial or object stimuli	Use words and actions Use humor, narration, personal experience, and fantasy Cooperative work	Through storytelling and the use of legends Simplify problems Cooperative work

Identity	Group membership (status) Group-based motivation (e.g., "Get all A's for my family")	Position in a group Motivation derived from group	Membership in a group Group-derived motivation (work for and with a group)	Membership in a group Group-derived motivation (work for and with a group)
Cognitive Style	Global or overall approach to conceptual thinking Less emphasis on detail-specific thinking Combine the cognitive with the affective (facts with feelings)	General or overall approach to conceptual thinking Less emphasis on detail-specific thinking Combine the cognitive with the affective (facts with feelings)	Global and overall approach to conceptual thinking Combine the cognitive with affective (facts with feelings)	Global and overall approach to conceptual thinking Combine the cognitive with affective (facts with feelings)
Communication Style	Indirect expression Emphasis on discretion Restrain strong emotions Use of formal or ritualized language	Verbal and nonverbal behaviors Stylized speech and delivery Spontaneous expression	Verbal and nonverbal behaviors Spontaneous expression Emphasis on being a good listener	Verbal and nonverbal behaviors (not language dependent)

Note: Information was synthesized from Carter and Sequra (1979); Gay (1978); Hsu (1982); John (1985); Levine and Havighurst (1989); Ramirez and Castaneda (1974); Richardson (1981); Ruiz (1981); Smith (1981); Solomon (1988); and Sue (1981).

unlike the children of mainstream culture, young people from the shared-function groups must deal with at least two different sets of rules and codes of behavior. In general, members of the shared-function groups see the relationships among human beings as central to their world. These relationships are more or less hierarchical, and individuals tend to see each other in terms of the positions they occupy in the hierarchy. Whereas some groups define the rules of behavior and language usage very rigidly, others are more flexible in specifying their role expectations. In any event, the shared-function groups place a much greater emphasis on each person's duties and responsibilities than on rights and privileges. For example, the duties of parents are to nurture and guide their children by making wise decisions. The duties of children are to follow parental decisions without questioning.

Regarding values, respect for authority and concern for group harmony are promoted in the shared-function groups. Members generally express these two qualities by not challenging the decisions made by authority figures and by conforming to the established group norm. For this reason, young people from the shared-function groups are not likely to be vocal in school or to raise questions to teachers, counselors, and administrators. They tend to restrain from having intimate or informal personal conversations or relationships with school personnel. Consequently, many culturally different children follow the instructions given by their elders and teachers without raising many questions; observation and emulation, or "watch and do," characterize their learning style. These young people's hesitancy in sharing their thoughts and feelings with others and in public reflects the cultural norm that encourages discretion and humility. But more often than not, this attitude is viewed by school personnel as a sign of non-responsiveness or disinterest or even as an intellectual deficit.

Members of the shared-function groups develop their self-identity not so much in terms of personal competence and achievements but more in relation to their positions in the family and community. In this context, the term *member* should not be understood as meaning an autonomous individual joining a group. Rather, self-identity is inextricably tied to the individual's position in a group. In a real sense, the individual is not only an integral part of his or her group; the group is an indispensable aspect of the individual. From this perspective, one who follows the group norm without questioning should not be viewed as an "outer-directed-person," for the group is an organic part of that person. *Outer* and *inner* are terms that reflect the assumptions underlying the Western concept of a person who is considered an entity separate from the group or nature. For those students whose identity is group-based, motivation to work or study hard comes not so much from the desire for self-improvement as from their concern for how their achievement may affect the group to which they belong. Even competition for high honors may be carried out for the sake of the group. This implies that school failure of culturally different children should not always be attributed to the lack of individual learners' self-motivation.

Of the many cultural differences already discussed, variations in the cognitive styles of the mainstream society and the shared-function groups may most affect the performance of culturally different young people in the school. In contrast to the importance the school places on objective, analytic, and detail-specific thinking, children from shared-function groups are inclined to think globally about concepts, events, and other subject-matter-related activities. In other words, they are more interested in getting an overall or general picture of the objects of their thinking than the minute details and their relationships. Consistently, their responses to queries that require specific, step-by-step answers tend to be rather general. This may be one of the reasons why many students from the shared-function groups encounter difficulties in conceptual analysis or reducing a complex problem to its minute constituent parts.

Communication in groups that emphasize hierarchical human relationships tends to move from higher to lower positions in the form of commands or demands. In such a communication mode, there is little giving and taking of ideas. Moreover, limits are often set as to what individuals in lower positions can say to persons occupying higher positions. For example, in some Asian languages, there are no expressions children can use to directly praise their parents because it is simply not appropriate for children to praise their elders. Although the directness with which people communicate with others varies greatly, members of the shared-function groups generally do not communicate as directly as individuals belonging to the mainstream culture. However, spontaneous and frequent exchanges are commonly practiced with peers in the shared-function groups. This practice radically differs from the implicit school requirement that the speaker must first be recognized by the teacher and that each person take turns speaking and listening. When seen from the school's perspective, spontaneous expression of thoughts by several students at the same time is considered undisciplined or disorderly conduct. This kind of judgment reinforces whatever negative images teachers and counselors may have about students from certain ethnic groups.

A primary purpose of the foregoing discussion is to point out that learning and behavioral difficulties may arise out of cultural differences, but that group identities are "interactive/dynamic (not universal and fixed)" (Cornbleth, 2003, p. 4). What is necessary for the school and the teacher is neither to dismiss the legitimacy of other cultures nor to encourage the culturally different to tenaciously stick to their own ways regardless of their own purposes or the context in which they must live and work. Insofar as minority children must function as members of the dominant and their own societies, they must acquire the skills necessary for functioning in both environments. Although limited space does not allow us to discuss how teachers and counselors could relate effectively to individuals from several distinct cultural groups, some general suggestions are given.

First, teachers should provide opportunities for the culturally different to display their special skills, talents, and achievements to others in the class so that they may gain group approval as well as self-confidence. One author recalls observing a third-grade teacher asking a non-English-speaking immigrant child to come up to the board to solve several difficult arithmetic problems the class had not yet studied. The teacher already knew that the child understood well the particular math problems. The student's success at this task helped the child win many friends and placed her in an environment that enabled her to participate in many other classroom and school activities. Due to the teacher's sensitivity to the child's emotional and social needs, the child was able to learn both the English language and the social skills to become an active and contributing member of her class and the school. What this episode illustrates is that whereas an enriching social environment helps a child to do well in school, social isolation becomes a serious barrier to a child's educational development. To many culturally different children, social isolation is one of the most painful and educationally damaging experiences. Having a teacher who establishes a close personal relationship through expression of approval and support and who uses personalized means of rewarding children's accomplishments is important to all learners. But these measures are particularly reassuring to minority children, who tend to have a sense of fear and uncertainty about mainstream teachers and students as well as themselves.

Students who come from cultures in which hierarchical human relationships, respect for authority, docility, and conformity are prized tend to experience difficulties in loosely structured learning situations. They need step-by-step instructions for carrying out a particular task. For this reason, teachers should be mindful of giving clear-cut explanations of what is to be done and how the work can be accomplished by providing specific instructions. As these students learn to do their work successfully, teachers may gradually relax their instruction-giving practice. In general, students from shared-function groups require a much more tightly structured or directive learning situation than their counterparts in the mainstream culture. We should keep in mind that providing a tightly structured learning situation is not the same as "having stricter disciplinary measures." Learning through modeling (imitating) can be an effective way for children to acquire the necessary skills and eventually develop their own unique ways. This approach is useful not only in performing arts but also in learning new languages and even in essay writing. Finally, having culturally different students in the classroom affords an excellent opportunity for mainstream students to learn about other cultures and about their own as different but legitimate ways of dealing with essentially similar human problems.

The goal of this culturally responsive teaching is to "increase the academic achievement of students by making learning more relevant to their experiences and frames of reference" (Conrad, Gong, Sipp, & Wright, 2004, p. 188). Such teaching rests on teachers being knowledgable about cultural diversity and then using that knowledge, as Geneva Gay (2002) outlines, in the development of curriculum, selection of teaching methods, interactions with students, and in the construction of a classroom community (p. 106). Thus, bringing an understanding of the cultural foundations of education to the classroom begins with "a humble sense of self-scrutiny" (Wlodkowski & Ginsberg, 1995, p. 258). Learning about who we are as educators and who our students are as learners needs to engage us with a profound awareness of the dimensions of culture in the classrooms where we meet.

Cases For Reflection

The following is a father's description of his son's struggle in school.

CHRIS'S STRUGGLE

Chris was a wonderful, social person. He was at ease with people of all ages. It was not unusual for him to drop in to visit a friend and, if the friend were not home, spend many hours visiting with the parents. He was an outgoing young man. On a number of occasions he spoke his piece in formal sessions with adults. Visiting tradesmen have been impressed with his willingness and ability to help. In the ninth grade, he was active and effective in contributing to his school's seventy-fifth anniversary celebrations. And then there was his sense of humor. Ah, yes, beware his sense of humor! He was a master of situational comedy. The Hunch Back of Notre Dame, the outrageous statement with a straight face, the aggressive bully, the voices of many characters, especially the menacing organized-crime thug and the village idiot—all were staples of his repertoire. Chris was a warm, convivial and funny person to be with.

But schoolwork was not Chris's forte. His success began to wane once he moved into the secondary grades. Indeed, in the eighth grade, he began to experience notable learning difficulties. In high school, as he sat in the third row, second seat from the back, he was required to listen to his teacher's lecture, ask questions, and place notes on the blackboard for copying into notebooks. Duplicated note sheets and worksheets filled his binders. Seldom was he invited to participate in group discussions, make choices, voice his opinion, or engage in learning that was in any way connected to his life. Chris experienced increasing frustration and generally disliked school. He finally made it through high school but what about life for Chris after school? He left school feeling no good, I suspect even incompetent. He shied away from learning, unless he really wanted to do it. Engaging in new learning to enrich his life required risk-taking; something he was hesitant to do. He expected he would fail.

Source: Waldron, Peter W.; Collie, Tani R.; Davies, Calvin W.; *Telling Stories About School: An Invitation,* 1st Edition, © 1999. Reprinted by permission of Pearson Education, Inc., Upper Saddle River, NJ.

DISCUSSION QUESTIONS

1. What can you surmise about Chris's ability to communicate with others? What can you reasonably say about his preferred style(s) of communication?
2. To what would you attribute his learning difficulties in school? What kind of learning style might he have had? Why?
3. To what extent do you think the school and his teacher were responsible for Chris's failure? Why?
4. If you had been his teacher, what would you have done to help Chris learn and grow? Is there a lesson to be learned from Chris's experience?

REFERENCES

Au, K. (1980). Participant structure in a reading lesson with Hawaiian children: Analysis of a culturally appropriate instruction/event. *Anthropology and Education Quarterly, 11,* 91–115.

Banks, J. A. (1988). Ethnicity, class, cognitive and motivational styles: Research and teaching implications. *Journal of Negro Education, 57,* 452–466.

Bennett, C. (1997). Teaching students as they would be taught: The importance of cultural perspective. In B. J. R. Shade (Ed.), *Culture, style, and the educative process: Making schools work for racially diverse students* (2nd ed.; pp. 129–142). Springfield, IL: Charles C. Thomas.

Beresin, A. R. (2002). Children's expressive culture in light of September 11, 2001. *Anthropology and Education Quarterly, 33*(3), 331–337.

Bergstrom, A., Cleary, L. M., & Peacock, T. D. (2003). *Seventh generation: Native students speak about finding the good path.* Charleston, WV: ERIC Clearinghouse on Rural Education and Small Schools.

Bruner, J. (1966). *Toward a theory of instruction.* Cambridge: Harvard University Press.

Bruner, J. (1996). *The culture of education.* Cambridge: Harvard University Press.

Carroll, T. G. (1981). Learning to work: Adaptive communication of the organization of the organizing principles of work in a suburban elementary school. In R. T. Sieber & A. J. Gordon (Eds.), *Children and their organizations: Investigation in American culture* (pp. 44–57). Boston: G. K. Hall & Co.

Carter, T. P., & Segura, R. D. (1979). *Mexican Americans in school: A decade of change.* New York: College Examination Board.

Castro, F. G., Boyer, G. R., & Balcazar, H. G. (2000). Healthy adjustment in Mexican American and other Hispanic adolescents. In R. Montemayer, G. R. Adams, & T. P. Gullotta (Eds.), *Adolescent diversity in ethnic, economic, and cultural contexts* (pp. 141–178). Thousdand Oaks, CA: Sage Publications.

Collins, J. (1988). Language and class in minority education. *Anthropology and Education Quarterly, 19*(4), 299–326.

Conrad, N. K., Gong, Y., Sipp, L., & Wright, L. (2004). Using text talk as a gateway to culturally responsive teaching. *Early Childhood Education Journal, 31*(3), 187–192.

Cornbleth, C. (2003). *Hearing America's youth: Social identities in uncertain times.* New York: Peter Lang Publishing.

Cushner, Kenneth. (1994). Cross-cultural training for adolescents and professionals who work with youth exchange programs. In Richard W. Brislin and Tomoko Yoshida (Eds.), *Improving intercultural interactions: Modules for cross-cultural training programs.* Thousand Oaks, CA: Sage Publications.

Dao, M. (1997). Acculturation issues for at-risk Southeast Asian-American students. In B. J. R. Shade (Ed.), *Culture, style, and the educative process: Making schools work for racially diverse students* (2nd ed.; pp. 51–59). Springfield, IL: Charles C. Thomas.

Dobbert, M. L., & Cooke, B. (1987). Primate biology and behavior: A stimulus to educational thought and policy. In G. D. Spindler (Ed.), *Education and cultural process* (2nd ed.; pp. 97–116). Prospect Heights, IL: Waveland Press.

Dumont, R., Jr. (1985). Learning English and how to be silent: Studies in Sioux and Cherokee classrooms. In C. B. Cazden, V. P. John, & D. Hymes (Eds.), *Functions of language in the classroom* (pp. 344–369). Prospects Heights, IL: Waveland Press.

Eggen, P. D., & Kauchak, D. P. (1996). *Strategies for teachers: Teaching content and thinking skills* (3rd ed.). Boston: Allyn & Bacon.

Erickson, F., & Mohatt, G. (1988). Cultural organization of participant structures in two classrooms of Indian students. In G. D. Spindler (Ed.), *Doing the ethnography of schooling* (pp. 133–174). Prospect Heights, IL: Waveland Press.

Fitzberg, G. J. (2001). Less than equal: A former urban schoolteacher examines causes of educational disadvantage. *Urban Review, 33*(2), 107–129.

Foster, M., Lewis, J., & Onafowora, L. (2003). Anthropology, culture, and research on teaching and learning: Applying what we have learned to improve practice. *Teachers College Record, 105*(2), 261–277.

Friedrich, O. (1985, July 8). The changing face of America. *Time, 36.*

Gay, G. (1978). Viewing the pluralistic classroom as a cultural microcosm. *Educational Research Quarterly, 2,* 45–49.

Gay, G. (2000). *Culturally responsive teaching: Theory, research, and practice.* New York: Teachers College Press.

Gay, G. (2002). Preparing for culturally responsive teaching. *Journal of Teacher Education, 53*(2), 106–116.

Grossman, H. (1995). *Teaching in a diverse society.* Boston: Allyn & Bacon.

Gutmann, A. (2003). *Identity in democracy.* Princeton, NJ: Princeton University Press.

Heath, S. B. (1984). Linguistics and education. *Annual Review of Anthropology, 13.*

Heath, S. B. (1986). Sociocultural contexts of language development. In Bilingual Education Office, California State Department of Education, *Beyond language: Social and cultural factors in schooling language minority students* (pp. 143–186). Los Angeles: Evaluation, Dissemination and Assessment Center, California State University–Los Angeles.

Hofstede, G. (1991). *Culture and organizations: Software of the mind.* London: McGraw-Hill.

Hollins, E. R., King, J. E., & Hayman, W. C. (1994). *Teaching diverse populations: Formulating a knowledge base.* New York: State University of New York Press.

Hsu, F. (1982). *Chinese and Americans.* Honolulu: University of Hawaii Press.

Ibarra, R. A. (1999). Multicontextuality: A new perspective on minority underrepresentation in SEM academic fields. *Research News on Minority Undergraduate Education, 1*(3), 1–9.

Ibarra, R. A. (2001). *Beyond affirmative action: Reframing the context of higher education.* Madison, WI: University of Wisconsin Press.

John, V. P. (1985). Styles of learning—styles of teaching: Reflections on the education of Navajo children. In B. Cazden, V. P. John, & D. Hymes (Eds.), *Functions of language in the classroom* (pp. 334–340). Prospect Heights, IL: Waveland Press.

Joos, M. (1967). *The five clocks.* New York: Harcourt Brace & World.

Kneller, G. F. (1984). *Movements of thought in modern education.* New York: Wiley.

Kochman, T. (1972). *Rippin' and runnin'.* Urbana: University of Illinois Press.

Korn, C., & Bursztyn, A. (Eds.). (2002). *Rethinking multicultural education: Case studies in cultural transition.* Westport, CT: Bergin & Garvey.

Leong, F. T. L., Chao, R. K., & Hardin, E. E. (2000). Asian American adolescents: A research review to dispel the model minority myth. In R. Montemayor, G. R. Adams, & T. P. Gullotta (Eds.), *Diversity in ethnic, economic, and cultural contexts* (pp. 179–207). Thousand Oaks, CA: Sage Publications.

Levine, D. U., & Levine R. F. (1996). *Society and education.* Boston: Allyn & Bacon.

Levine, D. U., & Havighurst, R. J. (1989). *Society and education.* Boston: Allyn & Bacon.

Markus, H. R., Steele, C. M., & Steele, D. M. (2002). Color blindness as a barrier to inclusion: Assimilation and nonimmigrant minorities. In R. Shweder, M. Minow, & H. R. Markus (Eds.), *Engaging cultural differences: The multicultural challenge in liberal democracies* (pp. 453–472). New York: Sage Foundation.

Martin, J. N., & Nakayama, T. K. (1997). *Intercultural communication in contexts*. Mountain View, CA: Mayfield.

Mitchell-Kernan, C. (1985). On the status of Black English for native speakers: An assessment of attitude and values. In B. Cazden, V. P. John, & D. Hymes (Eds.), *Functions of language in the classroom* (pp. 195–210). Prospect Heights, IL: Waveland Press.

Nieto, S. (2004). *Affirming diversity: The sociopolitical context of multicultural education* (4th ed.). New York: Pearson.

Oaks, J., & Lipton, M. (2003). *Teaching to change the world* (2nd ed.). Boston: McGraw-Hill.

Pang, V. O. (1997). Asian-American children: A diverse population. In B. J. R. Shade (Ed.), *Culture, style, and the educative process: Making schools work for racially diverse students* (2nd ed.; pp. 41–50). Springfield, IL: Charles C. Thomas.

Pearce, W. B., & Kang, K. (1988). Conceptual migrations: Understanding "travelers' tales" for cross cultural adaptation. In Y. Y. Kim & W. B. Gudykunst (Eds.), *Cross-cultural adaptation: Current approaches* (pp. 20–41). Newbury Park, CA: Sage Publications.

Pepper, F. C., & Henry, S. (1997). Social and cultural effects on Indian learning style: Classroom implications. In B. J. R. Shade (Ed.), *Culture, style, and the educative process: Making schools work for racially diverse students* (2nd ed.; pp. 168–177). Springfield, IL: Charles C. Thomas.

Pewewardy, C. (2002). Learning styles of American Indian/Alaska native students: A review of literature and implications for practice. *Journal of American Indian Education, 41*(3), 22–56.

Philips, S. (1972). Participant structures and communicative competence: Warm Springs children in community and classroom. In B. Cazden, V. P. John, & D. Hymes (Eds.), *Functions of language in the classroom* (pp. 370–394). Prospect Heights, IL: Waveland Press.

Pickering, M. (2001). *Stereotyping: The politics of representation*. New York: Palgrave.

Ramirez, M., & Castaneda, A. (1974). *Cultural democracy, bicognitive development and education*. New York: Academic Press.

Reyhner, J., & Eder, J. (2004). *American Indian education: A history*. Norman, OK: University of Oklahoma Press.

Richardson, E. H. (1981). Cultural and historical perspectives in counseling American Indians. In D. W. Sue, *Counseling the culturally different: Theory and practice* (pp. 224–227). New York: Wiley.

Rist, R. C. (1985). On understanding the process of schooling: The contributions of labeling theory. In J. H. Ballantine (Ed.), *Schools and society* (pp. 88–106). Palo Alto, CA: Mayfield.

Ruan, J. (2003). Toward a culture-sensitive pedagogy: Emergent literacy learning in Chinese-English bilinguals in America. *Language, Culture, and Curriculum, 16*(1), 39–47.

Ruiz, R. A. (1981). Cultural and historical perspectives in counseling Hispanics. In D. W. Sue, *Counseling the culturally different: Theory and practice* (pp. 186–215). New York: Wiley.

Samovar, L. A., & Porter, R. E. (Eds.). (1997). *Intercultural communication* (8th ed.). Belmont, CA: Wadsworth.

Saracho, O. N. (1997). *Teachers' and students' cognitive styles in early childhood education*. Westport, CT: Bergin & Garvey.

Schunk, D. H. (2004). *Learning theories: An educational perspective* (4th ed). Upper Saddle River, NJ: Pearson Education.

Shade, B. J. R. (Ed.). (1997). *Culture, style, and the educative process: Making schools work for racially diverse students* (2nd ed.). Springfield, IL: Charles C. Thomas.

Shade, B. J. (1997). The culture and style of Mexican-American society. In B. J. R. Shade (Ed.), *Culture, style, and the educative process: Making schools work for racially diverse students* (2nd ed.; pp. 35–39). Springfield, IL: Charles C. Thomas.

Shapiro, J. P., Sewell, T. E., & DuCette, J. P. (1995). *Reframing diversity in education.* Lancaster, PA: Technomic Publishing Company.

Sieber, R. T., & Gordon, A. J. (1981). Introduction: Socializing organizations—Environments for the young, windows to American culture. In R. T. Sieber & A. J. Gordon (Eds.), *Children and their organizations: Investigations in American culture* (pp. 1–17). Boston: G. K. Hall & Co.

Simon, H. A. (1979). Information processing models of cognition. *Annual Review of Psychology, 30,* 363–396.

Smith, E. (1981). Cultural and historical perspective in counseling blacks. In D. W. Sue, *Counseling the culturally different: Theory and practice* (pp. 141–185). New York: Wiley.

Smith, M. E. & Shade, B. J. R. (1997). Culturally responsive teaching strategies for American Indian students. In B. J. R. Shade, (Ed.), *Culture, style, and the educative process: Making schools work for racially diverse students* (2nd ed.; pp. 178–186). Springfield, IL: Charles C. Thomas.

Solomon, R. P. (1988). Black cultural forms in schools: A cross-national comparison. In L. Weis (Ed.), *Class, race, and gender in American education* (pp. 230–248). Albany: State University of New York Press.

Spindler, G. D., & Spindler, L. (1987). Do anthropologists need learning theory? In G. D. Spindler (Ed.), *Education and cultural process* (2nd ed.) (pp. 53–69). Prospect Heights, IL: Waveland Press.

Stefani, L. A. (1997). The influence of culture on classroom communication. In L. A. Samovar & R. E. Porter (Eds.), *Intercultural communication* (8th ed.). Belmont, CA: Wadsworth.

Sue, D. W. (1981). *Counseling the culturally different: Theory and practice.* New York: Wiley.

Suzuki, B. H. (1980). Education and socialization of Asian Americans: A revisionist analysis of the "model minority" thesis. In R. Endo, S. Sue, & N. N. Wagner (Eds.), *Asian-Americans: Social and psychological perspectives* (Vol. 2; pp. 155–175). Palo Alto, CA: Science and Behavior Books.

Swisher, K., & Deyhle, D. (1992). Adapting instruction to culture. In J. Reyhner (Ed.), *Teaching American Indian students.* Norman, OK: University of Oklahoma Press.

Thomas, E. (2000). *Culture and schooling: Bridges between research, praxis, and professionalism.* Chichester, England: Wiley.

Ting-Toomey, S. (1999). *Communicating across cultures.* New York: Guilford Press.

Triandis, H. (1995). *Individualism and collectivism.* Boulder, CO: Westview Press.

Wlodkowski, R. J., & Ginsberg, M. B. (1995). *Diversity and motivation: Culturally responsive teaching.* San Francisco: Jossey-Bass.

Epilogue

This is not a book about culture and education. Rather, it is about education as a cultural process. Implicit in this statement is the view that almost every aspect of education and schooling is influenced by culture. How we teach, what we teach, how we relate to children and each other, what our goals are—these are all rooted in the norms of our culture. Our society's predominant worldview and cultural norms are so deeply ingrained in how we educate children that we very seldom think about the possibility that there may be other different but equally legitimate and effective approaches to teaching and learning. In a society with as much sociocultural and racial diversity as the United States, the lack of this wonderment about alternative ways often results in unequal education and social injustice.

In general terms, the late 1960s to the late 1970s represents a period in which many attempts were made to provide equal education to the children of minority cultures and lower socioeconomic classes. A wide range of programs in compensatory education, bilingual/bicultural education, ethnic studies, multicultural education, and school desegregation was tried. However, the findings regarding the impact of these measures are inconclusive, even today.

The two decades following the 1980s, on the other hand, represent a time when renewed emphasis was placed on what has been termed *educational excellence* and *accountability*. In an effort to raise standards, concerns about equity and diversity were often lost. Although the rhetoric of reform from this period emphasized the need to raise standards for all children, less emphasis was put on finding ways to provide equal educational opportunity.

This period also represents a time when technological developments grew exponentially. What was unknown or nonexistent in 1980 (e.g., the Internet and all its connections on the World Wide Web) was becoming commonplace. The percentage of schools with Internet access increased from 50 percent in 1995 to 99 percent in 2004, with approximately five students for every Internet-connected computer (U.S. Census Bureau, 2004). While technological changes had made their way into schools, they still had had little effect on the ways day-to-day schooling was actually conducted. On the other hand, technology was having a profound effect on the ways young people could learn outside of school. Because education must be thought of more broadly than schooling, we find that equal educational opportunity was being further undermined by unequal access to technology. While young people from more affluent homes had easy access to the wealth of information (and misinformation) found on the Internet, those from poor homes and poor schools found themselves with less access to information and modern tools of communication.

Midway through the first decade of the new century, large gaps still existed between our knowledge of cultural differences and the way such understanding can be utilized to help the culturally different learn and live more effectively in their own community and the school. The need to do a great deal more research into the ways diverse cultural factors influence the process of learning and teaching in the context of schooling continues into this third millenium.

Schooling always occurs under complex cultural as well as sociopolitical and economic conditions. These conditions in turn affect how well the school can function. Schools in the twentieth century were a product of the late nineteenth and early twentieth centuries. Basic school organization and structure were developed in an industrial age. Schools would equalize educational opportunity by providing access to basic literacy. They would also serve to sort and select those who would be future leaders in society. Other institutions, particularly the family, were seen as playing a major role in the socialization of youth. But by the late twentieth century, we had entered the "Information Age."

American culture is different in many ways from what it was when accepted forms and functions of public schooling were taking root in the twentieth century. Basic literacy is no longer sufficient for economic success or equal educational opportunity. The roles the family and the church play in the socialization of children has declined. Mass media and popular culture have become powerful socializing agents. Immigration is on the rise, and the proportion of the population who are minorities is increasing. The U.S. Census Bureau (2004) reports that of the nearly 54 million students enrolled in K–12 schools, almost 20 percent speak a language other than English at home, and 21 percent have at least one foreign-born parent. In brief, American society and culture are rapidly changing. With these changes the role of schooling, as well as the tools of learning, change as well. How effectively we can utilize our understanding of the connections between culture and education and schooling will have a profound impact on the future of American school as a social institution.

USES OF "CULTURE"

Although the usefulness of the concept of culture has been discussed elsewhere in this book, a brief review of several key points may be helpful in examining the implications cultural diversity has for classroom teachers and counselors. Through the use of our knowledge about cultures of other people, we may be able to understand them better and more accurately. Such an understanding in turn breaks down barriers to effective communication, thereby improving our interactions with individuals from different sociocultural groups. Our appreciation of other cultures tends to prevent us from misinterpreting the behaviors of others by putting ourselves in their place. This kind of sensitivity to other cultures may minimize the possibility of making unfair evaluations of culturally different individuals.

CONCLUDING THOUGHTS

As Giroux and others have admonished, we need to educate children of all sociocultural backgrounds, not just give them credentials. We may not all agree with Giroux's conviction that our schools oppress women, ethnic groups, and other minorities by disconfirming and marginalizing their experience. But at the least, educators need to experience the pain and joy of being different from others and to understand how such differences can give us greater options for doing things. In this way we may learn about ourselves and others while discovering new ways of helping all young people to fulfill their dreams.

REFERENCES

U.S. Census Bureau (2004, July 6). *Facts for features: Back to school.* Available: http://www.census.gov/Press-Release/www.releases/archives/facts_for_features_special_editions/00263.html

Glossary of Key Concepts

Acculturation   The process of learning cultural change or learning another culture (e.g., a minority child learning the ways of the dominant culture is being acculturated)

Ageism   The process of stereotyping individuals based upon age and the perceived deficits that accompany aging

Age-stage linkage   The mistaken belief that children's ages are necessarily connected with certain pathological stages (e.g., adolescence anywhere at anytime is necessarily a period of storm, stress, and confusion)

Americanization   Historically, schooling that involved helping children learn to think, believe, and behave according to the white Anglo-Saxon Protestant ways while divesting non-WASP children of cultural practices that differed from the mainstream

Anthropology   A science *(logos)* of man *(anthro)* concerned with describing, analyzing, and comparing the physical, social, psychological, and linguistic aspects of human behaviors as they manifest themselves in different cultural patterns

Assessment models   Different approaches to pscyhoeducational assessment, including (1) the medical model, (2) the social system model, (3) the ability training model, (4) the task analysis model, (5) the pluralistic model, and (6) the authentic/performance model (see *Psychoeducational assessment*)

Authentic assessment   The process of obtaining information about students' learning activities and their products (e.g., journals and portfolios), reflecting specific objectives that have been set for them; this approach avoids comparing individual learners with a group norm

Bilingual education   An approach to learning English that would enable limited-English-proficiency students to maintain their primary languages and develop pride in their cultural heritages, as well as master the English language

Charter schools   Publicly funded schools that are not under the direct control of the local board of education but rather may be managed by any interested group

Cognitive style   A person's way of responding and performing in diverse situations

Compensatory education   A means of helping educationally disadvantaged children of poor and ethnic minorities to acquire the necessary cognitive skills to enable them to find and keep better-paying jobs and thereby eventually lift them out of their low socioeconomic status

Concepts of childhood   Definitions of childhood that are constructed by societies at various times and in different contexts; the meanings vary from one historical period to another and from culture to culture (e.g., children have been seen as "victims," "adults," and "underdeveloped adults")

Constructive postmodernism   This perspective is based on the belief that all living and non-living things in the world are interconnected and unified. Further, human existence has a purpose as well as a direction and that there is a universal basis for knowledge and meaning. The holistic view of education is rooted in this worldview.

Core values   A set of fundamental values of a society; the traditional core values of the dominant culture in the United States are said to be (1) Puritan morality, (2) work–success ethic, (3) individualism, (4) achievement orientation, and (5) future-time orientation

Credentialing   Requiring credentials such as diplomas, licenses, and certificates for entrance into certain high-status occupations (e.g., managerial or professional positions); the credentials are awarded upon completion of specialized training in appropriate fields

Critical theory   The view that reality is social, political, and economical in nature and that knowledge comes from critical analysis of class conflicts

Cultural anthropology   The study of cultural patterns or complex systems of human behaviors that represent people's attempts to solve the problems arising out of nature and human beings' associations with each other

Cultural capital   The ability to understand and practice the norms, discourse modes, language styles, and language modes of the dominant culture

Cultural deprivation   The belief that families who were culturally different or poor were generally unable to provide their children with adequate language, perceptual, and other cognitive experiences to succeed in school and in modern society

Cultural pluralism   As an ideal, the belief that America can be a cohesive society enriched by shared, widely divergent ethnic experiences

Culture   A system of norms, standards, and control mechanisms with which members of society assign meanings, values, and significance of things, events, and behaviors; culture includes patterns of knowledge, skills, behaviors, attitudes, and beliefs, as well as material artifacts produced by human society and transmitted from one generation to another

Culture of childhood   The child's-eye view of children's experiences and the world

Deconstructive postmodernism   A perspective that denies that there is an objective and real basis for knowledge and truth; deconstructive postmodernists argue that there are many ways of knowing and that truth and meaning are constructed and reconstructed as societies and social structures change, insisting that the meanings that have been taken for granted should be deconstructed. Through this deconstructive process, the marginalized and oppressed people can be empowered to be liberated from their status quo.

Deficit view   The notion that what is different is inferior or pathological in nature (e.g., black English dialect may be viewed as inferior to Standard English; children may be seen as inferior or inadequate adults)

Discovery learning   Jerome Bruner's view that learning is the process of discovering regularity and relatedness by ordering and organizing one's experiences for solving problems

Education   The deliberate means by which each society attempts to transmit and perpetuate its notion of the good life, which is derived from the society's fundamental beliefs concerning the nature of the world, knowledge, and values; societies carry on this process informally or formally—the latter is called *schooling*

Educational development   From a societal perspective, this represents the movement of young people toward becoming full-fledged members of society, which implies changes in cognitive competencies, acquisition of knowledge and social skills, cultivation of certain attitudes, and the formation of moral values and attitudes

Enculturation   The process of learning one's own culture

Ethnicity   The complex of interrelated factors such as nationality, language, cultural tradition and values, religion, socioeconomic status, and educational level

Ethnography   The study of a culture through observation and interviews

Exceptional learners   Gifted learners and learners with disabilities who may suffer alienation from mainstream society because they are viewed in terms of the extent to which they deviate from the standards of "normal" people

Generalization   The result of the process of drawing conclusions about an entire class or group based on samples; generalizations indicate certain group characteristics without implying that every member of the class or group has the same traits

Genres of language   Forms, schemas, or molds of language that have varied linguistic functions; the genres include (1) label quests, (2) meaning quests, (3) recounts, (4)accounts, (5) eventcasts, and (6) stories

Guided learning   The process of breaking down a learning objective into a set of specific skills or bodies of information so that the learner is able to achieve the objective by mastering each of the components according to a carefully prearranged sequence

Hidden curriculum   An indirect means of teaching norms and values without explicitly stating what is being taught (e.g., students may learn the principles of democracy from the participatory ways in which the teacher works with the students)

Holism (Holistic view of education)   Founded on constructive postmodernism, this perspective considers the discovery of the wholeness of the universe and the interrelatedness of all disciplines as well as the development of a global outlook and a sense of harmony and spirituality for building world peace as the central aims of education

Intercultural competence   Knowledge, attitudes, and skills necessary for effective communication with members of different cultural groups

Interpretivist theory   The view that an understanding of the relationship between school and society requires an analysis of the interactions among students, teachers, administrators, and various peer groups

Learning as information processing   Theory by which learning is viewed as a goal-oriented, problem-solving process in which the learner copes with simplified models of real problems, as with a computer; this approach focuses on cultivating skills that will enable the learner to (1) represent the problems schematically and (2) identify relations among the problem elements and recombine them into new patterns

Learning styles   Individual learners' consistent patterns of processing information

Lived curriculum   Another expression for *hidden curriculum* emphasizing that informal sets of practices define the day-to-day experiences of students and often assume a greater importance than the formal, official curriculum

Marxist conflict theory   A form of conflict theory that holds that the private owners of the means of production maintain their economic domination of the working class by controlling the process of allocating roles, social status, and rewards; in this way, social and economic inequities are perpetuated

Melting pot ideal   The view according to which ethnic differences that were "melted" into a single "pot" would produce a synthesis—a new homogeneous and superior culture

Moral development   The process by which children learn their moral beliefs and develop moral reasoning for making decisions regarding what is right or wrong

Multicultural education   A process by which individuals can develop a critical understanding of their own cultures and those of others, thus becoming more effective decision makers

Neo-Marxist theory   A form of conflict theory that argues that capitalistic societies perpetuate social and economic inequities and the privileged upper class maintains these inequities by controlling the lower class through noneconomic means of domination; the class differences are maintained by teaching common cultures, styles of language, manners, conversational topics, values, and preferences of all kinds to the upper-class children

Operating culture   In interacting with others in various contexts, a person shifts from one culture to another within his or her repertoire (private culture). But the person tends to use the cultures in which he or she is already proficient. The particular culture selected is his/her operating culture.

Postmodernism/poststructuralism.   See *deconstructive postmodernism, constructive postmodernism,* and *holism*

Private culture   A person's private culture consists of the generalized view of the culture of the one's own community, that is, public culture, as well as the awareness of several distinct cultures of other individuals. This cultural awareness within a person's private culture represents the individual's perceptions of how other human beings have organized their experiences based on the standards by which others perceive, predict, judge, and act.

Psychoeducational assessment   A process of obtaining information about the learner and communicating it to the intended users for making the best possible decisions about the learner's education

Psychological anthropology   A field of study that examines the relationship between culture and human nature

Schooling   A form of education that occurs in specialized institutions (e.g., schools); although education occurs in all societies, some societies may not have schooling

School vouchers   A tool through which parents can apply the amount of public money a school district would receive to educate their child toward the child's tuition at a private school

Sexism   Discrimination based on culturally assigned gender roles

Shared-function groups   Groups in which group interests rather than individual rights and goals are emphasized and personal identities of individuals are defined in terms of their positions in the group

Social structure A complex of formal and informal role relationships that exist among individuals in different positions (e.g., students, teachers, counselors, and administrators)

Status culture A sum total of such common cultural elements as styles of language, manners, opinions, values, conversational topics, and preferences of all kinds belonging to different occupations and/or social classes

Status groups Associations whose members share a common status culture

Stereotyping An erroneous manner of thinking in which group characteristics are assumed to be possessed by all members of the group (e.g., that all Asians are good in math is a stereotype)

Structural/functionalist theory The view that the school is a microcosm of the larger society; as such, the school should reproduce and perpetuate the established social, cultural, economic, and political structures and norms and young people should be educated to function effectively in society

Styles of communication Consistent patterns of communicating with other individuals

Styles of language Five major ways of using language, including (1) the intimate style, (2) the casual style, (3) the consultative style, (4) the formal style, and (5) the frozen style

Symboling The process of assigning meanings and significance to objects, events, and behaviors within a specific culture

Syncretism The process by which a person may change his or her operating culture by combining elements from different cultures into one's own private culture.

Name Index

Subject Index